How India Sees the World

How India Sees the World

Kautilya to the 21st Century

Shyam Saran

juggernaut

JUGGERNAUT BOOKS
C-I-128, First Floor, Sangam Vihar, Near Holi Chowk,
New Delhi 110080, India

First published in hardback by Juggernaut Books 2017
Published in paperback 2018

10 9 8

The international boundaries on the map of India are neither purported to be correct nor authentic by Survey of India directives.

ISBN 9789386228857

Typeset in Adobe Caslon Pro by R. Ajith Kumar, New Delhi

Printed at Thomson Press India Private Limited

Contents

Foreword

We live in an increasingly interdependent world. Therefore, developments in the outside world can have a profound impact on the evolution of our polity as well as our economy. It is the task of our foreign policy establishment to ensure that our engagement with other countries takes place on as favourable terms as is possible, in a manner that is consistent with our national interests.

Shri Shyam Saran, who has a wealth of experience with regard to the formulation and implementation of Indian foreign policy, is highly qualified to evaluate India's foreign policy in the post-Independence period. He considers the search for strategic autonomy – the ability to take relatively autonomous decisions on matters perceived to be of vital interest to India – as a running and consistent theme of our foreign policy. In this context, interestingly, Shyam Saran believes that the Indo-US nuclear deal – in whose negotiation he played a very important role – was significant precisely because it expanded India's foreign policy options.

In any study of India's foreign policy, India's relations with other countries of the subcontinent – Pakistan, Bangladesh, Nepal, Bhutan and Sri Lanka – and our big neighbour China must figure prominently. I have always believed that without the normalization of our relations with these countries, India cannot realize its full developmental potential. Shyam Saran's analysis of India's relations with China, Pakistan and Nepal is thought-provoking. In his scrutiny of the issues of energy security and climate change he lays emphasis on the orderly and equitable management of globalization processes. His observations on the role of technological changes in shaping the new international order are also very educative.

Altogether, Shyam Saran has produced a book which offers a lot of food for thought and is very informative in its content. For this he is to be commended.

Dr Manmohan Singh
Former Prime Minister of India

Introduction

This book is not a typical memoir. Neither is it a thesis on India's foreign policy. It is an endeavour to find the hidden strands that could tie together my varied experiences representing India in the foreign policy sphere for over four decades and see what recognizable patterns they yield. This book is therefore a recounting which seeks to place events I participated in (or witnessed) against the backdrop of India's history. It is partly introspective, partly reflective, re-examining some of the key happenings of my time from a perspective unclouded by the passions of the day. This recounting also rediscovers templates that are ancient in origin but more enduring than one would have believed.

Hindu cosmology locates India, or Bharatvarsha, on the southern petal of the four-petalled lotus that floats on the surface of the cosmic ocean. The petal is broad as it emerges from the central axis of the blossom, and narrow towards the tip, tracing in its sacred form the physical shape of the subcontinent. This geography constitutes the stage on which the story of India has unfolded over many aeons. It is this geography that greatly influences India's foreign policy behaviour.

In writing this book I wanted to demonstrate that India is heir to a very rich and sophisticated tradition of statecraft and diplomatic practice, and that this legacy continues to shape its current strategic culture and diplomatic behaviour. It may not always be explicit but it does constitute a mental prism through which the nation assesses and acts upon situations. It is important to study this intellectual heritage and its evolution over the ages, not only because it may explain our own foreign policy behaviour in some respects but also because it provides a set of principles that remains remarkably relevant in tackling contemporary problems. I have tried to use these principles in my own analysis of the many foreign policy challenges I had to deal with.

In studying Indian foreign policy since Independence, I consider the search for strategic autonomy a running and consistent theme. This objective may have been pursued through non-alignment in the post-Independence years, but even if its pursuit is happening under another label today – some call it 'multi-alignment' – the aim has remained unchanged. Strategic autonomy is the ability of a state to take relatively independent decisions on matters of vital interest. Expanding the scope for such autonomy is the hallmark of a successful foreign policy.

For instance, India did not sign the nuclear Non-Proliferation Treaty (NPT) in 1968 because it would have divided countries into a privileged group of a handful of states with nuclear weapons while permanently denying the others the right to acquire such weapons. This was unacceptable both for reasons of having to acquiesce to a subordinate status vis-à-vis nuclear weapons states and also because it would have closed India's option to become a nuclear weapons state in the future should this be demanded by its security interests. In becoming a declared nuclear weapons state in 1998, India exercised its nuclear option without violating any treaty commitment. Similarly, I believe the Indo-US nuclear deal was significant precisely because it expanded India's foreign policy options. I have tried to show this in the chapters describing the deal.

The book has a strong focus on China, reflecting my belief that China is, and will remain for the foreseeable future, the one country that has a direct impact on India as far as international relations go. It is already expanding its economic and military presence in India's subcontinental neighbourhood, and not only in Pakistan. Its naval forces now make frequent forays in the Indian Ocean, so far dominated by India. But China remains poorly understood by India, and this lack of familiarity can be costly when it comes to safeguarding India's interests. It is my hope that this book will trigger greater interest in what is a fascinating country with a civilization as complex and layered as our own.

India may have a rich tradition of statecraft that offers good advice on how a state can go about protecting and promoting its interests. One could claim that, on balance, the Indian state has been reasonably successful in this endeavour, despite the constraints it has faced since Independence. However, the nature of the challenges that are now emerging, and whose importance is likely to increase in the future, demands a template different from the narrower interpretation of Kautilya's principles. Technological change is driving globalization and there are new activities (such as those relating to cyberspace and outer space) which lie beyond the control of nation states.

The planet is also facing an ecological emergency. The scale of the loss of biodiversity, depletion of natural resources and environmental pollution is creating a health crisis. None of these problems can be tackled at the national or even regional level. They are global in scale and demand global responses. But nation states compete fiercely for political and territorial gains; this pursuit of selfish interests by each country can only yield minimal, least-common-denominator results when we need urgent, collaborative and maximal interventions. Here, too, I find there is a deep-rooted Indian cultural tradition that looks upon nature as a source of nurture rather than as a force to be conquered and harnessed to meet human greed. Drawing upon this ancient value system, India could take the lead in restoring the ecological integrity of our planet, not least because its own destiny is organically linked to it.

There is also the paradox of rising nationalism and fragmentation of countries based on community and regional identities, precisely when there is a pressing need for institutions and structures to manage an interconnected and globalized world. I argue that India is a rare example of a country that has been successful in managing diversity and a plural society. It has the civilizational attributes, honed over centuries, thanks to its 'crossroads' cosmopolitan culture, to help it deal with the polarization of today. But it must remain true to its precious heritage of celebrating diversity. It must resist the temptation to follow the current negative, divisive trends sweeping country after country.

~

The book is in four sections, each representing a seminal theme. The first, titled 'Traditions and History', explores the origins of India's world view and explains how they evolved into the template through which Indians look at the world around them. The experience of foreign invasions and colonial rule has also shaped independent India's foreign policy, as have post-Partition happenings in the subcontinent. These are covered in the two chapters on Indian foreign policy in the pre- and post-Cold War periods.

The second part, 'Neighbours', focuses on our complex and troubled relationship with three of our neighbouring countries – Pakistan, China and Nepal. I have not covered our other neighbours, only because I did not have much exposure to them and not because India's relations with them are less important. In analysing our relations with Pakistan, China and Nepal, I have drawn heavily from my own personal experience and understanding of the cultural and psychological factors behind these countries' perceptions of India. This section reflects my view that the Indian subcontinent is a single, interconnected geopolitical entity and ecological space with a shared history, strong cultural affinities and dense economic interdependencies. The eventual integration of this space, transcending national boundaries, will remain an enduring objective of Indian foreign policy.

Part Three explores the borderless world that is emerging in the virtual sense, driven by technological change and globalization. Energy security and climate change are twin challenges for India, requiring negotiations spanning national, regional and international concerns. Enhanced relations with individual countries have improved India's access to and participation in international arrangements. This in turn has helped improve its individual relationships with the major powers. These developments also underscore how, in the current international landscape, the line between domestic and external has become blurred. These issues have been dealt with in the chapters which describe the Indo-US nuclear deal, India's obtaining of a waiver from the Nuclear Suppliers' Group (NSG) which helped it participate fully in international civil nuclear commerce, and the negotiations over a new climate change agreement.

The Indo-US nuclear deal is an example of how India enhanced its energy security and expanded its strategic space. Meanwhile, the Copenhagen climate change summit marked the beginning of a downward slide for India, when it had to agree to a global climate change dispensation that limited its energy options. Its hopes for a strong climate change framework were dashed. Such an outcome would have minimized the adverse fallout for India. Both the nuclear deal and climate change episodes have been lessons for Indian foreign policy. This section is rounded off by a chapter titled 'Shaping the Emerging World Order and India's Role'. It offers a broad survey of the changing geopolitical terrain, the drivers of a new world order and India's place in that order.

Last in this book is an epilogue. It looks at future trends and their impact on India. Three cross-national domains are examined – the maritime, cyber and space worlds. These domains need new international institutions and governance processes for their careful regulation and management.

Most of all, there is a need for a new spirit of international collaboration that can rise above narrow national interests so that the new institutions and arrangements can be effective. And yet the world is moving in the reverse direction, with the resurgence of nationalist urges and the hardening of opposing attitudes across countries. The question is whether India will be able to draw upon its innate civilizational strengths, explored in the earlier chapters of the book, and point the world towards a future of sanity and common humanity.

Part One

Tradition and History

1

Sources of India's World View

In the Mahabharata, the narrator, Sanjaya, recalls for King Dhritarashtra the vision of the entire cosmos as a vast circle of seven concentric oceans separating six regions or *varshas*, each with its own mountains and river systems. At the centre lies Jambudvipa, described in other sacred texts as a four-petalled lotus floating in the ocean, with our own *varsha*, Bharata, defined by the southern petal. It has the Himalayas for its mountain system and mighty rivers, as do the other *varshas*, and seas surrounding its triangular shape. This is a landscape that is mythical yet hallowed, and also recognizably physical. It is a template ingrained in the collective Indian consciousness that continues to shape our view of the world around us – as it has through the centuries, irrespective of the rise and fall of empires. This vision has endured in our subconscious, prevailing over the political, social and cultural particularities that make India such a diverse country.

There are many in the West, and some in India too, who consider India an artificial construct. The British colonial administrator John Strachey declared in 1888:

> The first and most important thing to learn about India is that there is not and never was an India.

And yet India had a centralized empire under the Mauryas, covering much of the subcontinent at least a century before the Qin united only part of Han China. The distribution of Ashoka's pillars and rock edicts traces much of the same geography as the India under British colonial rule.

Alexander Cunningham, the British archaeologist who served in colonial India, cites the Greek historian Strabo on how the country beyond the Indus was described to Alexander of Macedon by those well acquainted with it:

> These learned men described the land known as India as a rhomboid, an unequal quadrilateral, in shape, with the Indus to the West, the mountains to the North and the sea on the East and the South.

Cunningham goes on to write:

> The close agreement of these dimensions, given by Alexander's informants, with the actual size of the country is very remarkable and shows that the Indians, even at that early date in their history, had a very accurate knowledge of the form and extent of their native land.

I cite this historical and, yes, mythological, background to dispel the notion that Indians have never had a shared identity beyond a certain cultural and religious affinity, or that this affinity never found political expression rooted in a defined geography.

The Mahabharata and the Ramayana also unfold across what may be called a 'sacred geography'.[1] The invading Mughals

[1] Diana Eck, *India: A Sacred Geography,* Harmony, 2012.

and then the British (notwithstanding Strachey) assumed the mantle of rule over a land and people that for millennia had had a universally acknowledged identity as India. Mughal emperors like Akbar and Jehangir commissioned Persian translations of the Mahabharata and the Ramayana. These translations contained commentaries that sought legitimacy for Mughal rule as positioned in a long line of empires and kings dating back to remote antiquity; rulers of the geographic space called India. Akbar's conquests were compared to Yudhishtira's and Lord Rama's *asvamedha* sacrifices as the indispensable ritual for a *chakravartin* or universal ruler.[2]

~

We are familiar with Kautilya's *Arthashastra* of the fourth century BCE, but *arthashastra* or the science of governance draws on even older treatises. Kautilya himself refers to them. A later work in Sanskrit, the *Nitisara* of Kamandaki, probably dating to the fourth or fifth century CE, more specifically refers to several older works and authors, as also to the different theories propounded by them.[3] Interstate relations figured in these works as an essential part of statecraft.

There are other texts, such as the *Bhagavata Purana*, which are in the nature of discourses by ancient sages or

---

[2]The *asvamedha* sacrifice involved letting loose a royal horse and claiming for the king the territory it covered uncontested or the lands in its path that were under local rulers who surrendered to the overlordship of the king. If any ruler resisted the king's army was at hand to subdue him. On the Mughal fascination with *chakravartin* and the *asvamedha* ritual, see Audrey Truschke, *Culture of Encounters: Sanskrit at the Mughal Court*, Allen Lane, 2016.

[3] *The Nitisara of Kamandaki*, Asiatic Society, Kolkata, 1st ed. 1849–1884.

scholars focused on the nature, role and responsibilities of kingship. The sage Naradmuni was no less than a celestial diplomat, ranging between heaven and earth, sometimes acting as a conciliator, sometimes a wise counsellor, but often as an instigator of conflict and dissent. The *Narada Purana* is a massive repository of his exploits. The management of interstate relations also figures in some of these texts.

The *Arthashastra* of Kautilya[4] is undoubtedly the most important Indian treatise on statecraft. Kautilya, also known as Chanakya, may have served as a counsellor to Chandragupta Maurya, founder of the Mauryan empire. He declared in this work that 'the welfare of the State depends on an active foreign policy'. What is of interest to geopolitical strategists and foreign policy practitioners is the extraordinarily detailed section on foreign policy in the *Arthashastra*, which provides a flexible and dynamic theoretical framework for the conduct of interstate relations.

The setting is, in modern terms, a multistate or multipolar landscape of contending states. The perspective through which foreign policy options are evaluated is that of a *vijigisu* – one desirous of conquest. But the principles on which the options are based can apply to any state. The basic template, as per which progressively more complex interrelationships are explored, is an elementary *mandala*, which Kautilya describes in this way:

> The Conqueror shall think of the circle of states as a wheel – himself as the hub, and his allies, drawn to him by the spokes though separated by intervening territory, as its rim.

---

[4] Kautilya, *The Arthashastra*, trans. L.N. Rangarajan, Penguin India, 2000.

The intervening territory may contain hostile, neutral, strong, weak or even vassal states, their precise pattern in the territory defining the *vijigisu*'s foreign policy strategy.

When setting out to expand his empire, the *vijigisu* must ensure that he possesses the seven constituents of state power, which have a surprising contemporary resonance and are echoed in the modern concept of 'comprehensive national power'. These are:

- Political leadership – *svamin*
- Good governance through counsellors – *amatyas*
- Territory and people – *janapada* or *rashtra*
- The economy – *kosha*
- Fortifications – *durga*
- Military power – *danda*
- Allies – *mitras*

Taking an approach rooted in prudence, Kautilya then goes on to formulate foreign policy options for an active and expanding state in a multistate setting when confronted with a hostile state (*vigraha*). The options are:

- Seeking peace through treaty – *sandhi*
- Staying neutral – *asana*
- Marching on an expedition – *yana*
- Seeking protection from stronger states – *samshraya*
- Pursuing a dual policy of war with one state and peace with another – *dvaidhibhava*

Based on these categories of states (hostile or friendly, for example) and actions, which can exist or take place in several permutations and combinations, Kautilya builds his international relations theory along the form of the *mandala* or organizing principle. One must be careful not to become mechanistic in applying this template to contemporary situations but there is no doubt that as a method of managing a multipolar, multistate scenario the *Arthashastra* has much to teach us.

The Kautilyan tradition of statecraft was acknowledged and elaborated on by several later masters. For those in the world of diplomacy, the *Nitisara* of Kamandaki is also a truly remarkable text. It builds on the work of Kautilya and earlier scholars, and also uses the *mandala* as a conceptual framework for examining interstate relations. At the most basic level is the state, which has a set of immediate neighbours and a set of neighbours' neighbours. This is the elementary *mandala*. The states that are immediate neighbours have an inherent tendency to be hostile towards the protagonist state in question. The immediate neighbours' own neighbours, in turn, are likely to be potential allies to the protagonist state since they are subject to the same dynamic with respect to their own immediate neighbours. But these categories are not immutable and can change depending on the circumstances.

The 'instruments' to be used in handling situations involving neighbouring states are the same as in the *Arthashastra*: *sama* (conciliation or alliance), *dana* (placating and winning over with gifts), *danda* (punishing through the use of force) and *bheda* (sowing dissension). The *Nitisara* clearly lays down that *danda* – the use of coercive power or war – is the last resort after all other options have failed. The tradition also attaches higher value to wise counsel (*mantra-shakti*) than to the power of the king based on his treasury, his army (*prabhava)* or his own energetic temperament (*utsaha-shakti*). It enjoins the ruler to make a clear determination between what is attainable and what is not through cool and intelligent deliberation, that is, through the application of *mantra-shakti*.[5]

Kamandaki devotes a separate chapter to the role of diplomats and diplomacy titled 'Dutapracana'.[6] This is an ancient Indian version of British diplomat Ernest Satow's *A Guide to Diplomatic Practice* first published in 1917. Satow's book, regarded as a classic, was our bible when I joined the Indian Foreign Service in 1970. At that time, unfortunately, neither my colleagues nor I knew anything about India's own fascinating and still very relevant contribution to the theory and practice of diplomacy. We only turned to British sources.

Kamandaki lists three categories of royal ambassadors: the first is empowered by the king to take decisions while on a mission, something like a plenipotentiary these days; the second has limited and specific powers, perhaps like the ranking diplomat of today who is assigned specific representational responsibilities; and the third has the role of an envoy who is only an emissary with the task of delivering and receiving messages on behalf of his king. The *Nitisara* goes into considerable detail about the qualities of a royal ambassador and the manner in which he should conduct himself while on a mission. The following quotes give a flavour of Kamandaki's precepts:

> A royal ambassador should be an expert debater with a good memory and eloquence and well versed in military science as well as in the *sastras* and sufficiently experienced in ambassadorial functions.
>
> He should patiently bear with abusive words (of the

[5] *Sarga* XII, *Prakarana* 7, *Nitisara.*

[6] *Sarga* XIII, *Prakarana* 18, *Nitisara.*

> adversary) and himself avoid sensual impulses and anger as well as sleeping in the company of others. He should by all means maintain the secrecy of his own feelings (or plans of action). On the other hand he should ascertain the feelings of others.[7]

These are wise words of advice which our diplomats today would do well to follow even if their predecessors often did not.

~

India's world view is worth examining within the framework of the *mandala* as described in the old treatises on Indian statecraft. Studying the Jambudvipa *mandala* from our ancient texts, one is struck by the fact that it does not ascribe centrality and superiority to Bharatvarsha, which is only one among the lotus petals that make up our universe. Each of the concentric circles in the *mandala* that radiates outwards is superior to the preceding one. This is the reverse of the Chinese world view, which sees the Han core as the most advanced, with the increasingly larger circles symbolizing the more barbaric and the less civilized. India will never have a 'middle kingdom complex'. It accepts a world in which there are other *dvipas* or islands with their own characteristics and values.

The Jambudvipa *mandala* has a more direct bearing on how India looks at the Indian subcontinent in the modern context. The Indian subcontinent and the eastern and western reaches of the Indian Ocean surrounding it are reflected in the Jambudvipa as a single, interconnected geopolitical and

---

[7]I am indebted to Ambassador A.N.D. Haksar for bringing the *Nitisara* to my attention in his contribution to Vol.1 of the IDSA publication *Indigenous Historical Knowledge: Kautilya and His Vocabulary*, Pentagon Press, 2015.

geo-economic unit with a common history. It is considered a shared cultural space with its constituents enjoying significant economic complementarities.

In the past, political divisions tended to be more diffuse. The current theory of international relations takes the Westphalian state as its basic unit – an independent political entity with sovereignty over its territory and domestic affairs. But this became the norm only after the mid-seventeenth century, when the more nebulous and shifting frontiers of the past began congealing into rigid national boundaries. In an earlier age, successive empires reinforced the multiple networks binding the Indian subcontinent together. Invaders, migrants and traders soon became absorbed in these networks, enriching them and being enriched in return.

This closely interconnected entity is fragmented today, with the subcontinent divided into several sovereign, independent states, India being by far its largest and most powerful entity. This being so, the country's strategic compulsions are still defined by subcontinental concerns that override existing political divisions. It cannot insulate its security from developments within its neighbouring countries. Jawaharlal Nehru was reflecting this reality when he said that the Himalayas constituted India's security perimeter even though some sections of the range fell within the territory of other states such as Nepal. Equally, the country's influence cannot expand beyond the subcontinent without first transcending the political boundaries that divide the subcontinent. India is unable to connect with its extended neighbourhood in the Gulf and Central Asia because its historical contiguity with these geographies is interrupted by Pakistan. In the east, Bangladesh forms a political barrier to India's seamless linking with the South East Asian neighbourhood, although this is gradually being overcome as relations between India and Bangladesh improve.

The situation is complicated by the overlapping ethnicities, kinship and linguistic ties that spill across national boundaries in the subcontinent. People living in West Bengal and Bangladesh share a common language and culture. Tribal communities like the Nagas and the Mizos reside on both sides of the boundary separating India and Myanmar. There are disputes over the divided use of shared natural resources such as rivers and forests.

Since Independence, the persistent challenge for India is the reconciliation of its security interests – which cover the entire subcontinent – with the reality of a divided polity. There are only two ways that an analyst can see India restoring a coherent, unified and effective strategy for the subcontinent given its geographic, historic and cultural reality. One is by being powerful enough to impose its security perspective on other countries in the subcontinent in the manner of a Pax Indica. The other is by designing political, economic, cultural and security policies to create a web of interdependencies. These approaches can help the country work around, though not erase, the existing subcontinental political boundaries. If it chooses to create a web of interdependencies, India could take advantage of its size and its asymmetrical strengths vis-à-vis its neighbours to achieve a level of interconnectedness that would render borders irrelevant.

The positive experience of dense engagement and productive cooperation would, over time, create a common strategic perspective encompassing the subcontinent as a whole and be reflected in a shared regional identity and the pursuit of shared political, economic and security interests vis-à-vis the rest of the world. At least that is the hope. Whatever be the approach – overwhelming dominance or cooperative engagement – the enduring challenge is the same, though it has manifested in different ways during different historical phases. India's challenge is to transform the contested territory into one aligned with its own more expansive and expanding global objectives. The status of being the largest country in the subcontinent still resonates with the mental map that lies embedded in India's consciousness. There is a constant effort, even if only at the subconscious level, to rise above the political divisions in the subcontinent so that the ancient geography becomes whole again.

There is another unique element in India's world view that is shaped by its geography and history. India is a classic example of crossroads culture. Its peninsular character put it astride the major maritime routes dictated by the monsoon winds, both east and west. It also lay at the intersection of caravan routes linking Central Asia and China to distant nations in the Mediterranean. Its traders were a familiar sight in ancient Greece and Rome, as they were in South East Asia and China. When Ashoka sent Buddhist missions to foreign countries in the third century BCE, he was doubtless reaching out to those with whom India already had trade and even political links. In Edict XIII, Ashoka refers to missions he sent 'to the Yona (Greek) king Antiyoka (Antiochos II of Syria, 261–246 BC), Turamaya (Ptolemais II Philadelphos, 285–247 BC), Antikini (Antigonos Gonatas of Macedonia, 276–239 BC), Maka (Magas of Cyrene, 300–250 BC) and Alikasudara (probably Alexander of Epirus 272–255 BC)'.

In South East Asia we still see the deep imprint of the long-standing and close interaction that took place with India for centuries, until these links were severed by the rise of European colonialism. India's engagement with its South East Asian neighbourhood was extraordinary in its scope, covering political, economic, cultural, religious and social activity. It spanned a vast expanse of time, resulting in a rich layering of mutual influences. The Bali Yatra in Odisha still celebrates what must have been regular sailings from India to the Indonesian archipelago in the past.

There is a misperception in some circles that South East Asia got all its culture and art from India. Throughout the region one does encounter the colours and sounds of India but the cultural assets borrowed from it were transformed into exquisite works of local genius and creativity. Each side stimulated the imagination of the other, each encounter triggered an efflorescence of creative innovation. For India, much of South East Asia was 'Suvarnabhumi', the land of gold. Indian textiles and designs travelled to the region, and designs and motifs from the region influenced Indian designs and techniques. The Ramayana and the Mahabharata became popular in Myanmar, Thailand, Cambodia and Indonesia, their basic narratives often embellished with local legends and characters. One can see this in the spectacular performance of the Ramayana at the Prambanan temple in Jogjakarta, where local genius has added flavours and colours that are uniquely Indonesian.

It is only now that India is reconnecting with this neighbourhood, at once familiar yet with a proud identity of its own.

Indian engagement over the centuries has stretched to China's eastern seaboard and to Japan and Korea. In the eighth century CE, it was an Indian Brahmin priest, Bodhisena, then serving in the kingdom of Cambodge (Cambodia), who was invited by the Japanese emperor for the consecration of the great Buddha statue at Nara. He is credited with writing down the rituals for the ceremony and composing the sacred music. (Several Buddhist kingdoms in South East Asia retained Brahmin priests for their court and religious rituals, and one sees this practice even today in Thailand.) Bodhisena's musical score is still preserved in the royal palace, and the music is performed once a year by royal musicians. It is known as *gugaku* (ancient music) and a trained Indian ear can discern that it is based on the classical Carnatic raga Mohanam, whose north Indian version is known as Bhupali. Even today the Koreans celebrate an Indian princess who married a royal ancestor. The Buddhist heritage continues to generate a strong affinity for India in these countries.

Our ancient and rich seaborne trade with these nations is seeing a contemporary revival. Today the Asia-Pacific region is the most dynamic component of India's external economic relations, whether in terms of trade, investment or tourism. India is beginning to reconnect with Asia.

Central Asia too was once part of India's extended neighbourhood, and the string of Buddhist monasteries that flourished along the caravan routes over several centuries is testimony to this. These routes traversed some of the highest mountain ranges in the world – the western Himalayas and the forbidding expanses of the Karakoram range. Despite its difficult terrain, remoteness and generally inhospitable environment, this mountain zone has nurtured extraordinarily rich and culturally diverse communities, constituting a veritable ethnic mosaic. The Uighurs, Uzbeks, Tajiks, Kirghiz, Kazakhs and Afghans who travelled along these caravan routes mingled with pilgrims, traders and adventurers from both India and China. These communities have for centuries inhabited the fertile valleys and oases that dot this mountain zone. Ancient trade and pilgrimage routes also criss-crossed the length and breadth of this immense cluster of the world's highest peaks. The myriad communities who call this land their own have long coexisted with one another. Empires and powerful states may have put markers all over this region, staking their claims and demanding allegiance, but the region has been throughout history a zone of shifting political tides, not amenable to the concepts of boundaries or lines that nation states are built upon.

India's extended Central Asian neighbourhood is an ethnic jigsaw bearing overlapping footprints of the world's major religions – Hinduism, Buddhism, Islam and even Zoroastrianism. The great city of Bukhara derives its name from the Sanskrit word *vihara* and the large number of Buddhist monasteries it housed. It is also through Central Asia that Indian mathematical treatises, medicine systems and astronomy travelled to the Arab world, and later to Europe.[8] In addition, India still bears the imprint of its Mughal emperors who came from Central Asia in the fifteenth century CE.

Like India, this mountain region too is home to a veritable crossroads culture that cannot be easily uprooted.

~

At its height, the British Indian empire inherited the historical and cultural legacy that bound India to its extended neighbourhood. Delhi ruled from Aden in the west to Singapore in the east on behalf of London, and sought to safeguard northern India from the threatening advance of the Russian empire. Indian currency, particularly the silver rupee, was in use across this neighbourhood. When I visited the ancient caravan town of Kashgar in Chinese Xinjiang in 1984, the silversmiths in the older part of the town still carried a large hoard of Indian silver rupees, which had been the preferred medium of exchange even in the early 1950s.

It is likely that as India's economic and security capabilities increase, its influence will expand into the extended

---

[8] S. Frederick Starr, *Lost Enlightenment*, Princeton University Press, 2015.

neighbourhood of the past, along the remembered pathways of its old crossroads encounters. Throughout history India was a remarkably cosmopolitan place with diverse ethnicities, religions and cultures. And its embrace of plurality is not contrived. This makes the Indian remarkably adaptable, at ease in the world and accepting of its diversity. Maybe this is the Indian diaspora's secret of success. Twenty-first-century India's acceptance of globalization, though still somewhat hesitant, is a reassertion of the historical trend.

What then can be described as an Indian world view? What is the template that influences India's relationship with the rest of the world? The answers to these questions will sum up this chapter.

One, there is an immemorial and abiding sense of affinity drawn from a geography cosmic in origin but reflected in the physical attributes of the subcontinent. This is intrinsic to the sense of being Indian and is anchored in the geography of the subcontinent. This sense of affinity is overlaid by a modern nationalism but has echoes of the mental map inherited from the past. Overcoming the fragmentation of this historical and cultural space is the challenge. The idea of making the subcontinent whole again is a powerful driver of India's foreign policy behaviour.

Two, India's location at the intersection of major caravan and maritime routes in the past has afforded a certain innate cosmopolitan outlook and comfort in dealing with diverse cultures and peoples. Its embrace of pluralism is deeply rooted, almost instinctive, and this is an asset in an increasingly globalized world.

Three, India will reach out along the very same remembered pathways traced by its history – extending to the eastern and western reaches of the Indian Ocean and to the Central Asian neighbourhood to the north and west – as its economic and security capabilities expand. In Central Asia, India still echoes in the cultures of the erstwhile states of the former Soviet Union and Afghanistan, where Indian traders and Buddhist missionaries have left their imprint upon the mountain and desert landscapes. To the west, Indian influence radiates along the Gulf and the eastern seaboard of Africa. To the east, India will retrace its historical footsteps to South East Asia, the eastern coast of China and as far as Japan. Beyond the subcontinent, all this is India's extended neighbourhood.

2

Foreign Policy from Independence to the End of the Cold War

The world view and principles laid down in India's classical treatises on statecraft are in many ways still evident in the conduct of independent India's foreign policy. I must repeat here that we should be careful not to mechanistically apply these principles to contemporary situations. The principles are best seen as a frame of reference that influences decision-making in foreign policy.

Before we analyse independent India's foreign policy and its resonance with the past and the present, we need conceptual clarity on what constitutes foreign policy and also what constitutes diplomatic practice.

~

Foreign policy guides a state's relations with other states, its relations with regional and multilateral organizations and, increasingly, in our globalized and interconnected world, with non-state actors and civil society organizations that recognize no borders. In a broad sense, foreign policy is the strategy a state adopts to advance its national interests as articulated by its political leadership but within a contested geopolitical space characterized by complex interstate relations. There is a degree of relativity to the calculation of national interests which must take into account the interests of other states. There is a constant process of bargaining and seeking trade-offs between competing objectives. National interests, therefore, cannot and should not be ascribed absolute values. It is within a zone of relativity that diplomacy can enable accommodation, compromise and conciliation among states. Assigning absolute values to perceived national interests may undermine rather than enhance national security. It can pre-empt cooperation with other states or lead to situations that adversely affect the interests of the state.

For instance, while negotiating the Indo-US nuclear deal, the question of future nuclear weapons testing by India was a contentious issue. There were arguments insisting that the right of India to test such weapons in the future should be incorporated in the agreement. On the other hand, the Americans wanted a specific provision that the cooperation would come to an end if India did indeed carry out a nuclear test in the future. India could not accept a legal undertaking not to carry out nuclear tests at a future date; equally it would have been unreasonable for it to insist that its right to test be legally recognized by states which had, in the Comprehensive Test Ban Treaty (CTBT), given up their legal entitlement to test. We found a compromise whereby our right to test was left to our sovereign decision even though we implicitly acknowledged we could not insist on our partners continuing their civil nuclear cooperation with us if we ever decided to test. To insist that our right to test be explicitly acknowledged in an international instrument would have been in the nature of a demand based on an absolute interpretation of our national interest and would have precluded a creative compromise which retained this right for us even while recognizing the interests of our partners.

There are situations when public opinion is inflamed and the people demand action by the state without regard to the 'prudence' that Kautilya considers a key principle of statecraft. We see this often in Indian media coverage of Chinese activism on our borders or in our neighbourhood. The state should not allow itself to be pressured by public opinion into actions that may lead to consequences worse than the original problem.

Foreign policy seeks to safeguard and, wherever possible, expand a country's strategic space. This concept is best understood as the capacity of a state to take relatively autonomous decisions on matters of vital interest. The more the options or alternatives available to a state to achieve its objectives, the more this capacity is enhanced. In international relations, the fewer the alternatives available to you, the more likely that friends will take you for granted and adversaries will be emboldened to undermine you. Therefore a successful foreign policy is one that provides a country's political leadership with a range of options or alternatives to draw from to achieve its defined objectives.

~

Diplomacy concerns the implementation of foreign policy objectives using a range of instruments, such as interstate dialogue; negotiation of treaties, rules or norms; and the influencing of external political and public opinion. To borrow a military analogy, foreign policy may be likened to a weapon and diplomacy to its delivery system. If diplomacy is weak then even the best foreign policy would be ineffective. Diplomacy must not be confused with foreign policy, and the shortcomings of one should not be ascribed to the other.

What does a diplomat do? He is the *duta* or envoy, and his role has been described in Kautilya's *Arthashastra* and Kamandaki's *Nitisara*.

In his celebrated book, *The Principles and Practice of Diplomacy*, K.M. Panikkar relates an episode from the Mahabharata to illustrate an envoy's role:

> Sri Krishna, when he was being requested by Yudhisthira to go as a special envoy to the Court of the Kauravas, was asked by Draupadi what his purpose was in undertaking so hopeless a mission. He replied, 'I shall go to the Kaurava Court to present your case in the best light; to try and get them to accept your demands, and if my efforts fail and war becomes inevitable, we shall show the world how we are right and they are wrong so that the world may not misjudge between us.' All the secrets of diplomacy are contained in this statement of Sri Krishna.

One should also be aware that in the practise of diplomacy, it is important to separate the substantive content of policy from its public projection. For a diplomat, the first order of business is to determine the substance of a policy measure based on India's national interest. How it is to be packaged for the public is to be determined thereafter, taking into account the public opinion environment both at home and abroad. For example, the competitive relationship between India and China is a reality that Indian foreign policy will have to contend with. However, it has so far been convenient for both countries to show that neither is a threat to the other and that there is enough space in Asia and the world for both India and China to rise together.

In other cases, public projection may serve to reinforce the substantive policy. For example, in post-Independence India, non-alignment was, in substance, a policy assuring relative autonomy to a newly emerging country in a polarized international environment. However, non-alignment was also presented to the public as an ethical posture contributing to international peace and promoting solidarity among countries emerging from colonial rule. The public posture reinforced the substantive policy. The diplomat must be constantly aware of this and never confuse policy with rhetoric.

To quote Nehru: 'Every nation places its own interests first in developing foreign policy. Fortunately, India's interests coincide with peaceful foreign policy and cooperation with all progressive nations.'

I believe India's foreign policy is well thought out and crafted, and a reasonably 'potent weapon'. It is our delivery system that leaves much to be desired. There is also a tendency among political leaders and often even among professional diplomats to confuse rhetoric with substance. Whether Indian foreign policy should be based on unalloyed 'realpolitik' bereft of any moral or ethical anchor or whether it should aspire to a higher purpose, transcending in some way the essentially competitive character of interstate relations, is a matter of debate.

There is the starkly utilitarian, even brutal world of Kautilya's *Arthashastra*, with its reliance on *sama, dana, danda* and *bheda*. There is also the world of Ashoka's Dhamma with its novel view of state policy, infusing it with a moral obligation for the welfare of the people. Chanakya's theories were from the perspective of an aspiring hegemon in a multistate environment. His client is a revisionist state trying to overthrow the existing order. Ashoka's approach was more appropriate to a self-satisfied hegemonic state trying to preserve the existing order – a status quo power, in contemporary parlance. The appeal to higher principles is often the hallmark of a hegemonic state.

But there is also a sense of common humanity in the Indian temperament. There is an echo of a more ancient Hindu concept of *vasudhaiva kutumbakam*, which translates to 'common humanity'. These contrasting strains, often intertwined, have been a constant feature of Indian foreign policy since Independence.

Foreign policy in the Indian context is deeply influenced by the world view I have written about in the first chapter of this book. It is also influenced by history, particularly the bitter experience of foreign rule and humiliation. There is a political consensus in India that the country must never again allow the subordination of its people to alien rule or domination. This underlies India's search for autonomy in all its activities in the global arena, a running theme in post-Independence foreign policy behaviour. This is also the essence of non-alignment, as promoted by India's first prime minister, Jawaharlal Nehru, and remains the underpinning of our current foreign policy, even if the label of non-alignment is no longer favoured.

Nehru was also convinced that the extent of India's territory, its large population, its civilizational identity and its growing economy marked the country for a global role and influence. It was his conviction that a non-aligned foreign policy would enable India to pursue its destiny as a great power.

~

Non-alignment as a guiding principle of Indian foreign policy was adopted by Nehru soon after Independence. It is important to understand the domestic and international setting in which this policy was enunciated. The end of the Second World War brought with it the hope of enduring international peace and the end of colonial rule across the world. The creation of the United Nations (UN) heralded a more inclusive and relatively democratic pattern of global governance. Even though it did not find a place in the exclusive club of the UN Security Council, where the five victorious nations constituted a privileged global steering committee with veto power, India welcomed the new institution as a platform for newly independent countries such as itself to participate in the shaping of the post-war international order. To leaders of the new India, particularly Jawaharlal Nehru, the coincidental dawn of the atomic age with the threat of mass annihilation placed a very significant responsibility on the UN to maintain peace and international security. So, for the time being, the UN Security Council and the facts of its permanent membership were tolerated as a practical response.

The relatively swift advent of the Cold War put newly independent India and the other developing nations emerging from colonial rule in a dilemma. There were now two military blocs in the world, one led by the United States (US) and the other by the Soviet Union, whose growing ideological differences were threatening world peace. To become part of one or the other alliance would inevitably lead to the subordination of national interests to the demands of the alliance, particularly to the demands of the alliance leader.

Thus if India had become an ally of the US during the Cold War, it would have had to treat the Soviet Union as an enemy state despite there being no threat to Indian interests from the latter. It may have had to fight alongside the US in the Vietnam War despite having no stake. This would be a negation of the very independence India had fought for. The concept of non-alignment was a response to this dilemma. India decided, rightly in retrospect, that its interests would be better served by staying out of the competing alliance systems. On the contrary, the country would have a better chance of preserving its precious political freedom and promoting its economic development by maintaining friendly relations with both blocs.

For Nehru, non-alignment was different from neutrality, which would have meant not taking a position on issues under dispute between the competing powers. Non-alignment meant active engagement and a role in dealing with the key regional and international issues of the day. India's delegation to the UN had a big hand in drafting the historic Declaration of Human Rights. And it was India that mobilized the UN against apartheid in South Africa. It emerged as a relentless champion in the early global movement for creating a world free of nuclear weapons despite opposition from the nuclear weapons states.

India has not hesitated to play an active role in several regional conflicts and to undertake UN peacekeeping missions, a tradition that continues to this day. In the early post-Independence period, for example, India was the country of choice to head the International Control Commission on Laos, Cambodia and Vietnam. It also served on the Korean Armistice Commission after the Korean War. This was the result of non-aligned India being seen as a credible and trusted international actor, able to work as a bridge between the Cold War rivals. The growing ranks of countries emerging from colonial rule placed great confidence in India.

This reputation may have diminished somewhat after India's defeat in the border war with China in 1962 (see Chapter 7). But India continued to be a champion for the cause of developing countries in the succeeding decades too. Under Indira Gandhi, and later under Rajiv Gandhi, India regained a prominent international profile in areas such as disarmament, environmental affairs, international economic governance and the North–South dialogue.

As a young diplomat representing India at the Conference on Disarmament in Geneva and at the UN in New York in the early 1980s, I observed with great pride the respect shown to India by the large constituency of developing countries. They often took their cue from us in articulating their own positions and sought our advice on various topics. We were called upon to help draft UN documents and to speak on behalf of developing countries at many international events. This profile is less sharp now as we seek to pursue a foreign policy more narrowly focused on our own interests. The developing world too no longer stands as one, its diversity of interests making it difficult to arrive at common positions.

There is a perception that non-alignment restricted India's security choices during the Cold War. The record shows otherwise. Non-alignment assured the country its autonomy in the realm of international relations.

Despite being outside military alliances, India was able to pursue security arrangements with several friendly countries, even for the acquisition of defence hardware and technology. When access to Western arms was restricted after the India–Pakistan War of 1965, India was able to craft a partnership with Moscow, which enhanced its long-term military preparedness. A strategic partnership is different in nature from a military alliance because it is based on an equal relationship anchored in shared interests. Both India and the then Soviet Union had shared concerns about China and Pakistan, which enjoyed the support of both the US and China. This alliance also helped India deflect growing pressure from the West to make concessions to Pakistan on the Kashmir issue. The West made this a condition for its continued supply of arms to India in the wake of the India–China border war.

It is important to make a distinction between non-alignment as a foreign policy choice for India and the Non-Aligned Movement (NAM). As pointed out earlier, India became a natural leader among the newly independent countries across Asia and Africa, many of which wished to preserve their hard-won political independence. They wanted to join hands for a more equitable international order that would also support their development aspirations. The Afro–Asian conference in Bandung in 1955, which was initiated by Nehru and supported by the Indonesian president Sukarno, was a precursor to the NAM. It was the first major gathering of developing nations across ideological and political affiliations and had even China among the participants. The conference consolidated the role of uncommitted nations that saw themselves as agencies for peace between the Cold War rivals and their respective military alliances.

In 1961, led by Nehru, Egypt's Gamal Abdel Nasser, Ghana's Kwame Nkrumah and Yugoslavia's Josip Broz Tito, the NAM was born as a movement of developing countries that shunned military alliances and wished to jointly play a role in promoting peace, disarmament and development. Leadership of the NAM also fetched India great political leverage in its relations with the superpowers and their allies, compensating to some extent its lack of significant economic and military capabilities. While the NAM lost much of its relevance with the end of the Cold War, non-alignment as a principle governing Indian foreign policy remains relevant to this day.

Now it is fashionable to trash the idea of non-alignment these days as a moralistic posture that neglected India's vital interests. While it is true that India projected non-alignment as the expression of an ethical foreign policy favourable to international peace, this position was based on a realistic assessment of Cold War geopolitics and the requirements for maintaining the country's room for manoeuvre. In his 2014 book, *World Order*, Henry Kissinger has acknowledged the logic behind non-alignment, drawing an interesting parallel between India and the US's own early history:

> India's conduct during the Cold War was very similar to that of the United States in its formative decades. Emerging into a world of established powers and the Cold War, independent India, like the early United States, skilfully elevated freedom of manouevre from a bargaining tactic into an ethical principle. Blending righteous moralism with shrewd assessment of the balance of forces and the major powers' psychologies, Nehru announced India to be a global power that would chart a course manoeuvring between the major blocs.

Kissinger greatly appreciates this policy:

> The essence of this strategy was that it allowed India to draw support from both Cold War camps – securing the military aid and diplomatic cooperation of the Soviet bloc, even while courting American development assistance and the moral support of the US intellectual establishment. However irritating to Cold War America, it was a wise course for an emerging nation. With a nascent military establishment and underdeveloped economy, India would have been a respected but secondary ally in either superpower's camp. As a free agent, it could exercise a much wider reaching influence.

During the Cold War era, India pursued a policy of economic self-reliance, rejecting the export- and foreign-investment-led growth strategies favoured by the East Asian and later South East Asian countries. This did not prevent it from being a principal character in international trade negotiations for a new and more equitable international economic order. Its activism has continued at the World Trade Organization (WTO).

What drives India's increased influence as a major power today is the confluence of its tradition of global political engagement with the more recent global economic engagement. Increased participation in the global economy through trade and investment has also transformed the nature, scope and scale of its political engagement with the world. But it must be recognized that this new engagement is still aimed at increasing India's influence and relationships with other countries, multiplying its development and security options and preserving its ability to take relatively autonomous decisions on matters that are of vital national interest. In that sense, the spirit of non-alignment remains a compass for India's foreign policy, even though the original Cold War context no longer exists. This will be apparent when we later examine how India responded to a dramatically transformed international environment with the end of the Cold War.

~

India's overall foreign policy also took shape in response to the crucial challenges it had to confront following its birth as an independent nation.

In the early years of independence, two major developments occurred, which have remained the defining elements in India's foreign policy calculations. The first was the partition of India in 1947 and the attendant conflict with Pakistan over Jammu and Kashmir. A barrier now appeared, both political and geographical, in the form of Pakistan-occupied Kashmir, which includes the regions of Gilgit and Baltistan. This stood in the way of India's land access to Afghanistan, the Gulf, West Asia and Central Asia. While India was able to retain the major part of Jammu and Kashmir, it did not recover Gilgit and Baltistan, which would have at least assured access to Afghanistan and Central Asia. Till the present day, India's Afghan and Central Asian strategy is severely constrained as a result. In the east, the erstwhile East Pakistan reduced India's access to its north-east to a narrow and threatened corridor. The creation of an independent Bangladesh in 1971 reduced the security threat but the relative isolation of India's north-east is only now being tackled as relations between India and Bangladesh improve.

The second development was the annexation of Tibet by China, which for the first time in history, extended a relatively short border between China's Xinjiang province and India's Jammu and Kashmir state to a vast frontier between Asia's two largest countries. This impinged directly on India's strategic space.

Over the past seven decades, it is the impact and persistent consequences of these two developments that have greatly complicated India's foreign policy concerns at the subcontinental level. The China–Pakistan alliance, which crystallized over time, has only intensified this problem. I have discussed this in detail in Chapter 6.

China's occupation of Tibet in 1950 initially created the conditions for India to consolidate its presence and influence in the sub-Himalayan region. Nepal, Sikkim and Bhutan were, in the early years, fearful of China. India was able to continue with the traditional British policy of guaranteeing their defence and remained the dominant presence in these countries.

With respect to the island countries of Sri Lanka and the Maldives, India inherited the mandate of providing for their security as British power receded. Meanwhile, the overwhelming reach of the US Navy did create anxieties, which manifested in the advocacy of the Indian Ocean as a 'Zone of Peace'.

India's response to local crises in its neighbourhood that impinged on or had the potential to impinge on its security interests also influenced the evolution of its foreign policy. An example of this is India's intervention in Myanmar in the 1950s which enabled its prime minister U Nu's government to counter the Karen insurgency threatening the country's heartland.

In 1971, Indian prime minister Indira Gandhi dispatched security forces to assist her Sri Lankan counterpart Sirimavo Bandaranaike to tackle the JVP[1] uprising in the island country. The same year, Indian military intervention helped to create independent Bangladesh, a major strategic gain. In 1975, perceiving the threat of secession by Sikkim's ruling Chogyal (or king), that territory was incorporated into the Indian Union. In the 1980s too, India took decisive action by sending Indian Peace Keeping Forces to secure its interests in Sri Lanka, then embroiled in a violent civil war against Tamil militants. In the same decade, India intervened militarily in the Maldives to prevent an attempted coup against its president. And throughout the 1990s, it gave military and financial assistance to the Northern Alliance fighting the Pakistan-sponsored Taliban regime in Afghanistan.

[1]JVP: The Janatha Vimukti Peranuna led by Marxist youths which tried to overthrow the government through an armed insurrection.

Some Indian interventions have been political and diplomatic. India played a role in the restoration of multiparty democracy in Nepal in 1990–91, and also during the tumultuous events of 2004–05, when the Nepali monarchy was forced to yield to a civilian political coalition. The Maoist insurgency movement was brought into this coalition and into mainstream politics mainly through Indian efforts (see Chapter 5 for a detailed account).

If we examine these interventions from a broader perspective, they reveal a pattern of behaviour driven by the subcontinental imperatives described above, to ensure that Indian security interests in the subcontinent were not threatened. They flowed from an acknowledgement that while India would respect the independence and sovereignty of its neighbours, it would not hesitate to intervene if its security interests were threatened. There was also an implicit recognition that, in terms of the Kautilyan template, its neighbours would inevitably try to constrain India by engaging with more powerful countries both within and outside the region. This would remain an ever-present diplomatic challenge. But if this tendency created a threat beyond a certain threshold, India would take action. Of course, this went against the principle of non-intervention advocated by it on the international stage, but closer home, realpolitik would be ever the stronger driver.

The emergence of China as a united communist state, and its early and determined moves to establish and consolidate its control using military force over the vast territories of Xinjiang and Tibet, which bordered India, brought the two Asian giants to each other's doorsteps. Nehru had little doubt that China posed a threat to India but acknowledged that India did not possess sufficient military resources to confront China militarily over Tibet.

The response to the China challenge was therefore

initially focused on promoting a bilateral understanding that acknowledged China's assertion of sovereignty over Tibet but assured for Tibet a high degree of regional autonomy, its religious and cultural identity, and its special relations with India. There was also a calculated effort to promote China's political integration into emerging regional arrangements such as the Bandung process and to champion its permanent membership of the UN Security Council in place of Taiwan. Such a socialization process would restrain China's tendencies towards unilateral action, it was believed. This seemed to work initially in the period up to 1959, despite emerging differences over the alignment of the Sino-Indian boundary (see Chapter 6). It was the revolt in Tibet and India's grant of asylum to the Dalai Lama in 1959 that triggered a sharp downslide in the interaction between the two countries, culminating in the border war of 1962.

The confrontation between India and China created a steadfast convergence of China's and Pakistan's strategic interests, now targeted at their common adversary, India. India responded by aligning itself more closely with the Soviet Union, which, despite its ideological inclinations, shared its perception of China as a threat. The Soviet Union was willing to use its status as a permanent member of the UN Security Council to neutralize Western pressures on India on the issue of Kashmir by using its veto power.

In time, a strong and long-lasting defence partnership developed between India and the Soviet Union. This was further strengthened when the US and China established a virtual alliance in 1971. This is a textbook example of the dynamics of Kautilya's *mandala* of interstate relations. For India, a closer alignment with the Soviet Union was logical, given the superpower's own emerging adversarial, indeed hostile, relations with China. For the Soviet Union, India was its neighbour's neighbour, with the shared imperative of restraining China. Similarly, China saw in Pakistan a useful proxy against India – the pattern of allying with the hostile neighbour's neighbour coming into play. In 1971, during the Bangladesh war, India prevented China from intervening in support of Pakistan by signing the Indo-Soviet Treaty of Friendship.

The Sino-Pakistan alliance has persisted and narrowed India's room for manoeuvre in a very big way for over half a century and more. This may change only if the relations between India and Pakistan improve significantly, or if Pakistan's value as an ally diminishes in the Chinese calculations. Neither appears likely at present. In fact, the China–Pakistan Economic Corridor (CPEC) which traverses the Indian-claimed territory of Gilgit and Baltistan, presently under Pakistani occupation, has enhanced Pakistan's role in China's global strategy, particularly the aim of seeking an alternative land route to the Indian Ocean. The Chinese-built port of Gwadar on Pakistan's Balochistan coast, which is the terminus of routes across Pakistan from western China, is one of the points at which maritime and land connectivity under the ambitious Chinese project One Belt One Road come together. Over the past several decades, India's foreign policy makers have had to work around this fixed constant, even as almost every other regional and global equation has undergone dramatic transformation.

3

Foreign Policy in the Post–Cold War World

The end of the Cold War in the early 1990s and the collapse of the Soviet Union overturned the East–West balance, inaugurating a phase of US dominance that prevailed up until the global financial and economic crisis of 2007–08. This led to seismic changes in international affairs and of course impacted India, which now had to come to terms with the virtual evaporation of the Indo-Soviet partnership. That tie was rooted in a shared perception of threat from China. It had also supported India's pursuit of self-reliant economic growth and been a stable element in India's foreign policy, at least from 1960 to 1990.

India's balance of payments crisis coincided with the disintegration of this partnership, compelling India to embrace far-reaching economic reforms and liberalization. With this began the steady globalization of the Indian economy. Indian foreign policy too became more economic-oriented than in the past. Propelled by these powerful drivers, significant adjustments had to be made, which are still continuing.

I was serving as a joint secretary in the Prime Minister's Office (PMO) in 1991–92, handling external affairs, defence and atomic energy. I still recall how the rapidity of the Soviet Union's collapse shocked us all. There were now fifteen new countries to deal with, and the Soviet Union's successor, the Russian Federation under Boris Yeltsin, was mostly a closed book. There was great concern over how our long-standing defence relationship with them would be affected. In addition, the discontinuation of the rupee–rouble payment arrangement between the Soviet Union and India left on our hands a large rouble debt built over the years.

Trade between the two countries fell sharply as Indian commodities like tea, tobacco and textiles no longer enjoyed preferential access to the Soviet market and had to find new markets. Under Yeltsin, Russia came under the influence of the US and its European allies in a big way. This had adverse consequences on India's access to sensitive technologies. An early casualty was the supply of prototypes and designs for the more powerful cryogenic engines in India's space programme. The US was successful in preventing this on the grounds that it violated the Missile Technology Control Regime (MTCR).

The balance of payments issue brought the country close to bankruptcy. But in retrospect, the twin crises were handled with great skill and a nimbleness not usually associated with the Indian state. Prime Minister Narasimha Rao turned the dire economic situation into an opportunity by inaugurating a raft of economic reforms and liberalization measures. This shot India into a higher growth trajectory and transformed it into an outward-oriented economy.

The market-based reforms also projected India as a new and significant market opportunity for Western companies. The souring of relations between China and the West in the aftermath of the 1989 Tiananmen Square massacre helped India emerge as a democratic alternative.

The Russian turmoil was handled with patience and understanding. An early initiative was launched to reach out to the newly independent countries in Central Asia by putting to use the network of contacts and goodwill built up with Soviet republics in the past. The Look East Policy was announced, and India began engaging seriously with its South East Asian neighbours. Relations with Israel were normalized in 1992 without diluting India's traditionally close interaction with the Arab world. Rao played these cards well, and India's transition into the post–Cold War world appeared unusually smooth. It could have been a different story under a less pragmatic leader.

In my view, Narasimha Rao represented the Kautilyan mind more than any other Indian leader in recent times. He could be cold and calculating in handling the many challenges he had to confront but had an occasional streak of humour that took one by surprise. In one of his reflective moods, he turned to me and asked, 'Do you know the attributes of a successful leader in India?' Before I could respond to this unexpected query, he answered it himself: 'To be a successful leader in India you must be ruthless but also ascetic.'

~

After 1990, India began to improve its ties with the US as well as the European Union (EU). With the collapse of the Soviet Union, China's rise as an economic power began to be seen by the Western countries as a potential threat. The expectation that China's adoption of market economics and capitalist processes would transform it into a liberal democracy was belied by the brutal suppression of pro-democracy demonstrations in Beijing's Tiananmen Square in June 1989. By contrast, India was seen as a successful and politically stable plural democracy. And now, because of its accelerated economic growth, it appeared to be a major commercial opportunity too, rivalling China. India's nuclear tests in May 1998 may have retarded this realignment somewhat but by the turn of the century its relations with the US and the West in general had begun to crystallize into a mutually beneficial and substantive relationship.

In the subcontinent, the post-1990 period saw a steady shift away from a mainly defensive and reactive approach to a more active, coherent and focused posture. The far-reaching economic reforms and the economic growth and market globalization that followed also gave India greater political confidence in dealing with its neighbours. The alignment of security concerns of individual subcontinental countries was now sought through intensive and high-level political engagement, economic interdependencies, and the leveraging of shared cultural bonds. These can only crystallize over a long time, though.

As the largest country in the region, it is only India that can lead the South Asia project by establishing cross-border transport and communication links, opening up its own markets and transport system to its neighbours, and becoming the preferred source of capital and technology for their development. India is concerned about Chinese inroads into the subcontinent but it cannot deal with this by trying to compel its neighbours to keep China at bay or by urging China to stay away from what India regards as its backyard. The only effective solution is to build a countervailing presence superior to China's, a goal that is certainly attainable given how close we are, geographically and culturally, to our neighbours. Our security concerns, including Pakistan's cross-border terrorism and other hostile activities, are likely to be addressed with greater seriousness if we encourage our neighbours to build a stake in our own prosperity and capabilities.

The end of the Cold War was also the period when India began to re-engage with its East Asian neighbourhood. The Look East Policy inaugurated in 1992 made this region a dynamic economic partner for India in addition to providing great potential for robust security engagement.

While Russia continued to be an important partner and a significant source of advanced defence technologies and hardware, India now had to deal with the growing economic and security relationship among China and Russia. Russia was supplying the same advanced weaponry to China as it did to India. However, after 1989, neither the US nor its Western allies were supplying weapons or defence-related technologies to China.

The post–Cold War international environment remained this way for a whole quarter of a century, till the global financial and economic crisis that erupted in 2007–08. Under the near monopoly of power enjoyed by the US, there was relative calm in relations between the great powers. Neither Russia nor China was inclined to confront the US, even if there were perceived transgressions of their interests.

During the 1990s and the first decade of the new millennium, China and Russia mostly yielded to the unilateral American assertion of power, even though they often criticized the US for its role in many regional conflicts, such as the trouble in the Balkans, the Afghan War and the invasion and occupation of Iraq. On some controversial matters, like Iran's nuclear programme and North Korea's nuclear exploits, there was even a degree of coordination and cooperation among the major powers. This created the illusion that the end of the Cold War had led to a new phase in history, where there were no sharp ideological conflicts among them and that all these powers had accepted the logic of capitalist market economics. The norms of global behaviour laid down by the Western democracies appeared to be undisputed and universal in application.

From the perspective of the West, particularly the US, geopolitics had receded to the background, the probability of conflicts among the major powers had diminished, and the prospects of cooperation among the major countries on managing the global commons and other regional and global problems had significantly improved. But of course, from the perspective of the non-Western powers geopolitics had never gone away. In fact, disagreements had become sharper in West Asia and the Gulf, in several parts of Africa and in our own subcontinental neighbourhood, especially in the Afghanistan–Pakistan theatre.[1]

For Japan, South Korea and the South East Asian countries, the rise of China and its increasing assertiveness has raised new fears and tensions. China now makes claims to the entire South China Sea, and has made threatening moves to contest Japanese control over the Senkaku islands. So when the US and West European nations now speak about the 'return of geopolitics', as Walter Russel Mead has done in his celebrated essay in the journal *Foreign Affairs*,[2] it is from a very narrow, Western perspective.

Geopolitics has made a comeback, according to the West, because the unipolarity of the twenty-five-year period after the

---

[1] Af-Pak: Afghanistan–Pakistan, seen as an interlinked political and security challenge.

[2] *Foreign Affairs*, May-June 2014.

Cold War has come to an end. Rival powers like Russia and China no longer feel any need to submit to the US definition of global order. The global financial and economic crisis has severely dented the ideological orthodoxy enshrined in the Washington Consensus.[3] The US and Western Europe in particular find themselves on the defensive. Their own social and economic institutions are under heavy and debilitating stress, as in the case of Greece. The West was assiduous in propagating the virtues of globalization and free markets but only so long as its sway over the global economy was unchallenged. However, the economic crises afflicting the US, Europe and Japan show that it is they who are guilty of violating their own norms. The election of Donald Trump as president of the US, the vote in the UK to leave the EU (Brexit), and the rise of ultra-nationalism in several European countries reflect a gathering disquiet over this lost ascendancy.

For India, the quarter-century that followed the end of the Cold War was a relatively benign phase in favour of its economic advancement and security interests. With the exception of China, the members of the UN Security Council joined hands to make the Indo-US civil nuclear deal a reality in 2008. After the Ukraine crisis, which led to fresh tensions between Russia and the West, it is difficult to imagine that all the major powers could have come together to enable the consensus waiver in favour of India at the NSG in 2008. China had to relent because of the overwhelming support for India among the major powers. Even the middle powers like

[3]The Washington Consensus refers to the economic orthodoxy which puts free markets, global free trade and investment as the heart of economic success. In the post-1990 period, there was often a conflation of free markets with liberal democracy as the proven recipe for successful nationhood.

Argentina, Brazil, Mexico and South Africa supported India.[4] In the changed environment, China now openly opposes India's membership of the NSG.

All the major powers have also supported India's candidature for permanent membership of the UN Security Council, even though for some this support was only rhetorical and not a commitment.

In the Asia-Pacific, India's rise was welcomed, and during the two decades preceding and following the turn of the millennium, India moved from being a dialogue partner of the Association of Southeast Asian Nations (ASEAN) to a full dialogue partner, then a summit partner and finally, in 2012, a strategic partner. This status reflects the very broad-ranging relations which India has developed with the ASEAN over the past two decades, covering political, economic, security and cultural aspects. India is also a founding member of the East Asia Summit, which brings together the ten ASEAN countries, their summit partners – China, Japan, South Korea, India, Australia and New Zealand – and importantly, the US and Russia. In addition, India is a negotiating partner for the proposed Regional Comprehensive Economic Partnership, a free trade agreement between the ASEAN and its six summit partners. However, it has not yet succeeded in becoming a member of the Asia-Pacific Economic Community, the transregional consultative body that promotes greater economic engagement and the sharing of best practices among its members. But India is now firmly embedded in the region and will play a role in shaping its emerging economic and security architecture.

---

[4]The waiver approved by the NSG in September 2008 allowed its members to engage in civil nuclear energy cooperation with India despite it being a nuclear weapons state. The events leading up to the waiver are covered in Chapter 11.

The 11 September 2001 terror assault by the Al-Qaeda on the US significantly changed global attitudes towards Pakistan's cross-border terrorism. Earlier, this terrorism had been pursued with impunity under the guise of supporting a so-called freedom movement in Jammu and Kashmir. Pakistan could no longer rely on the ambiguity shown by the US and international powers towards its state-sponsored terrorism against India or its adventurist actions on the Line of Control (LoC), as it did in the Kargil War in 1999, and escape international censure. This was an important gain for India, a collateral benefit of the global war on terrorism unleashed by the US.

After the 26 November 2008 terrorist attack in Mumbai by the Pakistan-based Lashkar-e-Taiba (LeT) operatives and the assassination of Osama bin Laden, who was hiding in plain sight in the Pakistani cantonment city of Abbottabad, Pakistan could do little to protest that it was not a breeding ground for jihadi terrorism. The current level of counterterrorism cooperation between the US and India would have been unthinkable even a decade ago.

The relatively non-confrontational relations among the major powers helped India deal more successfully with its own challenges. It was able to leverage its improved relations with one major power to elevate its relations with the others in a cumulative way. This benign phase may be coming to a close as sharper contradictions come to dominate the evolving relations among the major powers. There is a new phase of competition in the international sphere and the current Modi government is faced with a far more complex and challenging international environment.

This new phase may be traced to the global financial and economic crisis of 2007–08, from which neither the US nor Europe has fully recovered (although the US appears to be in better shape today than its Western allies). The persistence of this crisis has meant that the relatively open and liberal trading environment in the West, which allowed the export-driven economies of China and East Asia to flourish as major manufacturing platforms supplying their markets, is now under threat. In responding to sluggish growth and shrinking markets, both the US and Western economies are increasingly bringing in protectionist measures in the form of non-tariff barriers, such as very strict environmental, labour or health and sanitary standards on imports.

For India, which adopted economic reforms and liberalization comparatively late, these protectionist trends come at a time when it is making efforts to establish itself as a globally competitive manufacturing hub. The Make in India scheme will not enjoy an international economic environment as supportive as the one China did in the post–Cold War period. There have been legitimate fears that the US-led Trans-Pacific Partnership (TPP) in the Asia–Pacific and the Transatlantic Trade and Investment Partnership (TTIP) might create a vast trading zone with restrictive norms and standards designed to keep away competition from countries like India. India will not be able to use its relative advantage as a low-cost country to increase its trade.

However, with Trump in the White House, neither of these mega trade arrangements appears likely since he has publicly attacked them. He has announced that the US will no longer participate in the TPP and will seek the renegotiation of other free trade deals it has with various countries. But the general trend towards more restrictive market access will continue. Trump will probably restrict visas for Indian IT professionals. India is likely to face the risk of being pushed to the margins of the global economy. Its strategic partnership with the US is now unstable. For a strong partnership, the economic and security pillars holding it up must be strong and mutually beneficial.

As pointed out earlier, the global financial and economic crisis has altered the equations between the major powers. Europe has turned inwards and is now dealing with multiple crises. Its economies remain stagnant, and social stresses and strains have begun to spawn ultra-right and xenophobic sentiments across the continent. Extremism among its deprived Muslim communities is becoming a worrying threat. These trends may worsen if Europe's economies continue to stagnate and unemployment remains high.

In 2004–05, India and the EU had forged a very strong partnership based on shared values as multi-ethnic, multicultural, multi-religious, multilingual plural democracies. Each side had a stake in the success of the other, and India looked upon a strong, united Europe as a pole in its own right in the global order. That has changed in the past decade, thanks to the Eurozone crisis, which has muted the voice of Europe in international affairs. With Brexit, this trend will only be accentuated.

The crisis has also led to the growing power and influence of Germany, which is now indisputably the strongest power in Europe. This has its own implications for the future of the continent since German interests may not always be aligned with the interests of other European countries or the US.

There is also no doubt that the West is divided over how to deal with Russia. Few wish to return to the dangerous tensions of a new cold war in Europe but the apprehension over Russian intentions is a legitimate one.

For India, the Ukraine crisis has introduced a new element of discomfort as it seeks to maintain its traditional relationship with Russia without spoiling its growing partnership with the US. It is also uncomfortable over the tightening embrace between Russia and China, which can only work to India's disadvantage. There is little doubt that the US actively encouraged dissidents in Ukraine to unseat a democratically elected government. The motive was to open the way for Ukraine to join the EU, and eventually the North Atlantic Treaty Organization. This inevitably led to a strong Russian reaction given the historic links between Russia and Ukraine. If these links were severed, Russia's Black Sea naval base at Sevastopol on Ukraine's Crimean coast would be under threat.

The Russian response of incorporating Crimea into the Russian Federation and supporting secessionist groups along the Russia–Ukraine border was therefore not unexpected. These developments led to the worsening of Russia's relations with the West, which imposed a number of sanctions on it. As a result, it is China that now holds the levers in the US–Russia–China triangle and not the US.

It will be interesting to see what happens to US–Russia relations under Trump's presidency. He has indicated that he wants better relations with Russia to fight Islamic fundamentalism. He may also seek to wean Russia away from too close a relationship with China. Should Trump do this there will again be a major geopolitical churn, especially in Europe. If the US removes sanctions against Russia, Europe will follow suit, boosting Russia's international profile. To the extent that the distance between Russia and China grows, these developments will suit India.

It is unfortunate that relations with Russia have become a major controversial issue in American domestic politics as a result of revelations that Russia may have been involved in influencing the presidential elections in favour of Trump. It seems unlikely that the positive shift in US–Russia relations anticipated earlier would in fact come about.

The Ukraine crisis has become interlinked with another recent trend – falling oil prices. This sharp and unexpected decline is attributed to oversupply, particularly from shale oil production in the US. The overall slowdown in the global economy, especially the Chinese economy, has also contributed to the excess supply. The current glut in the oil market is a temporary phenomenon. The growth in demand is currently one million barrels a day, and the natural decline in oil production from existing fields is about five million barrels a day. Moreover, every barrel of replacement oil is more costly to produce. Most analysts expect oil prices to rise sooner rather than later as supply falls short of demand. So if Russia can tide over its current crisis in a year or two, as appears likely, it will re-emerge as a key energy player, with all the influence that accompanies this status. It may already have begun to happen.

The implication for India is that it should not assume a prolonged decline in oil prices in drawing up its long-term energy strategy. However, this temporary phase of low prices should be leveraged to reform energy subsidies, acquire oil and gas assets abroad at more favourable prices and continue with its long-term strategy for an accelerated shift from its reliance on fossil fuels to renewable and clean sources of energy, such as nuclear energy.

India's energy security concerns are nevertheless currently tied to the situation unfolding in the Gulf and West Asia. Any major political upheaval in the region is likely to interrupt energy supplies to India. The diversification of supply sources away from the Gulf is an urgent necessity, as is ramping up domestic production.

Another related contingency to plan for is the impact of any political turmoil in this region on the welfare of the six million Indians and more who live and work there. As became apparent when Indian nurses and workers were abducted by the Islamic State (IS) terrorist group in Iraq, Indian expatriates are very vulnerable to shifting political changes in the region. India has few instruments of influence among the countries in this zone. The evacuation of a few hundred citizens during a crisis is a major operation and if larger numbers are affected, the country's own resources can be easily exhausted.

The other dimension to consider is the sharpening sectarian divide in the region and its fallout on our own Muslim population. There is a need to carefully study the attraction the IS holds for young Muslim men and women across the world, including India. It is paradoxical that an organization described as medieval in outlook is so compelling for the young. Strangely, it offers the Islamic youth an opportunity to break away from the conservative and repressive code of traditional Islam. The young women living together as 'temporary wives' of IS fighters find their experience liberating rather than oppressive. This emerged from several interviews of these young women which were carried in the British press.[5] This aspect has somehow been missed in the global discourse on the IS. Asking conservative family elders to warn their children against the barbarity and un-Islamic conduct of the IS is unlikely to work if the point of attraction lies elsewhere. The lure of the organization should be neutralized by encouraging a more liberal and accommodating Islam, such as that which prevailed before Wahabi influences crept into the subcontinent's Muslim societies.

If there is one international crisis that could derail India's economic prospects and dent its social cohesion and plural

---

[5] 'The Secret World of ISIS Wives', *Guardian*, 24 June 2015, www.theguardian.com/world/2015/jun/24/isis-brides-secret-world-jihad-western-women-syria.

culture, it is the very real likelihood of the current upheaval in the Gulf and West Asia spreading to the sheikhdoms and Saudi Arabia. Planning for this contingency should be a priority in our national security strategy.

India's China strategy will have to adjust to the growing power asymmetry between the two countries. While engagement as well as competition will continue to characterize the overall policy, their precise mix will vary according to changes in the regional and global situation. Prime Minister Modi went out of his way to accord an unprecedentedly warm welcome to Chinese President Xi Jinping in September 2015. But the visit coincided with renewed tensions on the border, leading to doubts about Chinese intentions. Perhaps this was a not-too-subtle action on China's part to test the new Indian political leadership. Modi reacted firmly, publicly announcing that such incidents were incompatible with the professed Chinese desire for closer relations. Subsequent summit meetings between Modi and Xi reflect the growing divide between the two countries.

On China's part there is less sensitivity to Indian concerns, while India under Modi appears to be more confrontational on such matters than it has been in the past. It is seeking to bolster India's defence preparedness to confront possible aggressive moves by China. At the same time it is exploring opportunities with China for mutually beneficial economic and commercial relations.

There was an expectation that with both India and China being headed by strong leaders, a window of opportunity for political resolution of the long-standing boundary dispute would open. The key question is, what are the terms and conditions under which the resolution could happen? The current reality is that the two sides have been sticking to the Line of Actual Control (LAC), which came into existence after the 1962 border war. To the east, the Indian side is in occupation of almost all the territory it claims, and to the west the Chinese side is occupying the territory it claims as its own. After more than half a century, it is difficult to visualize a boundary settlement very different from the current situation. To be politically acceptable in India, the solution would have to be LAC-plus, which means India retains the territory it holds in the eastern sector while China concedes at least some territory to India in the western sector. China's current posture does not appear to hold out such a possibility in the near future.

There is also the lingering issue of Tibet, which has cast a shadow on the relationship. All that is possible now is managing the dispute through confidence-building measures, reducing its salience in the overall relationship and continuing engagements at the summit level to ensure the relationship is stable despite the competitive undercurrents. A strong set of diversified relationships with the major powers, particularly the US, would also give India greater room for manoeuvre with China. This is preferable to provoking hostilities. So long as India refrains from becoming a member of an anti-China military alliance, China has more to gain by increasing its engagement with India than by confronting it.

It is inevitable that each side will continue to develop relations with the other's neighbours. India should implement its stated strategy of according priority to its subcontinental neighbourhood so that it does not leave gaps that China or others can take advantage of. Chapters 6 and 7 consider India–China relations in details.

What changes in international equations should one expect in the foreseeable future? How are they likely to affect India?

The first factor to consider is that, we have entered a phase of renewed rivalry and incipient confrontation among the great powers. India is coping with a more complex and polarized international environment as a result, which limits its room for manoeuvre.

Second, the global financial and economic crisis of 2008–09, which still has to run its course, has made the international economic environment less supportive of India's development ambitions than in the two preceding decades. Protectionist trends are gaining strength and new hurdles could limit India's market access to the developed countries.

Third, India could face a major crisis as a fallout of the intensified political turmoil and sectarian conflict in the Gulf and West Asia. It has few levers available to influence events. This could be a more immediate challenge.

Fourth, managing the rise of China qualifies as both an immediate and long-term challenge. The threat from Pakistan is a subset of this challenge, given the strong alliance between the two countries. For the foreseeable future, India will have to cope with its growing power asymmetry with China, whose economy is now four times the size of India's and still growing. At the same time, India is perhaps the only country that has the potential to draw level with and even surpass China over the longer term. This will only be possible if there is a determined leadership capable of making hard choices. Whether the current Indian leadership has that quality remains to be seen.

A key asset for India is its potential to become the world's fastest growing major economy as China's own growth decelerates. A period of sustained and high growth rate can bring India from the margins to the centre stage of the global economy. It will then be able to negotiate from a more favourable position. Its options, both Asian and global, will expand.

India's growing economic and security profile has found greater acceptance regionally and globally as the country is seen as a non-threatening, benign power. Its success as a liberal democracy helps it score over China, whose rise is already creating anxiety and concern both in its neighbourhood and among the major powers. India will continue to retain this perceptional advantage as long as it remains an open and plural democracy. The subcontinental view of India is more mixed as its neighbours respond to its power in terms of the Kautilyan dynamic and seek countervailing influences. India's difficult task of managing its neighbourhood is the subject of the next chapter.

Part Two

Neighbours

4

The Challenge of Proximity

With India's political independence in 1947 came the trauma of Partition. A vast subcontinent which had for long existed as an integrated and undivided entity and which carried the imprint of India's 'sacred geography' was torn apart. There are now several independent and sovereign states occupying this space with no shared vision of the future or a common view of the subcontinent's security challenges. Partition severed the transport arteries linking the different corners of the region. There was a growing assertion of nationalist sentiments and a drifting away from democratic freedoms in some states and soon the impact of Cold War rivalries threw this sacred geography into division and conflict. India and some of its neighbours felt a sense of siege begin to settle on them. The challenge for India is to transcend the political divisions in the subcontinent to restore its cohesiveness and make its borders increasingly irrelevant, drawing upon the enduring sources of affinity.

The defining feature of South Asia is asymmetry. India is by far the largest country in the region in terms of area, population, and economic and military capabilities, larger than all its neighbours put together. Each neighbour shares some significant ethnic, linguistic or cultural features with India but not so much with the others in the subcontinent. It is this asymmetry which shapes the neighbourhood's perception of India and vice versa. But India must recognize that the asymmetry is still not of a scale that can compel its neighbours to align their interests with its own. This is the challenge of proximity.

Apprehensions of domination by India are a given among its neighbours and this is hardly surprising, inherent in the reality of the above-mentioned asymmetry. The Kautilya *mandala* would show this as inevitable – the adoption of hedging tactics by India's neighbours to resist or counter Indian domination. An obvious illustration of this is Nepal's brandishing of the China card to offset what it regards as its excessive dependence on India.

The Kautilyan template would say the options for India are *sandhi,* conciliation; *asana,* neutrality; and *yana,* victory through war. One could add *dana,* buying allegiance through gifts; and *bheda*, sowing discord. The option of *yana*, of course, would be the last in today's world.

The Indian response to its subcontinental problems often departs from Kautilyan principles. It is frequently resentful at having to compete with other suitors for its neighbours' affections. This leads to either excessive and often misdirected generosity and accommodation, or harsh overreaction. There existed until recently in India a kind of being-under-siege mentality that regarded the neighbourhood as hostile and unfriendly, and a source of danger to Indian security. When the South Asia Association for Regional Cooperation (SAARC) was created in 1985 at the initiative of Bangladesh, India was a reluctant participant. It suspected this was a ganging up of mostly hostile smaller neighbours as a containment strategy against it. The motivations of some of the neighbours did justify this suspicion.

For example, the smaller states, including Pakistan, wanted SAARC to be a mediating forum to resolve interstate disputes. This would have put bilateral disputes – such as the India–Pakistan Kashmir problem or the India–Nepal or India–Bangladesh river sharing controversies – on the SAARC agenda. Some SAARC members advocated full membership of China in the organization – an obvious effort to counterbalance India.

At the thirteenth SAARC summit in Dhaka in November 2005, the Indian delegation had to tackle an obstructive Nepali delegation which held up consensus on admitting Afghanistan as the eighth member of the organization, insisting that China should be admitted too. This was the Nepali king Gyanendra's way of hitting back at India for its opposition to his assumption of absolute political power and for its suspension of arms supplies to his royal army (see Chapter 5). The matter was eventually sorted out with Afghanistan being welcomed into the fold while China, the US and Japan were accepted as 'observers'.

During the past decade there has been a visible change in India's approach to its neighbourhood and to SAARC. This is the result of a growing recognition that economic integration in South Asia is indispensable for the Indian economy as it globalizes. India has taken the lead in advocating a South Asia Customs Union, a common currency and even a South Asian Parliament. It is now accepted wisdom that the globalization of the Indian economy has delivered accelerated growth and relative prosperity. India sees itself as an integral part of the economic resurgence of Asia.

The much talked about shift of the heart of the global

economy from the trans-Atlantic to the Asia-Pacific is both a condition for as well as a consequence of India's own emergence as an economic powerhouse. The globalization process is pitching India into ever-widening concentric circles of economic cooperation. In this architecture of concentric circles, regional integration in South Asia may be seen as the innermost zone. India cannot take full advantage of the growing web of economic interaction and interdependence binding Asia together while remaining isolated from its own immediate periphery.

There is a political reason for this too. To keep its attention focused on achieving high and sustained economic growth over the next several decades, India will need to ensure a stable, peaceful and secure periphery. Crises in neighbouring countries, conflict situations or failed states may so completely engage the energies of the Indian state that other objectives may have to take a back seat. This is why the neighbourhood must rank as the highest priority in India's foreign policy strategies.

Prime Minister Modi appears to recognize this. He has placed it at the top of his foreign policy agenda with his invitations to SAARC leaders to attend his swearing-in in 2014 and his early visits to several South Asian countries including a more recent surprise visit to Lahore in December 2015. Despite some recent setbacks, including the postponement of the SAARC summit in Islamabad in 2016, this reorientation must be sustained and should be reflected in the deployment of resources, both human and material, in managing the neighbourhood.

In embracing regional economic integration as a key policy objective, there is an assumption that this is one way to overcome the political and psychological barriers dividing the region. Asymmetry in this context can be an advantage.

The very size of the Indian economy, the dynamism it has displayed since the adoption of reforms, its openness and increasing technological sophistication have transformed it into a potential and powerful engine of growth for all its smaller neighbours.

India is an opportunity and not a threat. Its free trade and comprehensive economic cooperation agreement with Sri Lanka, the enmeshing of the Indian and Nepali economies thanks to the open border and trade regime, India's expanding cooperation in the hydropower sector with Bhutan and the more recent advances in economic and trade relations with Bangladesh have lent a degree of political stability to our relations with our neighbours. Even with Pakistan there has been a significant increase in bilateral trade and cross-border transport links. These initiatives have resulted in a more positive and promising environment for the future of the subcontinent.

While these developments should be welcomed, they fall far short of creating a truly interconnected and interdependent South Asia, marked by a free flow of goods, peoples and ideas across borders, as it had been for most of the region's long history. This objective has been repeatedly articulated by India's leaders in recent years but the rhetoric has not always been followed by substantive action. Ingrained mental biases inhibit progress towards regional integration. And the lead has to be taken by India as the largest country in the region with the most powerful economy.

With the new focus on its immediate neighbourhood, there has been a simultaneous emphasis on cross-border connectivity and infrastructure development in the border areas. Progress has been slow and hesitant, though. In 2006, just before I retired as foreign secretary, I made a presentation on our neighbourhood policy at the Indian Council for World Affairs

(ICWA), in which I provided details of several cross-border transportation projects, including rail and road links and modern, integrated border checkpoints. It is depressing that even a decade later, very few of those projects have actually been implemented. This has eroded our credibility in the eyes of our neighbours.[1]

The actual roll-out of India's policy towards its neighbours has been hampered by slow delivery mechanisms. This is a systemic issue, needing urgent remedy. One problem is the lack of adequate numbers of trained professionals to manage relations with our neighbours across the political and economic spectrum. Despite the dramatic expansion in India's external engagement in recent years, its diplomatic personnel number just 900 today. Even the tiny nation of Singapore has a large diplomatic force.

In 2006, while I was still foreign secretary, the Ministry of External Affairs (MEA) recommended the creation of an autonomous Development Cooperation Agency under its overall supervision. The agency would have its own financial advisor to handle the many different components of India-assisted projects in developing nations, particularly the neighbouring countries. This was followed up for some time but eventually the perennial inter-ministerial turf battles ensured it did not see the light of day. Instead, the Development Cooperation Administration was set up within the MEA itself, but without the coordinating structure and financial autonomy that would be critical to its success.

The mindset of considering our borders as walls behind which we can protect ourselves against our hostile neighbours has changed only a little. We need to see our borders as

---

[1] 'Does India Have a Neighbourhood Policy?' Address to the ICWA, September, 2006.

'connectors', as transmission belts on which developmental impulses can travel without barriers. This also implies that we must stop treating our border states and border regions as buffer zones safeguarding the more populous and developed interior areas. Such an approach may have had a certain logic during British colonial rule but is irrelevant in independent India. All territory within our borders is national territory, after all, and all citizens living within these borders have equal status and equal right to development.

The hangover of British colonial attitudes still affects our administration of the border areas. It can be seen in the continuing Inner Line Permit requirement for visitors to several border states. (The Inner Line Permit is a travel document issued by the government not only to foreigners but also to Indian citizens to visit certain states or districts that lie on the international borders.) This permit is now mostly required for travel to India's north-east; it has heightened the sense of alienation among citizens living in these areas and affected both development and security along the borders.

Two kinds of connectivity are required in these areas. First, there has to be better connections between them and the rest of the country. The neglect of these places has resulted from the notion that our defence is best served by keeping them underdeveloped and remote, encouraging only defence-related infrastructure to be built in those parts. Second, any cross-border infrastructure must have rearward linkages to the interior. It is important to create both kinds of connectivity at the same time. Putting in place cross-border transport links without rearward linkages to the interior areas can potentially detach our border areas from the rest of the country. Economically, politically and psychologically, people living in the border areas may relate more closely to the neighbouring countries over time. This has happened in the ethnic regions of northern Myanmar, which are better connected with southern China today than with the rest of Myanmar.

India's north-east, which shares borders with Bangladesh, Bhutan, Myanmar and China, has become a key component of India's neighbourhood and the Look East Policy. To play its role as India's land bridge to the east, it needs infrastructure development in three interlinked categories, which are all to be pursued simultaneously.

One, there has to be significant improvement in connectivity between the north-east and the rest of India through the upgradation of rail and road links via the Siliguri corridor.

Two, connectivity among the different states of the north-east must be built. Currently it is at the barest minimum.

Three, cross-border links with China, Myanmar and Bangladesh should be pursued, including roads, railway lines and waterways.

The hardware of cross-border infrastructure must be fortified and made operational by the 'software' of better customs and immigration procedures, banking and financial services, trade facilitation measures, efficient quarantine facilities and tourism promotion. A modern highway traversing an international border is of no use if cumbersome border procedures grossly delay the movement of cargo and people. An impressive modern integrated checkpoint has been set up at Wagah on the India–Pakistan border but the procedures continue to be onerous and time consuming. The administration of cross-border movement has not kept pace with improvements in physical infrastructure.

SAARC leaders have declared the current decade (2010–2020) as the 'Connectivity Decade'. A multimodal transport network linking all the South Asian countries has been approved. The SAARC Motor Vehicles Agreement and the SAARC Railway Agreement are in place. Once implemented, they will provide for seamless travel across South Asia. But, like several other initiatives, these plans are now hostage to the political tensions between India and Pakistan.

Here one must acknowledge the progress achieved in sub-regional cooperation under the Bangladesh, Bhutan, India and Nepal (BBIN) framework, which too contains a motor vehicles agreement and a proposed railway agreement for smooth road and rail travel between the four countries. The recent improvement of relations between India and Bangladesh has also revived plans for a power grid. India is already supplying power to Bangladesh and to Nepal, while Bhutan is selling power to India. With the construction of some additional power transmission lines, a BBIN power grid could become a reality.

Proximity is the most important asset that South Asian countries possess, something partners in other networks outside the region do not have among themselves. Modern cross-border infrastructure and the smooth and efficient movement of people and goods can extract the best from this proximity, reducing the transaction costs of trade and sharpening the competitiveness of South Asian economies. Once this is understood and appreciated, regional integration can proceed rapidly.

Connectivity across the region cannot be leveraged fully unless mutual transit is permitted. India has sought transit across Pakistan to Afghanistan and across Bangladesh to its north-east but has itself not been very forthcoming in extending transit facilities to its neighbours. India is the largest and most critical transit country for the whole of South Asia. It is only through here that countries in the region can have the most direct and efficient access to one another.

The following situations make this plain.

- A container takes thirty-five days to move from New Delhi to Dhaka since the nearest maritime route is through Mumbai. From there it moves to Singapore or Colombo, then onwards to Chittagong. The final leg of its journey is by rail to Dhaka. A direct rail cargo service from Delhi to Dhaka would take the container in just five days.
- A container from Dhaka to Lahore would need to traverse only 2300 kilometres by rail across India. Currently it moves by rail and sea, taking the 7100 kilometre Dhaka–Chittagong–Karachi–Lahore route.

An important proposal that has been doing the rounds for several years is to convert most of the existing border trade points into regular trade points. There are several points where trading in goods from across the border is permitted. Only a designated list of so-called local commodities is allowed to be traded at each post, with either no duties or nominal duties.

The reality is that trade in regular items not included in the lists takes place illegally on a significant scale at these border points. In some cases third-country goods too find their way across. At the India–Myanmar border at Tamu–Moreh, for example, a very large volume of Chinese goods enters India as contraband. If we were to permit regular or MFN (Most Favoured Nation) trade through these points at normal duties – irrespective of where the goods are coming from or where goods from our side are eventually destined for – we would be able to prevent the criminalization of border trade. The government would also earn some badly needed revenues. The current border trade regime does not make much sense. While we resist overground economic integration, underground economic integration appears to be flourishing!

To advance regional integration, India should be prepared

to offer all its neighbours 'national treatment' on its transport network and access to its ports. This means entities from neighbouring countries can access our transport infrastructure on the same terms and conditions as our own nationals. The extra load on national infrastructure will be minimal but the positive political and economic impact on landlocked Nepal and Bhutan would be significant. Modern technologies like electronic and hologram seals, barcodes, and GPS-based systems to monitor cargo movement can fully enable cargo screening, taking care of security concerns. The cost of moving containers from Bangladesh to Pakistan or from Nepal to other South Asian countries would decline dramatically.

India should aim at positioning itself as the most convenient, efficient and cost-effective trade and transit hub for the entire subcontinent. It should not be a nation that appears to regard curbs on the access and transit of goods as its main leverage over its neighbours. In this context, India joining the UN's TIR (Transports Internationaux Routiers) agreement for enabling smooth cross-border transit of cargo is a welcome development.

A significant part of India's neighbourhood policy is based on the crucial role of cultural and people-to-people exchanges. There is so much in common among the South Asian countries. The ethnic, cultural and linguistic ties on either side of its international borders can be as much an asset as a complicating factor in interactions with neighbours. While India has a declared policy of aiming at the free flow of goods, people and ideas across its subcontinental borders, in practice it is restrictive and increasingly so. Exchanges among scholars, journalists, civil society representatives and artists have become rare because of India's extremely stringent visa policy. Some visa liberalization measures can be taken – even unilaterally – as greater people-to-people exchanges work to India's advantage. They create progressively larger constituencies in favour of closer engagement with India and correct misperceptions born of mutual ignorance and lack of exposure.

For example, the love of the Bangla language and literature and Rabindra Sangeet among the large number of young Bangladeshis who come to India for higher education has made for a potent mix. Over the years, this has created a more balanced and benign perception of India in Bangladesh. It has been one of the factors that led to a significant improvement in political relations between the two countries in recent years.

Even during periods of intense hostility with Pakistan, the pervasive popularity of Bollywood films and stars in that country has raged undiminished. This is also true of Sri Lanka, the Maldives and Afghanistan. Bollywood films, along with cricket, are a subcontinental passion, eclipsing borders and politics.

Today there is an even more compelling reason for India to take the lead in fostering South Asian cooperation. This region is a single, interconnected ecological space that is greatly under threat from the impact of global climate change. Seasonal monsoon winds sweep across the entire subcontinent each year, bringing life and sustenance to the hundreds of millions who inhabit this land. But climate change is causing alterations in weather patterns which are little understood – the monsoon patterns are changing, and the frequency of extreme climatic events such as floods or droughts has increased.

The entire Indo-Gangetic plain, home to over half a billion people, is watered by perennial rivers that spring from the glaciers of the Himalayas. As these glaciers retreat and melt due to global warming, the rivers may become only seasonally alive. Pakistan, India and Bangladesh will face food and water shortages. The mountain countries of Nepal and Bhutan and

India's hill states may become more vulnerable to glacial lake outbursts and flash floods. On the coast, rising sea levels could inundate our coastal plains and island territories. For a country like the Maldives, survival itself may be threatened. These are unprecedented dangers that recognize no national or regional boundaries. To tackle them with any degree of success will require equally unprecedented levels of collaboration among the South Asian states. Simply an awareness of these threats to ecological security would make our current political and psychological divisions appear self-defeating.

SAARC did adopt the Climate Change Action Plan in 2007 but its recommendations for collaboration remain on paper.

INDIA'S BOUNDARY DISPUTES

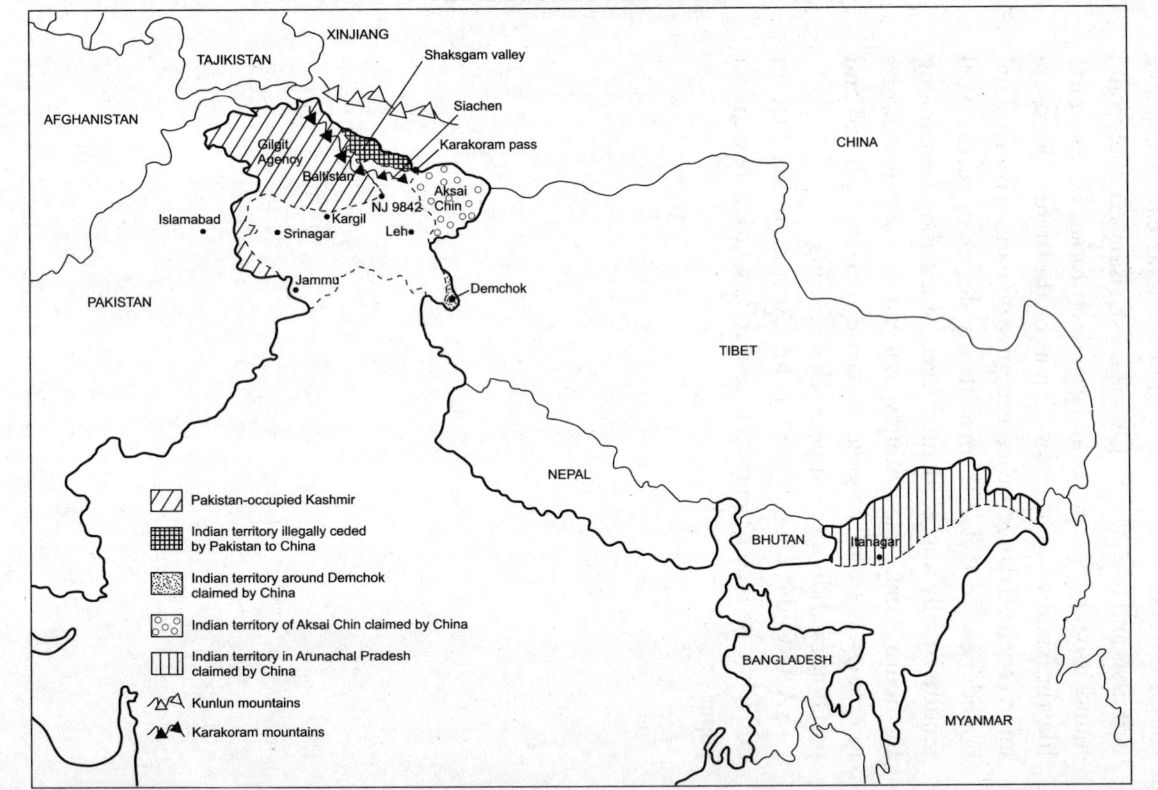

This map is not at scale and is for explanatory purposes only. It does not purport to reflect the official boundaries of India

5

The Pakistan Puzzle

India–Pakistan relations remain a prisoner of Partition. So even many years after 1947, Pakistan is still striving to separate itself from India, defining its still-evolving identity as 'not India'. It is struggling to subsume its own disparate ethnicities in a shared and often passionate adherence to Islam.

Over the past seven decades, India and Pakistan have composed widely different national and historical narratives. Each country has a different view on why Partition took place and what led to the dispute over Kashmir. Each has contrary views on the wars of 1965 and 1971 and the birth of Bangladesh, as they do over the later clash of arms in Kargil. The Indian expressions of shared history and culture reinforce the Pakistani fears of loss of identity. Until these contrary historical narratives are reconciled, it is difficult to see how an essentially antagonistic relationship can be transformed into even a normal one, let alone into friendship. Improved relations with Pakistan can only be the cumulative outcome of a series of modest and incremental steps rather than the result of any big-bang affair.

A sense of entitlement to equal status with India is also ingrained in Pakistan. As the economic gap between the two countries widens, Pakistan has nurtured its quest for parity with India through its large and powerful army, and now through an expanding nuclear arsenal. The use of asymmetrical warfare against India through state-sponsored cross-border terrorism is another example of its perennial ambition to be considered on par with India, bleeding our country using terror since it cannot do so militarily. Its willingness to become a client-state of the US, and now of China, arises from its obsession to constrain India. There is a fond belief in Pakistan that China's proposed $46 billion investment in the China–Pakistan Economic Corridor and in Gwadar port on the Balochistan coast will be a game changer for Pakistan and buttress its ambitions to become equal to India. These are deeply rooted fixations in the Pakistani psyche and will change only slowly, if they do at all.

I had limited exposure to Pakistan during my years in the Indian Foreign Service but had dealt with my Pakistani counterparts while serving in our missions – in Beijing, Geneva, Yangon and Kathmandu. Individual warmth and friendliness coexisted with collective antipathy and sometimes absurd competitiveness.

While I was posted in Yangon, my Pakistani counterpart asked me if I was planning to do anything special on our Independence Day on 15 August, lamenting that he would probably have to settle for another modest and boring reception to mark Pakistan's independence anniversary a day earlier on 14 August. In all innocence I mentioned that the Myanmar Army had very kindly agreed to depute a small band to play at our reception. On the day of the Pakistani reception, I was surprised to find a Myanmar Army band in attendance! There was a look of undisguised glee and triumph in the Pakistani envoy's eyes. Once again Pakistan was one up on India. I later found out that after our conversation that day, the Pakistani ambassador had made the same request to the Myanmar Army, arguing that their government would appear unfriendly if its military band played for India at its Independence Day reception but not at Pakistan's.

It was during my time as joint secretary at the PMO from 1991 to 1992 that I became more closely involved with our Pakistan policy. I had succeeded Ronen Sen at the PMO when Chandra Shekhar was the prime minister. The former prime minister, Rajiv Gandhi, had been killed in a terrorist attack on 21 May 1991, and his funeral in Delhi was a few days later. Several heads of state and government leaders came to pay their respects, among them the Pakistani prime minister, then a much younger Nawaz Sharif. Chandra Shekhar hosted a private lunch for him at 7 Race Course Road, which was followed by a one-to-one meeting, which I covered as a note-taker. A crisis had been building up on the LoC in Jammu and Kashmir, where a large number of Pakistanis were gathering, threatening to cross over to the Indian side to 'unite divided Kashmir' through 'people power'.

Nawaz Sharif tried to argue that the Pakistani government, despite its best efforts, may not be able to stop the groups from crossing the LoC. He said he expected restraint on the Indian side. Chandra Shekhar said it was the responsibility of Pakistan to prevent any crossing of the LoC from its side. As prime minister of India, he would have no option but to order his security forces to shoot anyone trespassing on Indian soil. This would be a violent act against unarmed people and would be condemned across the world, warned Nawaz. Chandra Shekhar said it was his responsibility to handle the fallout, but he wanted the Pakistani prime minister to be under no doubt that if one person crossed, one would be killed, and if a hundred crossed, a hundred would be killed. Nawaz hastily dropped the subject and moved on to less contentious issues. Over the next few days, Pakistani security forces moved decisively to prevent the gathering groups from crossing the LoC and soon they melted away.

When Narasimha Rao took over as prime minister after the general elections later that year, Nawaz Sharif sent Shahryar Khan, Pakistan's foreign secretary, as his special envoy to convey a message of peace and friendship to the incoming Indian government. The most important part of the message was an assurance that Pakistan would not permit cross-border terrorism and that India would see results 'on the ground' very soon. This did not happen. However, Rao kept his channels of communication open with Nawaz, meeting him on the sidelines of international meetings at Davos, Jakarta, Harare and Rio. These meetings, which I covered, were always cordial and helped keep relations on a relatively even keel but did not lead to any substantive improvement in the situation.

From my postings abroad between 1992 and 2004, I had watched the by-now familiar trajectory of India–Pakistan relations – what I describe as 'dialogue–disruption–dialogue' – repeat itself in endless cycles. There would be periods of engagement and a hope for better relations, only to be interrupted by cross-border terrorist attacks or tensions at the border. The pattern did not change even after the two countries became declared nuclear weapons states. India conducted its nuclear weapons tests in May 1998, and these were inevitably followed by Pakistan's. In its usual display of one-upmanship, Pakistan conducted six tests to India's five. Vajpayee's visit to Lahore in 1999 and the Lahore Declaration promised a new era of constructive relations between the two countries. There was an expectation that as nuclear weapons states, both

India and Pakistan could no longer afford to risk tensions and conflicts in their interactions.

The two sides agreed upon a number of confidence-building measures both with respect to their nuclear weapons programmes as well as conventional military forces and weapons. For example, both agreed to abide by their respective commitments to observe a moratorium on further nuclear testing. They also agreed to exchange views on their respective nuclear doctrines and take measures to minimize the risk of accidental use of nuclear weapons. The declaration envisaged the launch of intensive political engagement between the two sides on all issues of mutual concern and interest. There was optimism that the two countries, as nuclear weapons states, would finally overcome the negative legacy of the past and begin to develop a relationship of trust and cooperation.

However, the Pakistani occupation of the Kargil heights across the LoC later that year and the several major terrorist attacks that followed – the hijacking of an Indian Airlines plane on its flight from Kathmandu to Delhi in December 1999 and the attack on the Indian Parliament in 2001 – made it clear that Pakistan saw the nuclear overhang as a shield behind which it could not only continue cross-border terrorism but also escalate its attacks to progressively higher levels.

Each major terrorist attack would result in the suspension of dialogue between the two countries. After an interval, dialogue would resume, mostly at India's initiative. Given this pattern, there was no incentive for Pakistan to abandon what proved to be – from its perspective – a successful strategy of keeping India off balance, tying it down to the subcontinent and attempting to trade concessions on Kashmir for desisting from terrorist attacks. Pakistan also enjoyed a major advantage in the sustained support of both China and the US, whether the two major powers were in a hostile situation with each other or virtual allies. For China, at least since 1960, Pakistan has served as a very useful proxy against India. The Sino-Pakistan axis targeting India has been a nagging security challenge for us for the past few decades and is likely to remain so.

In the case of the US, Pakistan's relationship with it has been more complex.

Initially, the US saw Pakistan as a useful ally against the Soviet Union, located as it was on the latter's southern flank. Pakistan became the frontline state against the Soviet forces in Afghanistan in the 1980s. During this period the US was ready to overlook Pakistan's involvement in cross-border terrorism against India, both in the Punjab and Kashmir. It also turned a deliberate blind eye to its feverish and clandestine development of nuclear weapons capabilities and nuclear proliferation activities, despite compelling evidence of both. There was a quantum jump in Pakistan's military capabilities in these years, with supplies from both China and the US pouring in. For China, the anti-India focus was direct and deliberate; in the case of the US, India was often the victim of collateral damage – although one can't put it past that country to keep India off balance and assure a role for itself in intervening in India–Pakistan relations.

It took 11 September 2001 to bring about a change in American and Western attitudes towards terrorism. The terrorist attacks on the twin towers of the World Trade Center in New York and on the Pentagon in Washington that day were traced to Osama bin Laden, who was living under the protection of the Taliban in Afghanistan. Pakistan, as the patron of the Taliban, was now caught in American crosshairs. Once again geography came to Pakistan's rescue as it quickly gave in to US demands to abandon the Taliban and become its logistics base and transit corridor for its war against the

Taliban in Afghanistan. The self-declared US 'war against terrorism' did put pressure on Pakistan to wind down, though not abandon, its reliance on the terrorist groups it had nurtured to conduct cross-border attacks against India. It was no longer possible for Pakistan to claim that the so-called mujahideen engaged in terrorist attacks in Kashmir were local patriots fighting a war of independence.

This was also when it became known that Pakistan had been actively engaged in nuclear proliferation, sharing for a consideration its nuclear weapons know-how and even equipment with Libya, Iran and North Korea.

To let the Pakistani government off the hook, the US created a convenient myth that this proliferation was the handiwork of just one Pakistani, the scientist A.Q. Khan, the man credited with enabling Pakistan's nuclear weapons capability through stolen and surreptitiously acquired technology and components from across the world. The notion that Khan was running a private 'nuclear supermarket' without the knowledge and connivance of the Pakistani state beggars the imagination. Pakistan's cooperation in the US war in Afghanistan enabled it to get a pass for its nuclear misdemeanours. The US also relented when Pakistan refused to allow Khan to be interrogated by the US or the International Atomic Energy Agency (IAEA). Still, it came under intense international pressure over these two developments, giving India a window to engage with a politically more amenable Pakistan. The US too encouraged the resumption of the India–Pakistan peace process to make Pakistan focus on its western frontier with Afghanistan to support the US forces deployed there.

During the eight years of the Bush administration (2001–08), there was also a sharper interest in India as an emerging power and as a democracy that could be an important strategic partner to the US. The superpower was facing the challenge of a rising China and an altered balance of power in the Asia-Pacific region. The usual hyphenation between India and Pakistan, which has been a hallmark of US strategy in South Asia, was muted during this period. The new US line was that its relations with India and Pakistan would be based on their respective merits, and not on balancing one against the other. This too put pressure on Pakistan, which had always claimed parity with India in every respect. The most significant consequence of this altered US policy was the negotiation and successful conclusion of the Indo-US civil nuclear agreement, based on India's impeccable record in non-proliferation. Meanwhile, Pakistan was clearly told that its proliferation history had made impossible a similar initiative for it. The events leading up to the historic nuclear deal have been covered in Chapter 8.

My term as foreign secretary (2004–06) coincided with a relatively benign, and in some ways constructive, phase in India–Pakistan relations, though there were several ups and downs. This positive turn resulted from certain important initiatives taken by the Pakistani government including a declaration of ceasefire along the LoC and the assurance that terrorist groups operating from Pakistani soil and targeting India would be restrained. Prime Minister Vajpayee of India and President Pervez Musharraf of Pakistan met on the sidelines of the twelfth SAARC summit in Islamabad, and after their talks issued a joint press statement on 6 January 2004. This marked the beginning of a renewed process of normalization of the bilateral relations. The key paragraph in the statement read:

> Prime Minister Vajpayee said that in order to take forward and sustain the dialogue process, violence, hostility and

> terrorism must be prevented. President Musharraf reassured Prime Minister Vajpayee that he will not permit any territory under Pakistan's control to be used to support terrorism in any manner.

It is on the basis of this assurance that the two countries embarked on a peace process centred on the resumption of their Composite Dialogue, suspended since the terrorist attack on the Indian Parliament on 13 December 2001. (The Composite Dialogue was initiated in 1998 with an agenda comprising eight items – Confidence Building Measures, Jammu and Kashmir, Wullar Barrage/Tulbul navigation, Promotion of Friendly Exchanges, Siachen, Sir Creek, Terrorism and Drug Trafficking, and Economic and Commercial Cooperation. The resumed Composite Dialogue only lasted from 2004 to 2008.) The attack was traced to the Jaish-e-Mohammed in Pakistan, leading to a long, eyeball-to-eyeball confrontation between the armed forces of the two countries along their common border. Along with the dialogue process, transport and trade links were interrupted too. All this was now ready to be restarted.

Earlier, in November 2003, the two sides had agreed to a ceasefire along the three segments of the India–Pakistan border – the international boundary, the LoC and the Siachen area. This was the first time in nearly fourteen years that guns had fallen silent along the border.

Both countries agreed to pursue the proposal Vajpayee had made for a Srinagar–Muzaffarabad (in Pakistan-occupied Kashmir) bus service in his famous though controversial 'Hand of Friendship' speech at Srinagar in April 2003, calling for peace and friendship between India and Pakistan. This had gone against the prevailing sentiment that Pakistan had to be isolated and that there should be no engagement unless and until Pakistan abandoned its use of cross-border terrorism as an instrument of state policy. Many hours would be spent trying to work out the modalities of the cross-LoC service so that India's sovereignty over the whole erstwhile state of Jammu and Kashmir would not be compromised.

My first visit to Pakistan took place even before I assumed charge as foreign secretary. I was asked by the then external affairs minister Natwar Singh to accompany him to Islamabad for the 2004 SAARC ministerial meeting from 19 to 23 July. I was struck by the very positive and even friendly atmosphere that prevailed during the several bilateral interactions held on the sidelines of the meeting. It was apparent that the process initiated during the Vajpayee government was being enthusiastically taken forward by the Manmohan Singh government. This would be sustained over the next three years, until Musharraf ran into domestic political difficulties after the Lal Masjid affair[1] in July 2007 and had a confrontation with the chief justice of Pakistan, Iftikhar Muhammad Chaudhry. By then Shivshankar Menon was the foreign secretary. My term had ended on 30 September 2006.

While I was engaged in negotiations with the US on the nuclear deal, I was also, in parallel, involved in efforts to advance India–Pakistan relations on the basis of the agenda laid out at the Vajpayee–Musharraf meeting in January 2004.

---

[1] Pakistani forces were sent into the Lal Masjid in the centre of Islamabad to rescue several Chinese women who had been kidnapped by militant Islamist students attached to the Lal Masjid madrassa. The Chinese women, who were employed in a beauty parlour, were facing accusations of immoral activity. The kidnapping became a major issue, with the Chinese government demanding from Pakistan an assurance of their safety and return. The operation against the Lal Masjid kidnappers, in which several were killed, marked the beginning of the end of Musharraf's grip over Pakistan.

The Srinagar–Muzaffarabad bus service was discussed in great detail. The Pakistani side wanted the service to be limited to residents of the Kashmir Valley and the exclusion of the people of Jammu and Ladakh on the Indian side. We insisted that the service should be open to all residents of Jammu and Kashmir, including Gilgit and Baltistan. The reference to Gilgit and Baltistan was important because Pakistan had attempted to treat these areas as outside the boundaries of Jammu and Kashmir, designating them as 'Northern Areas' of Pakistan. We were able to prevail in this matter. The formulation adopted said the bus service would be available to 'all residents of the erstwhile state of Jammu and Kashmir, including Gilgit and Baltistan'.

There were also conflicting views on the travel documents to be used on the service. We held that each side should allow their respective passports to serve as the most convenient document for travel across the LoC. After all, there were Pakistani citizens from Pakistan-occupied Kashmir who sometimes travelled to Srinagar after entering India on a valid Pakistani passport. However, the Pakistanis were adamant that passports not be used because this may suggest that Pakistan accepted Indian jurisdiction over the parts of Kashmir under Indian control.

Eventually we accepted that travel across the LoC could be based on permits issued by the respective deputy commissioners or equivalent authorities to residents in their locality. Complicating matters, it was also agreed that the names of passengers travelling on the bus would be exchanged in advance for vetting by the security agencies of the two countries. While the bus service was an imaginative initiative, welcomed by people on both sides of the LoC, the cumbersome procedures and lengthy delays for security vetting diminished some of its political value.

After the Srinagar–Muzaffarabad bus service we were able to obtain fairly quick agreement on the Amritsar–Nankana Sahib, Amritsar–Lahore and Poonch–Rawalkot bus services, though these took time to materialize. A Kargil–Skardu bus service was proposed by India but rejected by Pakistan.

An important initiative on India's side was to open five new points for cross-LoC pedestrian travel within a limited zone in the wake of the terrible earthquake which hit both sides of Kashmir in late 2004.

During my tenure as foreign secretary, there were two bilateral issues for which the prospects for early agreement appeared to be relatively better. The first related to Siachen and the other to Sir Creek. It was my sense, after several interactions with my Pakistani counterpart, that there was a willingness on their part to arrive at a compromise on both issues. It was unfortunate that despite the significant progress on these issues, with mutually acceptable and politically sustainable agreements being worked out, the window of opportunity available in 2006 was allowed to close because of last-minute opposition from certain quarters. Here are my stories of Siachen and Sir Creek.

~

The ceasefire agreement between India and Pakistan in 1949 had marked out the line separating the forces of the two countries up to a point known as NJ 9842. Beyond this, said the agreement, the line would run 'north to the glaciers'. This formulation was repeated in the Simla Agreement of 1972, when the ceasefire line was converted into the LoC. Thus the area north of point NJ 9842 was left undemarcated.

In the late 1970s, official US maps, without explanation, began to show the line extending eastwards from NJ 9842 to the Karakoram pass. And now the Pakistanis too began to do the same in their maps. Slowly, the maps of several other countries adopted this version of the LoC as well. The entire glaciated area comprising the Siachen Glacier and the Saltoro Ridge, covering an area of over 2300 square kilometres, came to be shown as under Pakistani control.

In the early 1980s, Pakistan began to issue permits for international mountaineering expeditions to the Siachen Glacier area, thereby asserting its jurisdiction over it. In 1984, concerned about what this would mean for India's military position vis-à-vis both Pakistan and China, Indian forces were sent to occupy the glacier in a pre-emptive strike named Operation Meghdoot. Pakistani attempts to dislodge them did not succeed but they did manage to occupy and fortify the lower reaches. The Siachen conflict has been smouldering between the two countries ever since.

The first attempt to resolve the dispute was made in 1989 after a meeting between the then Indian prime minister Rajiv Gandhi and his Pakistani counterpart Benazir Bhutto in Islamabad in December 1988. An agreement was reportedly arrived at in subsequent talks between the defence secretaries. But it was not implemented because of Pakistan's refusal to delineate the actual ground positions of the two sides from which the mutual withdrawal of forces would take place. The Pakistanis contest this version of events and say that Rajiv Gandhi had committed to Bhutto that Indian forces would unilaterally withdraw from the positions they had occupied in 1984, and that no side would intrude into the resulting zone of demobilization.

Another attempt to resolve the dispute was made in 1992. In defence secretary–level talks held in November that year, Pakistan agreed to the Indian demand that the Actual Ground Position Line (AGPL) of the two forces in the area and the subsequent positions to which they would be redeployed be recorded. The vacated area would be monitored by both sides to prevent any intrusion, and a joint commission would draw the LoC beyond NJ 9842. The AGPL and the redeployment positions would be recorded in an annex to the main agreement.

N.N. Vohra, who was the defence secretary at the time, confirmed in a newspaper interview that an agreement on Siachen had been reached. At the last moment, however, a political decision was taken by the Narasimha Rao government to defer its signing to the next round of talks scheduled for January the following year. But this did not happen.

This background is important since a possible deal along the lines of the 1992 understanding was also worked out between my Pakistani counterpart Riaz Mohammad Khan and myself in 2006. We too agreed that the current positions of the forces of the two countries, the positions to which they would withdraw, a schedule for redeployments, and a joint monitoring mechanism to prevent mutual intrusions – all this would be recorded in an annex. However, to give the document additional strength, we insisted, and the Pakistani side agreed, that both the agreement and the annexure would be signed and that the main agreement would explicitly declare that the annexure had the same legal validity as the agreement itself.

Prime Minister Manmohan Singh had asked me to work on this agreement but had also insisted that I obtain a consensus on it from all the key stakeholders in our own system. I did many rounds of consultations, both at the senior bureaucratic and ministerial levels in the ministries of defence, home and finance (whose members are part of the Cabinet Committee on Security [CCS]). The army chief J.J. Singh and the intelligence chiefs were also brought on board.

The technical details of the agreement, including the points and timing of redeployment, the phases in which it would be implemented and the structure of the monitoring mechanism, were actually worked out at the army headquarters by the director-general of military operations. The draft agreement, along with the annexures, were then put together in a note to the CCS for approval so that it could be presented as a proposal from the Indian side at the India–Pakistan defence secretary level talks scheduled for May 2006. The note had been examined and agreed to by all the relevant stakeholders and agencies. The CCS approval was, therefore, expected to come as a matter of course.

When the CCS meeting was held on the eve of the defence secretary–level talks, the then national security advisor (NSA) M.K. Narayanan launched into a bitter offensive against the proposal, saying that Pakistan could not be trusted, that there would be political and public opposition to any such initiative and that India's military position in the northern sector vis-à-vis both Pakistan and China would be compromised. J.J. Singh, who had happily gone along with the proposal in its earlier iterations, now decided to join Narayanan in rubbishing it. The ministers of home (Shivraj Patil) and defence (Pranab Mukherjee) decided to play it safe and proposed the deferment of its consideration until further study. My defence of the deal became a voice in the wilderness.

The prime minister chose to keep silent and not step into the fray, perhaps for good reason. Narayanan, at one point, suggested that Siachen be taken off the agenda of India–Pakistan talks entirely and that this should be communicated to the visiting Pakistani defence secretary at forthcoming talks. I resisted this strongly, pointing out that this would mean the unravelling of the entire dialogue process of years, since Siachen had been on the agenda for over two decades.

At this stage Pranab Mukherjee fortunately stepped in to support me. He pointed out that Rajiv Gandhi himself had agreed to include Siachen in the India–Pakistan dialogue and it should remain part of the agenda. This was solemnly endorsed by the others. But the opportunity to finally resolve a long-standing issue and a constant source of bitterness in Pakistan was lost.

In 2007 I visited a couple of high-altitude posts on the Siachen Glacier as part of a border infrastructure survey I was asked to do by Prime Minister Manmohan Singh. I had hours of interaction with the younger officers stationed there. They were enduring extreme cold and unpredictable weather in these inhospitable areas, their psychological isolation just as bad as their physical hardship. Their living premises were fibreglass units heated with kerosene. The kitchen and toilets were outside in unprotected structures. Waste would collect just outside their units in ever-rising heaps, its smell sometimes overpowering. This was also a health hazard. Informally, I asked if they would support a mutual withdrawal by India and Pakistan from the glacier, and the answer was an unqualified 'yes'. I then asked whether we could risk Pakistani occupation of the area vacated by us. The officers replied that nothing better could happen because the Pakistanis would suffer 'what we have been going through these past several years'.

I made several recommendations to the then defence minister, A.K. Antony, to improve the living conditions of our troops deployed on the borders. I was pleasantly surprised to find, in a later survey, that several of the recommendations had been implemented, thanks to Antony's personal intervention.

~

Another long-standing issue between the two countries has been the alignment of Sir Creek, which flows out into the Arabian Sea through the Rann of Kutch. The creek flows north–south into the Arabian Sea. Pakistan claims that the boundary lies on the east bank as per a resolution of the Bombay government of 1914, which demarcated the internal boundary between the Sind and Kutch divisions. India insists that we should follow the international Thalweg principle, which would place the dividing line mid-channel in the river. The alignment of the creek affects the maritime boundary between the two countries and the ownership of potential gas reserves. This is because the usual practice is to extend the land boundary seaward.

The Indian Navy had come up with a very innovative approach which would have determined the maritime boundary from a point out in the sea on the edge of the countries' respective continental shelves, with equal lines drawn to points on each coast. This would have left a triangular zone of about a hundred square kilometres just at the mouth of the Sir Creek without a demarcation. One possible compromise was to divide this between the two sides in an agreed proportion.

For example, if we accepted the Pakistani alignment, with the east bank of the creek as the boundary, then Pakistan would get only 40 per cent of the triangle. If our alignment according to the Thalweg principle was accepted, Pakistan would get 60 per cent. There was keen interest in Pakistan to follow this approach but we were unable to explore this further when the Siachen deal fell through. Pakistan was no longer interested in a stand-alone Sir Creek agreement.

I do not believe that these two proposed agreements, if concluded, would have significantly transformed the bilateral relationship or opened the way to some 'grand reconciliation'. We are too far apart in how we view our respective histories, how we construct our respective national narratives and how we see our place in the world for that. We can only have a modest expectation of improvement in our relations.

However, I believe these two agreements would have been in our interest, given the enormous burden of sending troops to Siachen and the uncertainty and avoidable confrontations on our seas due to a non-demarcated maritime boundary. The rare window of opportunity in the 2003–06 period, when these incremental steps could have been taken towards some relief for us on the Pakistan front, is now closed. These initiatives are like 'perishable commodities', which rot if left on the shelf for future consideration. If they are not grasped when the time is opportune they quickly fade away, as they indeed did.

~

Musharraf and Vajpayee had agreed upon a back channel for confidential talks on Kashmir at their January 2004 meeting in Islamabad. Then NSA Brajesh Mishra was the interlocutor on our side and Tariq Aziz, a trusted aide of Musharraf's, on the Pakistani side. With the change in government later that year, Mishra's successor J.N. Dixit became Aziz's counterpart. Dixit's sudden and unexpected death from a heart attack in January 2005 caused a temporary hiatus until Prime Minister Manmohan Singh decided to appoint the veteran and thoroughly professional diplomat Satinder Lambah. He had significant experience in dealing with Pakistan, having been the prime minister's special envoy for Pakistan. Lambah continued in this position until the end of Manmohan Singh's government in May 2014. The Modi government has not indicated its willingness to resume these talks although the NSAs of the two countries remain in touch.

On the Pakistani side, Aziz continued to be the interlocutor until the end of the Musharraf regime in 2008. The Asif Ali Zardari government, which took office in 2009, continued the back-channel talks, with seasoned diplomat and former foreign secretary Shahryar Khan serving as his special envoy. When Nawaz Sharif became the prime minister in 2013, Riaz Mohammad Khan, another former foreign secretary, became the interlocutor on the Pakistani side.

As foreign secretary, I was kept posted on the broad contours of the talks but those were early days and positions were significantly distant. I gather that eventually a framework for an understanding on Jammu and Kashmir did emerge based on a pragmatic proposition put forward by Manmohan Singh in 2005. Dr Singh said that while he had no mandate to change India's borders, he did have the mandate to render them progressively irrelevant so that there could be a free flow of peoples, goods and ideas across them. Musharraf claims that progress was achieved in these back-channel talks on the basis of a new approach he had recommended in 2005, which he later formalized in his 'four-point formula' in December 2006. He had suggested that each party put aside what the other could not accept and try to find a compromise on the middle ground that remained. His other suggestions were the 'demilitarization' of Kashmir, beginning with major towns such as Baramulla and Sopore; the opening of borders for travel across the LoC; and finally, the 'joint management' of the two sides of Kashmir through joint mechanisms comprising representatives from the Kashmiris' 'self-governing bodies'.

I had, in fact, conveyed our reaction to this proposition in the foreign secretary–level talks held soon afterwards, when the 'four-point formula' was formally raised by my counterpart. I had pointed out that given the diametrically opposite positions the two countries had on Kashmir, there would be no room for compromise left if each side excluded what the other side could not accept.

As far as demilitarization was concerned, I said Indian security forces were deployed to protect the people of the state from cross-border terrorist attacks and hostile military actions from the Pakistani side. Once the threat of cross-border terrorism receded there would be no reason to deploy large security forces in the state.

On 'joint management', I said we could only consider joint consultative mechanisms on subjects of mutual interest, such as cross-LoC trade, travel and tourism, environment and health. As we did in the matter of the bus service, we insisted that the proposed consultative mechanisms cover the entire erstwhile state of Jammu and Kashmir. In this context, I pointed out that while we had duly elected representatives on our side, there were no counterparts to them in Gilgit and Baltistan, which was administered directly from Islamabad. However, I did convey our prime minister's view that the borders should be made progressively irrelevant and that we would pursue initiatives to that end, step by step. I do not know whether the framework agreed to in principle in the back-channel talks upheld our positions on these key questions. I understand that Musharraf did initiate action to create elected bodies in Gilgit and Baltistan so that they could be represented in the proposed joint mechanisms.

There was no doubt in my mind that any understanding on Kashmir had to be part and parcel of a larger peace process between India and Pakistan. So, whatever the understanding arrived at in the back-channel talks, it could only be implemented and sustained if there was, in parallel, a broader peace process. It was then agreed that the India–Pakistan

Joint Commission would be revived to pursue cooperation in a number of different areas. The joint consultative mechanisms on Kashmir would then fold into the larger rubric of India–Pakistan cooperation.

The India–Pakistan Joint Commission, headed by the foreign ministers of the two countries, was revived in October 2005 after a gap of sixteen long years. Eight subgroups were created for practical cooperation in areas of common interest – agriculture, education, environment, health, information and broadcasting, IT and telecom, science and technology, and tourism. These subjects could also feature on the agenda of the 'joint mechanisms' for Jammu and Kashmir. Unfortunately, the joint commission met only once again in 2007 because of another disruption in relations. It was revived in 2012 but has not met since.

The back-channel talks over the past several years have demonstrated the usefulness of parallel dialogue away from the glare of media and public perception. There should be a revival of this additional channel of communication. This kind of a political-level interaction will go beyond the contact (useful though it is) taking place under the Modi government between the NSAs of the two countries.

~

India has not been able to craft an effective strategy to deal with Pakistan's use of cross-border terrorism as an instrument of state policy. Each time there is a major terrorist strike by elements aided and abetted by the Pakistani state, the choice confronting our political leadership is whether to engage in a retaliatory military strike and risk possible escalation to a nuclear exchange, or do nothing more than suspend bilateral engagement and, in some cases, as after the attack on the

Indian Parliament, interrupt trade and transport links. Indian troops were mobilized and massed on the India–Pakistan border after this attack but no operations were undertaken. It is debatable whether this changed Pakistani calculations in any way. The troops were demobilized after a very costly standoff lasting several months.

India's basic weakness is that its political leaders have no credible response options between the extreme choices of military retaliation and appeasement when it comes to Pakistan-sponsored terrorism. What we need is a toolkit of options, short of war, that can inflict costs and damages on Pakistan. We need to have a series of pressure points on Pakistan to contain its hostile activities against India. These would need to be built up gradually. One pressure point, for example, could be Gilgit and Baltistan; we could pursue our claim on them more aggressively, highlighting the disaffection within the largely tribal population there. After all, technically speaking, they should be treated as our own citizens and their welfare should be a matter of concern to us. I had begun to receive delegations from these areas, even though many of them are now resident in other countries.

Human rights violations continue in Balochistan, and yet we have been hesitant to draw attention to them. On 27 December 2005 I had authorized this press statement to be issued:

> The Government of India has been watching with concern the spiralling violence in Balochistan and the heavy military action, including the use of helicopter gunships and jet fighters by the Government of Pakistan to quell it. We hope that the Government of Pakistan will exercise restraint and take recourse to peaceful discussions to address the grievances of the people of Balochistan.

The idea was to build up countervailing pressure on Pakistan whenever it raised Kashmir or any other matter to criticize India. But I was advised not to issue such statements any more because this could adversely affect the improvement of bilateral relations. My point was that despite the improvement, Pakistan was not shying away from regularly finding fault with India on Kashmir and a range of other issues.

It has also been my view that we should not be reluctant to leverage our presence in Afghanistan to pressure Pakistan even more. Pakistan has been making wild allegations that India has fourteen consulates in Afghanistan, some of which are being used to instigate the insurgency in Balochistan, and that India's cooperation projects in that country are a cover for more nefarious activities. In one of my meetings with my Pakistani counterpart, I had suggested a separate bilateral dialogue on Afghanistan. I had offered to give Pakistan a complete rundown on all the Afghanistan projects we were involved in. I had also said that since both India and Pakistan claimed they wanted to see a politically stable and economically prosperous Afghanistan, we could consider joint projects for the benefit of that friendly country. We could also jointly verify if Indian consulates existed in the locations that Pakistan claimed they did. But this offer was not accepted. I understand similar offers made by my successors came up against the same blank wall.

Given this situation, there is no reason why India should not raise its presence in Afghanistan, even on the security front. Short of putting Indian boots on the ground, we should do everything we can to strengthen Afghan security forces. Pakistan cannot have a veto over our engagement with Afghanistan. We will continue to be marginalized, as we have been in the ongoing quadrilateral peace process with the Taliban. The US, China, Pakistan and Afghanistan are the lead players. India will be considered a key player only if its profile in Afghanistan is significantly sharper than it is today.

We have so far discussed only the negative levers of influence for dealing with Pakistan. These must be combined with the positive levers. Precisely because India has a difficult and complex relationship with Pakistan, it must remain engaged continuously with it at all possible levels, both official and non-official. The lines of communication must never be interrupted. Halting talks whenever there is a serious terrorist incident that is traced back to Pakistan is not the answer; in any event, that has never stopped Pakistan's policy of cross-border terrorism. Any rupture in bilateral dialogue only creates a space for external involvement and activism, where the agenda may not be aligned to our interests. During previous India–Pakistan crises, there have been interventions by the US, inevitably hyphenating the two countries. This is welcome to Pakistan but not India.

It is in India's interests to promote trade and economic relations with Pakistan, even if this means some non-reciprocal measures from our side. There is significant complementarity between the two economies, and it is estimated that as much trade takes place between them through third countries like the UAE, Kuwait and Singapore as through direct channels. Converting this indirect trade into direct trade will benefit both countries.

During my time as foreign secretary, it had been agreed that India and Pakistan would allow direct banking relations. Each side would designate two banks to open branches in the other country on a reciprocal basis. This has still not been implemented. Off and on there have been proposals for India to supply power to Pakistan, and technical discussions on linking transmission lines have also taken place. On a request from Pakistan, India had agreed to supply it diesel using the land route. None of these agreements were followed up, mainly because of opposition from the Pakistani military.

An important instrument in India's diplomatic toolkit for managing its relations with Pakistan is the promotion of people-to-people relations, cultural relations and civil society dialogue. This would, over time, create interest groups in Pakistan that have a stake in peaceful and friendly relations with India. The greater the exposure of ordinary Pakistani citizens to the Indian reality, the less effective that country's official policy of cultivating hostile and negative attitudes towards India. A more liberal visa policy, implemented unilaterally if necessary, would allow Pakistani citizens to visit any part of India. Currently their visas are limited to only three cities. The burden – and often humiliation – of police reporting for Pakistanis travelling to India must be done away with. Even the limited visa liberalization of the past few years has helped Indians and Pakistanis connect with each other. Pakistani authors come to India to launch books, their artistes perform at concerts here and Pakistani actors appear in Bollywood films. These should be encouraged. Instead we resort to jingoism.

In Chapter 4, it was emphasized that the Indian subcontinent is a single, interconnected geopolitical entity. It is even more a single, interconnected ecological space – and a fragile and threatened one at that. Climate change has already begun to aggravate the stresses and strains arising out of rapid economic and social transformation and population pressure. The rivers of the subcontinent are natural systems that political boundaries have divided up. Now river basin management appears impossible.

The Indus Water Treaty between India and Pakistan, concluded in 1960, has been successful in upholding the two countries' respective entitlements to the waters of the Indus and its tributaries but has no provision for the collaborative management of the Indus river basin. Without such management, it will be difficult to ensure continued water security and food security for those dependent on its waters.

If sea levels rise, it will be a grave danger to the coastal plains of the subcontinent and the large resident populations. The most compelling argument for collaboration among South Asian countries would be the ecological challenge they share, particularly India and Pakistan. Putting these larger issues on the agenda of India–Pakistan dialogues will help bring a more balanced perspective to our pursuit of good relations.

India's Pakistan policy must be based on the recognition that India–Pakistan relations are deeply adversarial and likely to remain so for the foreseeable future. The policy objective should be the management of this adversarial relationship rather than any quest for a grand reconciliation. We can prevent tensions from escalating and avert violence. As we have seen, the adversarial nature of the relationship is rooted in the widely different and deeply entrenched historical and national narratives of the two countries. For example, even so-called liberal Pakistanis believe that cross-border terrorism, even if not justifiable, is not without good reason because of the power asymmetry between the two countries.

Competing and deeply held narratives change slowly and can only be reconciled over a long period of time with patient engagement. There must be a willingness to separate historical fact from politically inspired distortions. That not being the reality, only modest and incremental measures to improve relations are possible. Any suggestion of a path-breaking initiative to transform relations has inevitably led to a backlash from those who are deeply invested in the perpetuation of hostility and are profiting from it. A recent example of this is the 2016 terrorist attack on the Pathankot air base days after the unexpected but highly publicized visit of Prime Minister Modi to Lahore at the invitation of his Pakistani counterpart Nawaz Sharif.

Another factor that has influenced Indian policy towards Pakistan is the implicit but unarticulated anxiety that the latter's disintegration or descent into chaos will present India with an existential crisis. This fear inhibits Indian actions that may be seen as contributing to that denouement. The reality is that India is only marginally relevant to the domestic political dynamic in Pakistan. Whether it survives as a stable entity or disintegrates will depend upon what its people want. To refrain from rapping Pakistan's rulers for fear of destabilizing that country is a flawed proposition.

One should also take note of the fact that while Pakistan's fragility is advertised as a mitigating circumstance by one set of analysts, its resilience is lauded by another set. Pakistan is often described as being suicidal. But its record shows that its ruling elite has displayed a remarkable ability to cut deals to ensure its survival and maintain its privileges. We are, in fact, dealing with a state that is coldly calculating in pursuing its declared interests, and it must be confronted as such.

Pakistan also uses our shared language and culture to arouse sentimentality. This mawkishness camouflages its mostly unsentimental aims as a state with hostile intent. Indian civil society and political leaders fall prey to this tactic, having no clue about the ulterior intent. Our bonds of language and culture are very real and should be used to advance links but they must not influence the calculus of interstate relations.

Managing Pakistan will always be a challenge. But we must think of it as a state amenable to influence – economic, military and cultural. Once we see this, we must then throw off our self-imposed inhibitions and be open to all options, creating and using both positive and negative levers to yield the results we want. This is what we do in dealing with other states. And this is what we need to do with Pakistan.

As the back-channel talks progressed, it became clear that the Jammu and Kashmir problem could not be resolved, not for a very long time to come. But the discussion took for a starting point Prime Minister Manmohan Singh's declaration that while he did not have the mandate to change India's borders he did have the mandate to make those borders progressively irrelevant. Of course, his comment applied not just to Pakistan but to all our subcontinental neighbours. But this points us back to what I referred to earlier in this book – the need to restore the geopolitical integrity of the region.

The practical application of Dr Singh's statement to India–Pakistan relations did yield results. What was agreed in the back-channel talks has still not been revealed in reliable detail but enough is known to conclude that the two sides committed to an essentially open border between the parts of Jammu and Kashmir under their respective de facto jurisdictions. But the agreement could not be taken forward precisely because it was not part of the larger peace process between the two countries.

It has been argued that converting the LoC into an international boundary is the only realistic solution to the issue of Jammu and Kashmir. Even if that were the case, it can only be the end point of negotiations and not the beginning. For the present there is no reason to abandon our formal position that the whole of the erstwhile state of Jammu and Kashmir is the sovereign territory of India.

We must chip away at Pakistan's hostility because our current adversarial relations with it and its use of asymmetrical strategies do impose significant constraints on India. We may have to adopt counter-constraint policies to attempt to change the strategic calculus in Islamabad. This may include the option of inflicting pain on Pakistan if India's security is threatened. India must also include in its policies an uninterrupted, longer-term project to enhance people-to-people links, trade and commercial relations and cultural interactions at every opportunity.

6

Understanding China

China shares a very long border with India and is the power that has the most direct impact on India's strategic space. Its recent asymmetrical accumulation of authority cannot but constrain India's exercise of strategic autonomy, an abiding objective of our foreign policy. In dealing with the rapid rise of China and the challenge it poses to India, it is important to have a much deeper understanding of the nature of the Chinese civilization, its cultural particularities and the world view of people. One must appreciate that this is a country whose attitudes and ways of thinking have formed over millennia, layer upon layer; it has been less influenced by the outside world than any other major civilization.

Through much of history, India and China were only dimly aware of one another despite being the two major centres of Asian civilization. This is not surprising, separated as they were by the soaring, snowbound Kunlun and Karakoram mountain ranges in the west, the vast icy plateau of Tibet that divided them north to south, and the oceanic expanse to the east. Such interaction as did take place was through the caravan routes linking Kashmir with what is now Chinese Xinjiang.

One such route ran from Leh in Ladakh, and through the Karakoram pass to the oasis towns of Yarkand, Khotan and Kashgar. These towns were in turn linked through the well-known Kansu corridor in western China to the ancient Chinese capital of Chang'an, now known as Xi'an, home to the terracotta warriors unearthed in the tomb of the first Chinese emperor, Qin Shi Huangdi. Another caravan route ran from the Punjab, through Afghanistan and what are now the Central Asian republics of Uzbekistan, Turkmenistan and Kyrgyzstan, to Kashgar. From Kashgar there were two routes to Chang'an, one following a trail south of the great Taklamakan desert and the other a trail north of it. These were the paths through which trade caravans plied between India and China. Buddhist monasteries soon emerged in the oasis towns along them, serving both as caravanserais and as transmission belts for the Buddhist faith.

The ruins of these monasteries can still be seen today. Aurel Stein's *Serindia* is an encyclopaedic compendium of how art, culture, and religious and philosophical ideas travelled along these trails, providing glimpses of one civilization to the other.

During my assignment to China from 1983 to 1986, I once travelled to its western regions. I visited the cave temples of Dunhuang, which have wall paintings on Buddhist themes, the earliest dating back to the fourth century and the latest to the tenth. The earlier frescoes are simpler in conception, the facial features of the Buddha and the Bodhisattvas clearly Indian. As one moves to the later caves, the figures become steadily more Sinicized, as do the scenes depicted in the background.

In Xinjiang I visited the ruins of two prominent oasis towns with massive remains of ancient Buddhist monasteries and stupas. These towns are known by the Chinese names of Jiaohe and Gaochang. The ruins, spread over a very large area, convey some notion of how Indian influence spread across Central Asia and into China. Some memories of those ancient links still echo among the people in this part of China.

I also visited some of the oasis towns in Xinjiang, including Hami, famous for its honeydew melons, and Turfan, famous for its grapes that are dried into raisins on the rooftops of squat mud houses. Kashgar was easily one of the more fascinating stops, still retaining its picturesque Central Asian character. The main mosque in the city had an old imam who had studied in a seminary in Delhi and later in Bukhara. He spoke fluent Urdu. The old town was still divided into craft quarters of metalworkers, silversmiths, woodworkers, carpet weavers and tailors.

I was able to make a brief visit to the well-known Chini Bagh, for years the home of the British consul general and featuring in several accounts of European travellers who found it a haven of very English comforts after their arduous journeys. After the British left, it briefly housed the Indian and Pakistani consulates, one occupying the ground floor and the other the first floor. The Chinese closed the mission in 1956.

My visit to Kashgar coincided with the Muslim month of Ramzan. After sundown and through the night, the Kashgar bazaar would be alive and bustling with foodstalls selling naan, kababs and various kinds of sweets. There was much music and dancing too. One evening I was accosted by a group of young men who asked where I was from. When I replied 'India', they gave a spirited rendition of *'Awaara Hoon'*, an Indian film song popular in the 1950s, with much vigorous dancing to boot. It did not take long for the Chinese security who were shadowing me to put a stop to this memorable spectacle. The resounding success of the recent Indian film *Dangal* in China is also testimony to the continuing popularity of Bollywood in that country.

Buddhism entered China via Central Asia and also through the sea route linking its eastern coast with ports on the Indian peninsular coast. Chinese junks were a familiar sight at Calicut, long famous as an entry port for the spice and textile trade. Several Chinese pilgrims travelled to India in merchant vessels from China. The Zen patriarch Bodhidharma, said to be a prince of the ruling family at Kanchipuram, travelled in the fifth century to China using the sea route. So did several Indian monks who went there to preach and to help translate Buddhist texts into the Chinese language.

Tibet was a third source of transmission of Buddhist texts and philosophy from India to China, particularly during the reign of the Yuan dynasty in the thirteenth and fourteenth centuries, when the Mongols ruled China.

The regular traffic of pilgrims, traders and scholars between northern India and China declined once Muslim invasions and rule interrupted the existing patterns of trade and travel. For several centuries – between the fourth and the thirteenth centuries CE – the Buddhist monastery and University of Nalanda had attracted pilgrims and scholars from across South East Asia and China. Nalanda was the accepted knowledge capital of Asia. The Chinese monk Xuanzang spent several years at the university, marvelling at the depth and quality of scholarship on offer.

With its destruction by Bakhtiar Khilji in the thirteenth century, its intellectual and philosophical contributions came to an end. However, the Indian contact with China continued through the maritime route, especially the south. The port of Calicut had regular sailings to Guangzhou and Quanzhou on the Chinese coast. Quanzhou even had a resident community of Tamil traders, who established a Krishna temple that was later transformed into a Buddhist temple whose remains have survived. Its pillars have Hindu motifs and there is a stele on its premises bearing Tamil inscriptions.

This history of regular though limited engagement, the recognition of India as the source of Buddhism, the exposure to learned Indian scholars and the stories told by respected Chinese monks who travelled to India for studies – all this placed India in a category all by itself in the Chinese view of the world. India did not feature in the traditional Chinese political order, which considered China the civilizational centre with concentric rings of subordinate states paying tribute. India may have been considered a special case, a parallel centre of power and high culture, but situated a comfortable distance away.

China's next encounter with India came with the Qing dynasty's conquest of the 'New Territories' of Xinjiang and the extension of the Chinese presence in Tibet. The Manchus, who took on the dynastic name of Da Qing, or the 'great Qing', displaced the Junghar Mongols from their Central Asian lands in the middle of the eighteenth century. The proximity of India to these newly conquered areas revived ancient memories of the land famous in China as the birthplace of Buddhism and celebrated in ancient texts as the 'western paradise'. However, it was difficult to reconcile this with the reality of the Muslim empire then ruling northern India, even though it was crumbling by this time, and by the reported inroads of the British who were taking advantage of the fragmenting polity. There were attempts to adjust the Qing empire's geography by locating India (believing it was still a Buddhist country, 'Yindu', as described in the ancient texts) further south and east of the Mughal territories, now called Hindustan. It would be much later that the two would be recognized as one country that was now ruled by a European power – one that threatened the very survival of the Qing empire.

It is interesting to note that this reference to earlier accounts of India as a parallel and perhaps even superior locus of civilization was contested at this time, even as its location was being debated at the Qing court. In his fascinating study 'From Frontier Policy to Foreign Policy – The Question of India and the Transformation of Geopolitics in Qing China', Matthew Mosca refers to a Qing scholar's criticism of the Chinese pilgrim Faxian's account of fifth-century CE India in his *Foguo ji* (An Account of the Buddhist Country):

> This book takes India to be the Central Country (Zhongguo) and China to be a peripheral land, which is probably the Buddha boasting of his own religion – its absurdities are not worth arguing with.

During the age of imperialism and colonialism, India came into the Chinese consciousness as a source of opium, which the British insisted on dumping in China. The use of Indian soldiers in the various British military assaults on China and the deployment of Indian police personnel in the British concessions may have also led to a negative attitude among the Chinese towards India and Indians. In addition, the British empire in India was seen as a threat to Chinese control over its newly acquired domain in Xinjiang and its suzerainty in Tibet.

The government of independent India was suspected of having inherited similar motivations against the new communist China, particularly as China now sought to extend its presence right up to the frontiers of Xinjiang and Tibet with India. The comprehensive defeat of Indian forces in the brief border war of 1962 placed India in a subordinate position in China's own *mandala* of interstate relations. It was no longer even rhetorically acknowledged as a parallel centre of power and influence. These factors would influence later relations between the two countries as they embarked on building themselves into modern nations.

There are elements in Chinese culture which set it apart from others; these constitute a relatively stable prism through which the country interprets the world around it. Of course, one should be cautious in applying this template to modern China, which is undergoing a dramatic transformation. It is unclear how and to what extent the modern digital culture which has pervaded Chinese society, particularly its youth, is shaking the roots of its deeply ingrained traditional culture. However, as in every society, a change in mental attitudes usually lags behind economic and technological changes. It is still worth our while to examine some of the more deeply rooted elements shaping China's collective psyche.

China's world view is inherently hierarchical. It is a legacy of its history of relative pre-eminence in a neighbourhood populated by smaller and, in Chinese eyes, less civilized countries. China was mostly a self-contained and self-sufficient economy through most of its history, foreign trade being a marginal component of its continental economy. Unrest within China itself was associated with the breakdown of central authority – an interpretation in keeping with the principle of hierarchical order. The tributary system arose out of this notion, though in many instances it resulted from a self-entitled assumption of overlordship, declared with choreographed displays of pomp and ceremony by the central authority.

With the increase in its economic and military capabilities, China can see its return to the top of the emerging economic and security architecture in Asia, to the pre-eminence it believes it enjoyed for most of history. Such sentiments are reinforced by Western comments on China regaining the share of the global GDP it already had before the nineteenth century, which was close to 25 per cent.

China is failing to recognize that the contemporary landscape of international relations is very different from what it may have encountered in the past. Ancient China was a self-contained and insular economy, with a mostly domestic-driven prosperity. Today China's prosperity is linked to the globalization of its economy. It is deriving wealth through its positioning in the interconnected web of economic activity. But interdependence runs counter to the hierarchy principle.

The Asian landscape and interrelations too are very different from what China would have encountered in the past. It is populated by a cluster of major powers, and the US continues to deploy a formidable military presence in the region. The Japan of today is not the neighbouring country which once borrowed from China's resplendent culture and script. It is the third largest economy in the world and a substantial military power. The region also has several middle and emerging powers, including South Korea, Indonesia, Australia and India itself. They will resist any unilateral reassertion of Chinese dominance. A multipolar world, with its continuing diffusion of economic and military power, includes a multipolar Asia. This is one instance where the Chinese perspective derived from its past is in contradiction to the prevailing reality.

Another unique feature of China's rich civilization that distinguishes it from other major civilizations is the use of ideograms or characters rather than an alphabet for its script.

Each character represents a word or a concept and these have survived – even as they have evolved over time – since they first appeared on oracle bones some 3500 years ago during the Shang dynasty. There is no grammar but patterns of usage sanctioned over time. A decent vocabulary requires the memorization of more than 3000 characters, while a scholar may aspire to an arsenal of more than 5000. I spent two years learning to speak, read and write Mandarin in Hong Kong. It was like having an entirely new and fascinating world opened to me. I was fortunate to have teachers who were mostly from Beijing and who had come to Hong Kong to escape the rigours of Mao's China. They were from old, well-to-do families, speaking a language matching in courtesy and elegance the old-world Urdu of Lucknow. Mrs Chen was one of the more sophisticated of my teachers, a woman with a very aristocratic bearing and language to match. One day I invited her to dinner, and our Chinese conversation went something like this:

> SS: Respected Mrs Chen, may I be presumptuous enough to extend an invitation to you to have a very simple and frugal meal at my very humble abode?
>
> Chen: My esteemed friend, I do not deserve this honour. I cannot think of putting you to so much inconvenience as to lay out a banquet for my humble self in your most wonderful residence.
>
> SS: On the contrary, I would be deeply honoured if you could grace my humble abode with your kind presence and share a very sparse meal with only a few simple dishes.
>
> Chen: I really do not think I qualify for such a great privilege being extended to me. I do not want to be the cause of much inconvenience and discomfort to you.

SS: There is no inconvenience at all. It would give me deep satisfaction to have you as my respected guest and it will indeed be an occasion for me to cherish.

Chen: Even though I do not at all deserve this honour I very humbly accept in view of the extreme generosity and valued friendship I enjoy with you.

SS: I am overjoyed and filled with gratitude at your kind gesture and the rare honour you have bestowed upon me.

As I was walking away, my invitation accepted after an exchange that would have been easily appreciated in Lucknow, Mrs Chen called me back, and in a barely audible whisper said: 'This is the first time I will be going to a student's place for dinner in the several years I have taught at this school.'

I asked her why. She said, simply and politely, 'You see, we never get beyond the first sentence. As soon as I say this will be too much trouble for my intended host and that I do not deserve the invitation, they think I am politely saying no to the invitation and the conversation ends there. In fact, I would like nothing better than to have dinner with my students but in our culture it is rude and impolite to say yes immediately.'

I felt relieved that at least in some respects our cultures were similar.

I must add that the somewhat old-world and excessively polite Mandarin I learnt in Hong Kong is no longer in use in revolutionary Beijing. I had to relearn much of the language, with its new and proletarian idiom. An early call I made on a senior female functionary in the government nearly ended in disaster when I addressed her with the honorific '*Taitai*', which is a very polite way of referring to a married lady and, directly translated, means 'great-great'. Apparently it had now become associated with abuse! I was politely told that this was a term associated with the bad old feudal society and that in new China everyone was a comrade. The old forms of address are making a comeback as China drifts away from its revolutionary pretensions.

It was difficult learning Mandarin. Writing the characters was not only a novel experience but also a window to the thought processes that lay behind them. Some concepts were so different from one's own ways of thinking. I would always confuse the phrase for 'day before yesterday' (*qian tian*) with the phrase for 'day after tomorrow' (*hou tian*). *Qian* means 'in front', while *hou* means 'at the rear'. How could a day in the future be behind us and a day in the past in front of us? My teacher once asked me in frustration why I was always confused about something so logical and easy to understand. I replied somewhat disdainfully that for most people the future was in front and the past behind. And here this logic was reversed. The teacher explained patiently that the past, having been already experienced, lies in front of us; it is no longer a mystery. And the future is behind us since we cannot see it! There were several such concepts in the language so very different from what one was accustomed to that it took me some time to internalize them. But it did make me appreciate the many perspectives from which the same phenomenon can be viewed; one's own perspective is not the only valid one.

The Chinese characters functioned as a powerful instrument in forging a common identity among diverse peoples inhabiting a vast territory, even though their spoken dialects were as good as different languages. Over the centuries the Chinese script created a shared vocabulary and a relatively homogeneous culture, which has become the bedrock of Chinese identity. Peter Hessler, author of *Oracle Bones*, writes:

> Classical Chinese connected people over space and time. It provided a powerful element of unity to an empire that, from another perspective, was a mish-mash of ethnic groups and languages.

But for the same reason, it has been difficult for China to accept the separate identity of the Uighurs in Xinjiang and Tibet, who have rich, well-developed languages and scripts of their own.

The Chinese script, which has evolved along with Chinese culture over several thousand years, is integral to the latter. This has led to the importance that is attached to the written word in China. Chinese ideograms have also become an intrinsic element of Chinese aesthetics. Calligraphy is a much-admired accomplishment, and Chinese characters figure as embellishments in classical painting and high-quality Chinese ceramics. Classical prose or poetry, written or transcribed by famous calligraphers, were admired as much for their visual impact as for their content.

Indian culture, by contrast, gives greater value to the spoken word. The ancient Vedas were heard as '*srutis*', and memorized and chanted as '*smritis*'. Writing came much later; in fact, classical Sanskrit could be written in several ancient scripts, including Kharoshti, Brahmi and Devanagari. In reciting ancient Sanskrit hymns and prayers, meticulous rules for tone, pitch and rhythm had to be followed. *Mantras* are said to generate and transmit power only if their intonation is precise. Beauty is associated with and sought through pleasing arrangements of sounds which have a flow. Imagery is of lesser aesthetic value as it becomes static even as it is created. To an Indian, Chinese music may sound stilted and lacking in melody. Indian classical music, on the other hand, is a breathtaking permutation and combination of seven notes and the several microtones in between, blending mathematical precision into almost infinite improvisations.

Chinese culture is a predominantly visual one, a legacy of the ancient ideogram. India's is predominantly an aural culture, with the spoken word, the chanted *mantra* and vocal music as its defining characteristics. The different civilizational paths forged by the two great Asian countries have also shaped the prism through which our respective cultures perceive the world around us, and how we interact with each other. The emphasis on the written word led to an immense treasury of historical documentation in China. The Chinese pilgrims Faxian and Xuanzang have left us elaborate records of their travels in India. They translated the voluminous Buddhist *sutras* that they gathered from the great monasteries of Taxila, Nalanda and Vikramshila. These have been preserved in libraries across China.

Even though several thousand Indian monks and teachers travelled to China between the first and tenth centuries, preaching and helping translate Sanskrit scriptures into Chinese languages, they have left behind no account of their adopted country. We know of them only through accounts preserved in Chinese documents. One such master is Bodhidharma, the first patriarch of Zen Buddhism, who travelled to China in the fifth century and was honoured by the king of the ruling Liang dynasty. Legend has it that he meditated for thirteen long years facing a blank wall at the famous Shaolin monastery before achieving enlightenment.

The enormous corpus of detailed historical records in China provides a contemporary reference point to the Chinese. Contemporary events are often interpreted using the wealth of historical analogies in the corpus. Even to this day, much of Chinese political discourse is carried out through recourse to historical analogies. Some are well-known and explicit, others artfully coded in language that lends itself easily to ambiguity and innuendo.

The start of the Cultural Revolution in China was signalled by a critical article on a play written by Wu Han, a scholar and historian of the Ming dynasty, titled *Hai Rui Ba Guan (Hai Rui Dismissed from Office).* Wu Han's play appeared in 1961. It told the story of a Ming official, Hai Rui, who was dismissed by the emperor for his honest criticism of the monarch's policies and conduct. Criticism of the play appeared early in 1966, depicting it as a veiled attack on Mao himself. Mao had purged the well-regarded Marshal Peng Dehuai in 1959 for daring to criticize him for the disastrous failure of the Great Leap Forward. Wu Han was put in prison, where he died in 1969.

During my first assignment in Beijing (1974–77), Chinese media and journals carried an obscure debate on the merits of 'legalism' associated with the Qin dynasty philosopher Han Feizi (280–233 BC) and the much better-known philosophical principles advocated by the sage Confucius. Han Feizi insisted that power was the decisive factor in interstate relations and there was no room for sentiment or moral principles so far as a ruler was concerned. He insisted that a king should rule by ruthlessly enforcing laws. It is said that the Qin emperor admired Han Feizi's writings; they had guided him in his conquest of other warring kingdoms and in the rule of his own kingdom using terror. One can find echoes of Kautilya's *Arthashastra* in them.

Confucius, on the other hand, was considered a philosopher of the feudal order, preaching virtue and paternalism for both ruler and householder alike. Confucius may have been comfortable with Ashoka's Dhamma. The media debates on the merits of 'legalism' that I referred to above were an oblique reflection of the intense factional struggle then taking place between the radical left wing, associated with Mao's wife, Jiang Qing, and a more moderate faction associated with Premier Zhou Enlai. Mao was identified as the latter-day Qin Shi Huangdi, while Zhou was identified with Confucius. This is yet another example of how historical analogies become instruments of current political battles in China.

The contrast with India, where history is still mostly a distraction, will be obvious. As a young diplomat serving in China, this was for me a most fascinating and intensive crash course in the use of history in statecraft and helped me sharpen my capacity for political analysis.

Deception as an instrument of statecraft is common to several cultures. In India one will find its use being advocated in the *Arthashastra* and, later, in the *Nitisara*. There are innumerable examples of this in the Mahabharata and the Ramayana too. The Mughals used it to subdue their rivals. The British relied on it to extend their empire. But in China, deception is accorded a value more significant than in other cultures.

In the Chinese classic *Romance of the Three Kingdoms*, there is a famous story called 'Ruse of the Empty City'. Zhuge Liang, the famous general of the kingdom of Shu, was in danger of being besieged and overcome in the fortress city of Xicheng by the army of the rival Wei kingdom. His own forces were a good distance away and unable to raise the siege of Xicheng. Zhuge Liang ordered all the city gates to be opened. His soldiers were asked to dress as ordinary householders going about their daily chores. He himself went to the top of one of the city gates, and sat there playing the Qin, a Chinese string instrument. The Wei general, Sima Yi, confronted with this strange spectacle and suspecting that he would run into an ambush if he entered the fortress, withdrew. Deception saved the day for Zhuge Liang. The story is celebrated as an example of how a stronger adversary can be pulled down by playing on his anxieties or creating false confidence in him.

Two instances illustrate how India's lack of familiarity with Chinese strategic culture created a misplaced sense of assurance. During the early 1950s, Nehru took up with Zhou Enlai the matter of Chinese maps showing large parts of Indian territory as part of China. Zhou Enlai explained that they were old Kuomintang maps which had not been reviewed and revised. He did not acknowledge that they were wrong. Yet the impression created was that China accepted the boundary as drawn on Indian maps.

The other misunderstanding was about the Chinese position on Kashmir. Some months before the 1962 border war, secretary general in the MEA, R.K. Nehru, met Zhou in Beijing. Nehru drew Zhou's attention to reports that China was leaning towards the Pakistani position that Jammu and Kashmir was disputed territory. He reminded the Chinese premier that on an earlier occasion, when asked if China recognized Indian sovereignty over Jammu and Kashmir, he had replied, rhetorically, 'Has China ever said that it did not?' Now Zhou turned this same formulation on its head and asked Nehru, 'Has China ever said that it did recognize Indian sovereignty over Jammu and Kashmir?'

In both instances, the Indian side did not press the Chinese to convey categorical and unambiguous assurances. If the Chinese had demurred, as they might have, we would have at least been better prepared to handle the subsequent problems we had with them.

There is a certain subtlety to the Chinese use of deception, which escapes most Indians.

In the Chinese scheme of things, the use of force is an essential and accepted way of pursuing national interests; and war is not necessarily an unmitigated evil. The Indian attitude towards the use of force and war is more ambiguous; it is often seen as a failure of diplomacy rather than as its extension, at least in certain circumstances. It favours force as a last resort only. We come across this even in our treatises on statecraft, in the *Arthashastra* and the *Nitisara*.

When Jawaharlal Nehru visited Beijing in 1956, he had a most interesting exchange with Mao on the nature of war. Mao suggested that war was not necessarily a bad thing since revolutions took place through war, emancipating countries and peoples. He suggested that the Second World War had created conditions for China's liberation, just as it may have also allowed India's independence. Nehru, on the other hand, drew attention to the new situation created by the advent of nuclear weapons, which could, in a war, threaten human survival itself. It was at this point that Mao made the chilling statement that even if nuclear weapons were used, China and India would still have several hundred million people left.

In analysing China's foreign policy behaviour, and specifically its posture towards India, these elements of Chinese thinking must be always kept in mind. Without an understanding of China's world view and how it influences the country's associations with other nations, it would be difficult for India to confront the China challenge.

It is against this background that we should look at India–China relations, particularly our border dispute.

7

The India–China Border Dispute and After

India's border dispute with China has been a major sore point in relations between the two countries over the past half-century and more. The failure of several rounds of negotiations in 1960 led to the catastrophic border war in 1962. As we have seen, India found itself in an unexpected clash of arms mainly as a result of its unfamiliarity with Chinese culture and ways of thinking. Indian leaders failed to pick up cues and oblique hints which if understood accurately may have led to a different outcome than humiliating defeat. It is a defeat that continues to be a scar on the Indian psyche. It altered India's strategic perceptions, suggesting the possibility of it having to fight a two-front war, with Pakistan to the west and China to the north. This remains India's main security concern.

The Jammu and Kashmir state of India and the Chinese province of Xinjiang shared a boundary in the western sector but after Partition, a substantial part of this boundary fell within Pakistan-occupied Kashmir, constituted by Gilgit and Baltistan. In the eastern sector, India and China became contiguous neighbours for the first time in history in 1950, when Chinese military forces occupied Tibet and incorporated it as the Tibet Autonomous Region of the People's Republic of China. Chinese empires had claimed Tibet as a tributary state at various points in history, just as they had several other states on their periphery, such as Mongolia, Vietnam and Korea. However, the large territory of Tibet had maintained an independent identity. Its unique governance structure, which combined religious and temporal power, exercised real political and administrative jurisdiction over the country. The Himalayan mountain range formed its natural frontier with India, making for a border that was never contested even if it was not drawn as a line on modern maps.

This natural frontier, covering the entire eastern sector in what is now Arunachal Pradesh, was given legal status in the Simla Convention of 1914 as the McMahon Line; the agreement was signed by the representatives of Britain, Tibet and China, although the Chinese government at that time did not follow up with its ratification. But Chinese maps today show about 65,000 square kilometres of the 84,000 square kilometres that constitute the total area of Arunachal Pradesh as part of Chinese territory. However, China usually asserts its claim to the whole of Arunachal Pradesh, which it calls 'southern Tibet'; it says the dispute is over 90,000 square kilometres of territory. The Chinese have never been asked to explain this discrepancy, so far as I am aware.

In the central sector of this line covering the border between Tibet and the current Indian states of Uttarakhand and Himachal Pradesh, differences between the Indian and Chinese claim lines are not significant. They relate to the precise alignment to be followed in the Barahoti plains, which is a relatively low-altitude gap in the high mountains of the central Himalayas.

In the western sector, the Chinese were ceded 5180 square kilometres of territory by Pakistan from illegally occupied Pakistan-occupied Kashmir under their 1963 boundary settlement. This is the Shaksgam valley, west of Siachen. Our dispute with China in this sector is mainly over the Aksai Chin plateau, an area of 35,200 square kilometres. Another area of contention is near Demchok to the south, involving about 500 square kilometres of territory. Aksai Chin (an Uighur phrase which translates into 'desert of white stones'), which lies between the Kunlun and Karakoram ranges, had at various times been included by the British as part of their empire in India.

As early as 1865, a Survey of India official, William Johnson, had proposed a boundary which ran along the Kunlun range and put the whole of Aksai Chin in the state of Kashmir. The Johnson Line broadly conforms to India's post-Independence claim line. Later, in 1897, British military officer John Ardagh proposed a modification of the Johnson Line which still depicted the boundary as lying along the Kunlun range. Hereafter, this boundary was referred to as the Johnson–Ardagh line.

In 1893 the Chinese representative in Kashgar handed over a map to the British consul general, Macartney, which proposed a boundary following the alignment of the Laktsang mountains, which would have placed most of Aksai Chin in China, with a southern portion known as the Lingzi Tang plains in India. This would have made the Karakoram mountains the boundary, separating the watersheds of the Indus and Tarim rivers, the former in India and the latter in China. There was a debate within the British government about whether to persist with the Johnson–Ardagh line or accept the Chinese proposal. The argument in favour of accepting the Chinese proposal was that it would provide a Chinese buffer between the British empire in India and the expanding Russian empire in Central Asia. However, it was not until 1899 that the British acceptance of this line was conveyed formally to the Chinese government. There was, however, no official Chinese response.

In terms of historical evidence, the Chinese never exercised any jurisdiction south of the Kunlun mountains, even when their empire was at its most extensive under the Qing dynasty (1644–1911). This was officially acknowledged in successive editions of the Postal Atlas of China published between 1917 and 1933. It also figured in the Peking University Atlas of 1925. The Dogra rulers of Kashmir, on the other hand, did exercise jurisdiction over much of the territory claimed by India. But it must be acknowledged that the Survey of India maps inherited from the British show much of the area in the western sector as 'undefined'. It was only in 1954 that a decision was taken to replace these maps with new ones showing the boundaries as fixed, with an alignment that incorporated Aksai Chin in Indian territory. In retrospect, this may not have been a wise decision since it deprived the Indian side of flexibility in negotiating a compromise with the Chinese.

The Sikkim–Tibet boundary is a special case. It was first defined in the Anglo-Chinese Convention of 1890 but then redefined in the Anglo-Tibet Convention of 1904 and confirmed in the Anglo-Chinese Convention of 1906, which the Chinese implicitly accepted. The British had negotiated this boundary on behalf of Sikkim, then a British protectorate. However, China did not accept Sikkim's incorporation into the Indian Union in 1975.

It was only in 2003 during Prime Minister Vajpayee's visit to China that the Chinese agreed to acknowledge India's sovereignty over Sikkim. During Chinese premier Wen Jiabao's visit to India in 2005, the newly published Chinese official maps showing the state as part of Indian territory were handed over to India. Since then the Chinese have been sometimes suggesting in official talks that India and China sign a partial agreement confirming the Sikkim section of the border. The Indian side, however, still prefers a comprehensive agreement.

In the year 2000, I was serving as India's ambassador to Myanmar. Our chancery was located in the old Oriental Fire and General Insurance building in downtown Yangon (Rangoon), which we had inherited after the wave of nationalization that swept the country from 1961 to 1964 under General Ne Win's military rule. It was a sprawling old building, badly neglected over the years. There was a large room at the back on the ground floor where all the muck and detritus of decades awaited some determined spring cleaning. It was filled with broken furniture, discarded books and publications, and a mountainous pile of old and tattered files, which had been written off and should have been destroyed. The old books and files attracted my attention.

I found a few rare and out-of-print books on South East Asia and translations of Buddhist classics which I retrieved and put right back into our embassy library. Most of the files were on mundane administrative matters but one thin file caught my eye. It carried the enigmatic title 'Ambassador's Personal Correspondence'. In it were two letters, both from Jawaharlal Nehru to Burmese premier U Nu, one dated 22 April 1957, and the other 29 September 1959, after the Dalai Lama's entry into India following the Tibet revolt. Our ambassador in Rangoon at the time, Lalji Mehrotra, had been asked to convey these letters to U Nu, and that is how these copies were kept in the file. They were probably unthinkingly consigned for destruction because the file was not marked confidential or secret.

In the 1957 letter, Nehru expresses sympathy for Burma's difficulties in settling its own border dispute with China. He refers to Zhou Enlai's statement to U Nu that China could accept the McMahon Line as the boundary with Burma but that it should be called the 'traditional line'. The following extract from Nehru's letter is revealing:

> When Zhou Enlai was here last, we discussed many matters at great length. He referred to his talks with you and U Ba Swe[1] and indicated that a satisfactory arrangement had been arrived at. In this connection he said that while he was not convinced of the justice of our claim to the present Indian frontier with China (in Tibet) he was prepared to accept it. That is, he made it clear that he accepted the McMahon Line between India and China, chiefly because of his desire to settle outstanding matters with a friendly country like India and also because of usage etc. I think he added he did not like the name 'McMahon Line.'
>
> This statement he made to me orally was important from our point of view and so I wanted to remove all doubts about it. I asked him again therefore and he repeated it quite clearly. I expressed my satisfaction at what he said. I said that there were two or three minor matters pending between India and China on the Tibet border and the sooner these were settled, the better. He agreed.

Nehru goes on to advise U Nu that the term McMahon Line 'is not right' because it 'reminds one of British incursions

[1] U Ba Swe, then the Burmese foreign minister.

and aggression'. He says India has stopped using it. But he also adds:

> As far as we are concerned, we have maintained all along that our frontier with China, except for the two or three very minor matters, was a fixed and well-known frontier and there was no dispute about it.

What is interesting is Nehru's utter silence on the western sector and the border with Xinjiang. Does this mean that in his view the western alignment was not 'fixed' as it was in the east? On the other hand, as I have pointed out earlier in this chapter, it was in 1954 that new Survey of India maps showed the Indian boundary in the western sector as already fixed along our current claim line, replacing earlier British era maps that had shown much of the Aksai Chin area in a colour wash that conveyed it was undefined. At this time, the Indian side was unaware of the Xinjiang–Tibet road that China had built in the early 1950s traversing the Aksai Chin. Indian patrols became aware of the existence of this road only in 1957.

The tone of the next letter in the file, written by Nehru nearly two years later, in 1959, is very different. Nehru says that 'the border troubles with China have been distressing'. He clearly ascribes it to developments relating to Tibet:

> I can only imagine that this is, partly at least, due to Chinese resentment at India's attitude in regard to events in Tibet and the Dalai Lama, though India had tried to function as correctly as possible in this regard.

Other reasons for China's newly hardened attitude on the border issue mentioned by Nehru in this letter relate to the economic distress in China. This resulted from Chairman Mao's programme of extending People's Communes as part of his Great Leap Forward, and from a persistent drought that had severely affected food production. Nehru also refers to the Soviet Union's criticism of China's aggressive posture towards India.

In this letter, too, there is no specific mention of the western sector or of the Chinese claim to Aksai Chin. In describing the India–China border dispute to U Nu, Nehru says:

> I cannot discuss our whole border problems because that is a complicated matter. We have a border with China now of 2500 miles. Part of this is what is called the MacMahon Line which you have in Burma also. Other parts are governed either by very old treaties or conventions and usage. To us it does seem absurd that these major claims on large areas of our territory should be made by China now.

It is also worth noting that at this stage Nehru did not expect any large-scale hostilities to break out:

> I do not think there is any real chance of a major conflict on the border but there is a possibility of petty conflicts here and there. I hope even these will be avoided.

These remarks confirm that India did not expect the border conflict to escalate beyond minor skirmishes and was, therefore, totally unprepared to handle the major Chinese assault in 1962.

After the 1962 war, China ended up occupying nearly all the territory it claimed in the eastern sector – that is, up to the Himalayan foothills comprising Tawang, Bomdila, and other areas right up to Tezpur. It then declared a unilateral ceasefire and withdrew to the general alignment defined by the McMahon Line. In the western sector, the Chinese occupied some additional territory (other than Aksai Chin) – in the Pangong Lake and Spangur Lake area, and in the Chip Chap valley of Ladakh. They did not withdraw from these newly acquired areas. There were no operations involving the central sector along Tibet's border with Himachal Pradesh and Uttarakhand. There is, now, a post–1962 LAC along the India–China border, whose alignment is implicitly acknowledged by both parties. There are differences between the two countries as to where exactly certain segments of the line lie, and this sometimes leads to confrontations between the patrols of the respective countries.

It is not clear why the Chinese forces withdrew after their successful assault all along the eastern sector in 1962. Perhaps it was due to the coming winter, and the attendant logistical difficulties in the high mountains. Alternatively, this may have been a political signal that China was still ready to settle on the basis of what later came to be known as the 'package proposal', that is, China accepting the McMahon Line as the boundary in the east and India recognizing Chinese claims in the western sector, including on Aksai Chin.

The Chinese scholar Wang Hongwei, a recognized authority on India–China relations, corroborates what Nehru has said about Zhou Enlai having accepted the McMahon alignment in the eastern sector as the basis for the boundary in this sector.[2] He quotes Zhou as having conveyed to Nehru:

> . . . the Chinese Government felt it necessary to take a relatively realistic attitude to the MacMahon line and

---

[2] Wang Hongwei, *A Critical Review of the Contemporary Sino-Indian Relations*, China Tibetology Publishing, 2009.

act with caution. It will take a certain period to solve the problem. However, in line with Sino-Indian friendship we believe the problem of this section of the border will be solved friendly.'

Wang goes on to make the Chinese position explicit:

> The 'relatively realistic attitude' was a hint to India that if India and China held talks on a compromise settlement of the border problem, China would likely accept the MacMahon line as forming the east section of the Sino-Indian border.

This was China's position before the Indian government presented a memorandum to the Chinese side in 1958 claiming the Aksai Chin region through which China had built the Xinjiang–Tibet highway. This changed the situation even before the events in Tibet. Here is what Wang has to say:

> . . . Zhou Enlai still hinted, instead of speaking out clearly [i.e. he was no longer explicit] that China was prepared to accept the MacMahon line as forming the eastern boundary. The reason why he did it in this way, except that as stated above [sic], was because he took into consideration the coming diplomatic talks, particularly that the Indian Government had made a definite territorial claim on the area through which the Xinjiang highway passed just 3 months before in a memorandum to the Chinese Government on October 18, 1958. The Chinese Government would like to hold talks with India on all problems of the whole Sino-Indian boundary, but the Indian Government claim on the western section of the Sino-Indian border made the Chinese Government feel that the coming talks would be a difficult

> bargain. In such a case how could one hoped [sic] that China would have officially admitted the trend of MacMahon line as the forming of the eastern section of the boundary and therefore, given up an important counter for the bargain.

In other words, the Chinese side raised large claims on the eastern sector because of the objection India raised to its construction of the Xinjiang–Tibet highway and not because of doubts China had about Indian claims to the eastern section of the boundary.

This again is made quite explicit by Wang in a subsequent paragraph:

> However, facts proved that the Indian Government misunderstood this and instead thought that the Chinese Government refused the MacMahon line in a roundabout way in order to take back and occupy 90,000 square kilometres of land between the MacMahon line and the traditional line. The Indian Government [sic] unusual understanding of diplomatic remarks of the Chinese side was one of the reasons for the tragedy that might have been avoided.

As I have mentioned earlier, it was during the Qing dynasty (1644–1911) that the Chinese empire achieved its largest footprint, establishing administrative control over Xinjiang and laying claim, through a largely symbolic tributary relationship, to overlordship over Tibet. The China claim on Tibet did not involve direct exercise of administrative jurisdiction. In the Qing maps the frontiers of the empire never extended south of the Kunlun mountains. Towards the west from the Karakoram pass, in the area south of the Kunlun mountains, it was the Mir of Hunza and the Kashmir state which exercised authority. It was only after 1890 that the

British began to encourage China to extend its jurisdiction into the region; and soon this jurisdiction was being claimed by China right up to the Mustagh and Aghil ranges. This is the line conceded by Pakistan in its 'provisional boundary agreement' with China, concluded in 1963.

In the region east of the Karakoram pass, the Chinese never claimed any territory south of the Kunlun nor did they exercise any administrative jurisdiction until after the construction of the Aksai Chin road. As mentioned earlier, the British had considered various alignments in this section that would have conceded part of the territory lying between Kunlun and Karakoram, including part of Aksai Chin, to the Chinese. These moves were driven by the fear that Tsarist Russia might extend its southern territories closer to the British Indian empire, and by the notion that China could serve as a useful buffer.

It is indeed ironic then that China, which projected the McMahon Line as an imperialist imposition, sought to profit from the gratuitous proposals made from time to time by imperial Britain for delineating the frontier, but which were never formalized. It should be noted that if China was so convinced of the legality of its claim in this sector then why did it believe it was necessary to raise a tactical claim in the eastern sector, post-1958, to deflect Indian claims in the western sector?

As to the Ladakh–Tibet boundary in the western sector, this boundary was well known and acknowledged by the Qing administration in the 1842 treaty it signed with the Sikh empire ruling Kashmir.[3] This was reaffirmed when the British took over these territories after defeating the Sikhs in 1846. It extended from the Lanak La pass in the north at the head

[3] G.N. Rao, *The India–China Border: A Reappraisal*, Motilal Banarsidass Publishers, 2009.

of Chang Chenmo and Niagzu in the Pangong Lake area to Demchok in the south. The LAC in this area is the result of additional territory occupied by Chinese forces in the 1962 war.

In reviewing the archival material now available and the more contemporary Chinese narratives, the following conclusions may be made:

- Until 1958, when India formally conveyed to China that its territory in the western sector included the area between the Kunlun and the Karakoram ranges, including Aksai Chin, and that the Chinese had violated Indian territorial integrity by building the Aksai Chin road, the alignment in the eastern sector defined by the McMahon Line was not disputed. The subsequent claims in this sector were raised by China only as a bargaining chip to acquire territory in the west that did not belong to it in the first place. Had China been convinced of its claim in the west there would have been no reason to suggest this trade-off.
- The Chinese empire, even at its maximum extent under the Qing dynasty, did not claim territory south of the Kunlun range. On the other hand, the exercise of administrative jurisdiction over this territory by the Hunza principality west of the Karakoram pass and by the Kashmir state east of the pass is well documented. Even if the Indian claims are considered somewhat tenuous, there was no Chinese presence in these areas at all until the early 1950s.
- The Ladakh–Tibet boundary had been well established and acknowledged by the Qing administration. It was in the 1962 operations that Chinese forces created an alignment further west, which is, broadly, the current LAC.

It is important to underline these conclusions because of the revisionist interpretations of the India–China border issue, not only among foreign scholars but in India too. There appears to be an unstated attitude that since India lost the 1962 war, the Chinese territorial assertions stand validated. While Indian claims have been repeatedly and selectively subjected to close scrutiny, Chinese declarations have rarely come under unbiased and critical examination. In fact, they are not very different in nature and intent from China's current claim on the South China Sea as its 'historic waters'. Much of this is based on nothing more than accounts of the voyages of the Ming admiral Zheng He in the fifteenth century. This has been rightly and universally rejected by the International Court of Justice. And yet, in the case of the India–China border dispute, a similar recourse to manufactured history appears to raise few notes of dissent, even among Indian analysts.

Right up to 1985, China continued to propose that the border dispute be settled on the basis of the so-called 'package proposal' put forward by Chinese premier Zhou Enlai in 1960: China would be prepared to accept the alignment as defined by the McMahon Line in the east with some minor adjustments, while India should accept the Chinese alignment in the west, which would give China control over the whole of the territory between the Kunlun and Karakoram ranges, including Aksai Chin. On the central sector, there were only minor disagreements, and these would have been easy to resolve. There was a re-emphasis on this package by Chinese leader Deng Xiaoping in 1982. In an interview to the Indian journal *Vikrant*, Deng had said, '. . . for instance in the Eastern Sector, can we recognize the existing status quo, I mean the so-called McMahon Line? This was left over from history but in the western sector, the Indian government should also recognize the existing status quo.'

The same position was conveyed later that year by Deng to G. Parthasarathi, then chairman of the Policy Planning Committee and a former ambassador to China and a prominent advisor to Indira Gandhi.

In 1983 I was back in Beijing on my second assignment. A.P. Venkateswaran was the ambassador. I had become friendly with a Chinese scholar, Zhao Weiwen, a senior researcher and a specialist on India with the newly established think tank China Institute of Contemporary International Relations. During one of our many conversations, she suggested that Ambassador Venkateswaran meet with the head of her institute, Professor Ma, who she claimed had direct access to the senior leadership, in particular to Zhao Ziyang, then the Chinese premier. Through her good offices a series of informal and confidential meetings were held through 1984 between Venkateswaran and Ma, at which Zhao Weiwen and I were the only others present. At these meetings, Ma argued that there was a shift taking place in Chinese foreign policy. From too close a relationship with the US and a virtual alliance against the Soviet Union, China was moving towards a more centrist position. A decision had been taken to improve relations with Moscow. China would also lay greater stress on its third world credentials. In this context, Ma said relations with India were of particular importance because China, too, in effect, was becoming more 'non-aligned'.

These conversations led eventually to a query as to whether Indian prime minister Indira Gandhi would respond to an invitation to visit China in her capacity as India's leader and also as chairman of the NAM. Venkateswaran pointed out that she could hardly contemplate such a visit with the border dispute still unresolved and with the painful memories of what had happened in 1962. In response, Ma referred to Deng's 'package proposal' and said the border issue could be settled on that basis. Venkateswaran rejected the 'package proposal' saying it would legitimize the territorial gains achieved by China through force of arms. A deal could only be politically saleable in India if it was status quo-plus. This meant that India would retain the territory it claimed in the eastern sector while China would concede some additional territory in the western sector.

One possibility was that in the western sector, China would return the additional territory it had occupied as a result of the 1962 operations, thus restoring the status quo in this sector. With this additional territory in the west and the LAC in the east, there could be a basis for an agreed boundary. This would have meant China returning to India some 3000 square kilometres of territory in this sector. Ma said he would discuss this with his leadership. After several days he sought a meeting, asking whether the Indian prime minister would be ready to visit Beijing if the Venkateswaran proposition was agreed to. He added that he was posing this hypothetically, to see if things could move forward.

It just so happened that I was going on leave to India soon afterwards. Venkateswaran asked me to take the proposal confidentially to G. Parthasarathi on his personal behalf, and to request him to put it to Prime Minister Indira Gandhi. I met Parthasarathi at his residence in Delhi, armed with detailed maps to show what was being contemplated. I conveyed Venkateswaran's view, which matched my own, that if the proposal was accepted by the Chinese this would be the best deal we could hope to get. However, Parthasarathi was not convinced. He was in any case opposed to the idea of Mrs Gandhi visiting Beijing. He kept referring to Chinese hostility towards Nehru and claimed that Mrs Gandhi still nursed bitter memories on that score. When I gently suggested that he should at least put this proposition before her he refused.

I conveyed this to Venkateswaran, who said he would follow up the matter with Mrs Gandhi herself. I learnt later that the proposition had indeed been put to her but she wanted to wait until after the general elections in 1985 before responding. Unfortunately, Mrs Gandhi was assassinated by her own bodyguards on 31 October 1984.

In 1985 the Chinese side reworked the 'package proposal', significantly hardening their stand on the border issue. This followed the Wangdung incident in the eastern sector, where Chinese troops overran an Indian Intelligence Bureau (IB) post near the Thagla Ridge and set up a helicopter base at a point called Le. This post was usually left unoccupied in the harsh winter months and reoccupied in summer. When we protested, the Chinese side claimed they were well within their side of the LAC and were only strengthening their border management.

At the regular secretary-level talks that followed, the Chinese now conveyed to us that to arrive at a solution, India would have to make 'meaningful' concessions in the eastern sector, which was the largest area in dispute, involving 90,000 square kilometres of territory. In return China would make 'corresponding' but undefined concessions in the western sector. For the first time an explicit demand was made for the handing over of Tawang in Arunachal Pradesh as an indispensable component of any boundary agreement. When it was pointed out that this was contrary to what Deng Xiaoping had himself conveyed just a couple of years earlier, the response was that the Indian side had misread their leader's words. With this moving of goalposts, the likelihood of a settlement became even more remote.

The situation in the eastern sector worsened when Indian troops unexpectedly moved to occupy the entire ridge opposite Chinese positions across the Sumdorung river.

This was known as the Hathongla, Lurongla and Sulunga Ridge Line. Two forward posts, Jaya and Negi, were also established on the northern bank of the Sumdorung river. The Chinese retaliated by setting up their own forward post just ten metres away.

It is not entirely clear why the Chinese altered their long-standing implicit acceptance of the McMahon Line as the basis for the boundary in the eastern sector at this particular juncture. Perhaps they felt the power asymmetry between their country and India had moved decisively in their favour. They may have also been emboldened by the coming to office of a young and as-yet-untested prime minister in India following Mrs Gandhi's assassination. Another fact that explained the Chinese action was the diminishing strategic importance of the Aksai Chin road after their sustained building of infrastructure in Tibet and Xinjiang. There was now less reason to concede ground in the east to retain strategic advantage in the west. This post-1985 posture adopted by China has remained unchanged up to the present day.

Rajiv Gandhi's visit to Beijing in December 1988 was a major landmark in India–China relations, as was his highly publicized meeting with Deng. This was the first visit by an Indian prime minister to China since 1954. The border issue was high on the agenda. The Chinese side wanted an explicit reference to the principle of 'mutual understanding and mutual accommodation' as the basis for resolving the dispute. Mutual accommodation implied willingness on the part of each side to make territorial concessions. This would have gone against India's formal position that there was no dispute about where the boundary lay except for some minor adjustments. However, the Chinese principle was reportedly conceded to in private by Rajiv Gandhi but not acknowledged in public statements. In the Chinese foreign ministry documents on the visit, however, it is clearly mentioned:

> Premier Li Peng stated China's principled position on the boundary issue and stressed that to act in the spirit of mutual understanding and mutual accommodation is the only way to resolve this issue. The 2 sides agreed to settle the boundary issue through peaceful and friendly consultations.

During the Indian prime minister's visit, it was decided to set up a Joint Working Group on the boundary issue, with a mandate to promote an early settlement and to adopt measures to ensure peace and tranquillity at the border.

Li Peng visited India in 1991. I was at that time joint secretary in the PMO and was present as note-taker at the one-to-one meeting Prime Minister Narasimha Rao had with his Chinese counterpart. Rao tried to probe Li Peng on the possibility of a border settlement, drawing attention to Deng's remarks of 1982. Li Peng dodged the question, saying he would need to consult his colleagues in the leadership. The visit was nevertheless important for the understanding reached to maintain peace and tranquillity at the LAC. The two sides also agreed to withdraw their respective forward posts at the Sumdorung river in the eastern sector, thus ending the eyeball-to-eyeball confrontation.

When Narasimha Rao paid a return visit to Beijing in 1993, the Agreement to Maintain Peace and Tranquillity at the LAC was formally concluded. It was also agreed that the Joint Working Group on the border issue would take up the task of clarifying the alignment of the LAC.

It was during Prime Minister Atal Bihari Vajpayee's visit to Beijing in 2003 that significant progress was made on the border issue. The two sides agreed to appoint special representatives 'to explore from the perspective of the overall bilateral relationship the framework of a boundary settlement'. The state councillor on the Chinese side and the NSA on the Indian side have been the interlocutors.

During the Vajpayee visit, the Chinese side agreed to recognize Sikkim as a part of India and committed to changing the country's official maps to reflect this. However, this change was not reflected in the joint statement issued at the end of the visit. The Indian side responded with a stronger formulation on Tibet's status as a part of China. While earlier documents usually referred to Tibet as 'an autonomous region of China', the joint statement issued after Vajpayee's visit said:

> The Indian side recognizes that the Tibet Autonomous Region is a part of the territory of the People's Republic of China.

The special representatives' talks were successful in drafting the Political Parameters and Guiding Principles for Solving the Boundary Question,[4] and this document was adopted at the time of Chinese premier Wen Jiabao's visit to India in 2005. From the Indian point of view, these principles are important since they include references to 'easily identifiable geographic features' and mention safeguarding 'due interests of their settled populations in the border areas'. These formulations had been strongly resisted by the Chinese in earlier discussions. The reference to settled populations was particularly significant on account of Tawang, which China had laid claim to.

During Wen Jiabao's visit the Chinese also released a new official map clearly showing Sikkim as a part of India.

However, since 2005 there has not been much progress in

---

[4] www.mea.gov.in/bilateral-documents.htm?dtl/6534/Agreement.

talks between the special representatives. The Chinese side has proposed that we split the disputed area between us in some agreed proportion but given the large claim they have made in the eastern sector this may result in a major loss of territory for India. The late Brajesh Mishra, who was the NSA to Vajpayee, had once told me that the Chinese had informally indicated they would be prepared to settle for the return of about 10,000 square kilometres of territory around the Tawang tracts, including the Tawang settlement itself, in the eastern sector, thereby relinquishing their claim to the rest of Arunachal Pradesh. But I have not been able to find any corroboration of this.

Is a settlement of the border issue with China in the near future a realistic possibility?

Historically, the border dispute has been intimately linked with the Tibet issue. In fact, it is the Tibet revolt of 1959, the strong reaction against the repression of Tibet that followed, and India's grant of asylum to the Dalai Lama and then to a large number of Tibetan refugees that transformed the border dispute into a strategic confrontation. The series of skirmishes at the border began to be seen by the Chinese as an Indian attempt to dislodge them from Tibet, though this was hardly the intention. India did not even have the capability to do so.

Given this history, the border issue would be easier to resolve if a process of reconciliation between the Dalai Lama and the Chinese authorities got under way seriously. This seemed likely when Xi Jinping became the top party and state leader in China and several overtures were made on his behalf to the Dalai Lama. However, more recently, there has been a return to the hard-line position on Tibet and the recent white paper on Tibet issued by the Chinese authorities has belied any hope of reconciliation.

How the two countries regard the border dispute will be

influenced by their perceptions of the regional and global equations at play. Is there a strong enough incentive for the two sides to settle the issue on the basis of a mutually acceptable compromise?

First, as the current status quo on the border has been maintained for a very long time, it is difficult to contemplate any solution that departs significantly from it. This suggests that if China were to revert to its original 'package proposal' it would be a hopeful sign of its willingness to consider a settlement. There are some recent pointers in this direction. At Track-2 interactions, some Chinese scholars have pointed out that neither India nor China is likely to go to war to obtain the territory each lays claim to. If they are right, the status quo acquires a certain sanctity.

Second, China may calculate what the payoff will be in terms of its perceived interests if it were to accept a settlement broadly based on the status quo. The payoff may be in terms of the Tibet issue, or in terms of geopolitical advantage – for example, a loosening of ties between India and the US.

More probable, however, is that the current situation will continue fairly indefinitely, barring unforeseen developments. It is unlikely that either side will find any incentive to seek a border settlement that acknowledges the status quo as its basis with minor adjustments. In the meantime, therefore, it may be more realistic to seek to expand confidence-building measures, such as more frequent meetings among the border-guarding forces of the two countries at more locations, more border trade points and the promotion of cross-border travel. To strengthen peace at the border, regular dialogue at the level of the Central Military Commission of China and the Ministry of Defence in India would help manage the political fallout from confrontations at the border.

Given the importance of the Tibet issue in our bilateral

relations, we should explore whether a dialogue on the subject is possible. The Tibet question remains a fault line in relations between the two countries. It is in India's interest that there be a reconciliation between the Dalai Lama and the Chinese government. The deep influence of His Holiness on the Tibetan community in India and in Tibet itself has acted as a restraint on militant tendencies among the Tibetans, in particular the younger generation. The Chinese seem to believe that their troubles in Tibet will go away once the Dalai Lama is no more (he is over eighty years old now but in good health). No other Tibetan figure commands the respect and reverence that he does and no one can take up his role in the reconciliation process.

But for the Dalai Lama, India too would find it increasingly difficult to control militancy in the Tibetan community, given India's democratic political environment. Such militancy would lead to even greater mistrust between the two countries. It would be better to reach some understanding on this issue at an early date to avoid problems later. An informal dialogue, where neither side lapses into repeating their formulaic positions, would be a wise step.

At their meeting in New Delhi in April 2005, Manmohan Singh and Wen Jiabao spelt out the elements of consensus underlying the development of India–China relations in the new millennium.

First, they acknowledged that relations between India and China, the two rising powers in Asia (and in the world) had acquired a 'global and strategic character'. Both had a shared interest in the existing institutions of global governance such as the UN and in shaping emerging global systems to handle new fields such as climate change and cybersecurity. In declaring the Strategic and Cooperative Partnership, the joint statement issued at the end of Wen Jiabao's visit said:

> As two major developing countries, India and China acknowledged the importance of their respective roles in the shaping of a new international political and economic order.

Second, with this changed perspective the two countries would seek early settlement of the India–China boundary issue as a strategic objective. The Agreement on Political Parameters and Guiding Principles for Settling the Boundary Question was concluded during the Jiabao visit, so as to clear the decks for this purpose.

Third, both sides agreed there was enough room in both Asia and the world to accommodate the simultaneous and rapid rise of both India and China. Each welcomed the rise of the other and declared that neither posed a threat to the other.

Fourth, each would be sensitive to the other's concerns and, importantly, develop their relations on the basis of 'equality'. This was reflected in China's explicit acceptance of Sikkim as a state of India, while India adopted a more nuanced position on Tibet, accepting it as 'part of the territory of China', rather than as an 'Autonomous Region of China', which was the earlier formulation.

Despite its long-standing alliance with Pakistan, China appeared to accept India's pre-eminent role in South Asia. Wen Jiabao stated as much to Manmohan Singh on the sidelines of the Copenhagen Climate Summit in 2009. China adopted, at least rhetorically, a more balanced stand on India–Pakistan relations.

The symmetry this consensus imparted to India–China relations proved to be short-lived.

A decade later, there is a new dynamic in the equation. The power asymmetry between the two countries, in terms of military and economic capabilities, is steadily increasing.

China is today an \$11 trillion economy while India is barely at \$2 trillion. There is little doubt that China's regional and global profile will expand, narrowing India's own strategic space. China is determined to shape the international political and economic order in a manner aligned to its own interests. But in this quest it no longer regards India as a source of support. Under Xi Jinping, it seeks a new type of 'great power relations', benchmarking itself with the US.

At the Copenhagen Climate Summit, China had sought India's support against the pressures mounted on it by the Western countries. The Copenhagen Accord was a last-minute deal arrived at jointly by the US, on one side, and the BASIC countries – Brazil, South Africa, India and China – on the other. Contrast this with the US–China Joint Presidential Statement on Climate Change on 25 September 2015, in which China agreed to a peaking of its emissions in 2030 and the two countries committed themselves to a trajectory which would lead to each having a per capita emission of fourteen tonnes of CO_2 by the same year. In the matter of a few years, Chinese positions have diverged significantly from those of other emerging economies, including India.

As the strategic and global dimension of India–China relations has weakened, bilateral issues have regained importance. China no longer sees any urgency for resolving the boundary issue. The special representative talks have receded into the background even as Chinese activism at the LAC has increased. China is now actively seeking to advance its presence in countries in India's neighbourhood, and this is clearly evident in Nepal and Sri Lanka. China's relations with Pakistan have now gone beyond the latter's role as a proxy to constrain India. Pakistan is now a part of China's long-term and grand design called the One Belt One Road initiative.

Sensitivity to India's concerns is on the wane, with China not only shielding Pakistan on the issue of cross-border terrorism but also in blocking India's entry into the NSG.

In dealing with the changed dynamic in India–China relations, the application of Kautilyan principles may still be useful.

It is necessary to first build India's comprehensive national power in all the different attributes Kautilya has listed, in particular, political leadership, good governance, a strong economy and a strong military. This alone can chip away at the power asymmetry between India and China, bringing a degree of 'equality' in the relationship.

Next, India must seek to align with other powerful states to countervail the main adversary. This would mean closer relations with the US, Japan, Australia, Indonesia and Vietnam, all of which share India's concerns over China's unilateral assertion of power in Asia.

Lastly, one should remember Kautilya's advice to act with prudence, not provoking a conflict with a stronger power while building one's strength.

I believe that India is the only country with the potential to emerge as a great power in the same league as China and to even surpass it. But this will require leadership with vision and a people who aspire and work towards realizing that vision. India still falls short on this score.

8

India and Nepal: A Relationship of Paradox

Physical proximity often helps create positive bonds between countries but it may just as likely create misunderstanding and points of conflict that sometimes overwhelm strong and abiding political, economic and cultural connections. With no other neighbour is India so well bonded on these fronts as it is with Nepal. And yet there is a widespread perception in Nepal that India does not respect the country's sovereignty and independence, that it often intervenes in Nepal's domestic affairs and generally behaves like an overbearing Big Brother. In this respect Nepal is no different from several of our other neighbours but in its case there is a peculiar coexistence of sentiments of deep attachment to India and an equally deep fear of domination by India.

In India there is great bewilderment when expressions of hostility by Nepali leaders and even the Nepali populace come its way. This is happening despite India's generous support to the country's development! Nepal's attempt to balance the overwhelming presence of India next door by reaching out to

China is resented by India. Such actions heighten our security concerns. This paradox of affinity coexisting with hostility made my assignment as ambassador to Nepal (2002–04) one of the most difficult in my diplomatic career.

The extent of the closeness between India and Nepal is often not appreciated. Our historical, cultural, religious, ethnic and kinship ties go back a long way, and the traditionally open border between the two countries continues to reinforce these ties to the present day. The chief priests at the famous and sacred Pashupatinath temple in Kathmandu have traditionally been Bhat Brahmins from Karnataka; this practice goes back at least 350 years.

Nepal is also associated with the Indian epic Ramayana. Legend has it that Janakpur in Nepal's Terai region is where Sita wed Rama. Sita's father King Janak reigned in a kingdom located in these foothills of the Himalayas. Nepal is also sacred to the Buddhists. Lumbini in the southern plains of Nepal, just across the border from India, is where the Buddha was born. And the ancient city of Kapilavastu, which served as the capital of his Sakya kingdom, may well have been located within Nepal's current boundaries. There are ancient mounds and stupas in and around Kathmandu said to have been built by Ashoka.

And then there are the Himalayas themselves, which have as many ancient legends associated with them across northern Nepal as with the stretches ranged on the Indian side. People living on both sides of the border share tight ethnic and family bonds, and these connections continue to grow day by day. These links not only involve the people living in the Nepali Terai – the southern plains of Nepal adjacent to the Indian states of Bihar and Uttar Pradesh – but also those in the hill areas of Nepal. They have family and community bonds with their ethnic cousins residing in Sikkim, Uttarakhand,

Himachal Pradesh and West Bengal who are citizens of India. This is not counting the estimated six million to eight million Nepali citizens, almost all of them from the hill areas of Nepal, who live and work in cities across India.

The political discourse both in India and Nepal mostly ignores this reality. In Nepal, politics has traditionally been dominated by a high-caste elite made up of the Bahuns (Brahmins) and Chhetris (who identify themselves with Kshatriyas), which has consciously tried to project Nepal as a country with a distinctive mountain culture and identity. They have sought to impose this view upon a populace that is ethnically and culturally almost as diverse as India's. In Nepal's attempt to uphold its separate identity – as thrust upon it by its elite – India has become 'the other' from which it must be distinguished. The reality that Nepal has been home since ancient times to a very large Indian-origin population with its own culture, language and traditions is glossed over.

In India too there is mostly ignorance of the plurality of Nepal. Even seasoned politicians in India accept the notion peddled by the Nepali political elite that the Madhesis or the inhabitants of the Nepali Terai, who are ethnically the same as the people across the border in India, are immigrants into Nepal. In fact, the Madhesis are overwhelmingly the original inhabitants of the Terai, whose lands were conquered by Prithvi Narayan Shah, the Nepali king who unified the many principalities of Nepal into a strong kingdom in the eighteenth century. However, putting in place a political boundary did not and could not erase the age-old interconnections among people inhabiting the border region. This applies as much to the Madhesis as it does to the numerous hill tribes of Nepal.

There is another source of strong people-to-people ties between the two countries. During the British colonial period, the British Indian Army would recruit hundreds of Nepalis from across the hill areas to serve in its Gurkha regiments. After India's independence, the Indian Army has continued with this practice under an agreement between the two governments. Over the years, a very large number of pensioners from the Indian Army have been living in villages and towns across Nepal. Their pensions put them in a relatively higher income category, and they often become respected community leaders. They are patriotic Nepalis but also have a deep attachment to India and to the Indian Army, where they have served with great distinction. They constitute an invaluable bank and network of goodwill for India. They also represent the many ethnic groups that make up Nepal – the Magars, Rais, Limbus and Gurungs. The Tamangs constitute another important ethnic group in the Terai.

There have been attempts by Nepali governments to stop the annual recruitment of their citizens to the Indian Army but in a country where employment prospects for the youth are severely limited, this is one opportunity that remains much sought after. Closing it may invite a backlash, which no Nepali government has so far been willing to risk.

The border that separates India and Nepal is open, allowing for the free and unrestricted movement of people. This derives from tradition and usage. There is no legal sanction behind it. Many people, both in India and Nepal, believe the open border is part of the India–Nepal Treaty of Peace and Friendship concluded in 1950, but that is not the case.

Efforts have been made by the Indian government to regulate this traffic, especially because of concerns over terrorism, but the sheer numbers crossing the border has made this a mostly futile exercise. There have been demands from the more nationalist among Nepali leaders that the border should be closed and travel permitted only through the use of passports and visas. This has often been justified on grounds that there is a large-scale migration taking place into Nepal from the Indian border states. But the main beneficiaries of an open border have been Nepali citizens who have sought shelter or livelihood in India. This was particularly apparent during the several years of violent Maoist insurgency which ravaged Nepal. Ordinary citizens were often caught in the crossfire between the insurgents and Nepali security forces.

The India–Nepal treaty of 1950 has been criticized by the Nepali political elite as an unequal one. But no Nepali government has exercised its sovereign right under the treaty to abrogate it, which is possible after giving one year's notice. The treaty was unique in extending, reciprocally, the rights to residence, employment and purchase of property to each other's citizens – in other words, it extended 'national treatment' by each country to the other's citizens.

The treaty was concluded at a time when Nepal feared a Chinese threat, particularly after the Chinese occupation of Tibet. The treaty has an explicit reference to threats from third countries, which India and Nepal would cooperate in tackling. There was also a confidential exchange of side letters to the treaty, which obliged Nepal to seek India's consent for the import of arms from third countries. It is the security aspects implicitly and explicitly included in the treaty that became controversial in later years.

At least since 1960, when the China–Nepal boundary agreement was concluded, the security provisions in the India–Nepal treaty, which were the result of a shared perception of threat from China, became outdated from Nepal's point of view. At the same time the pursuit of a nationalistic policy, with India projected as a threat to Nepal's independence, made the treaty appear anachronistic. Adding to the sense of Nepali discomfort is the notion of being under siege as the country is landlocked and dependent on transit through India for trade with third countries. The virtual blockade imposed on Nepal in 1987 when King Birendra began to lean more towards China and purchased arms from it reinforced the sense of siege.

This could be seen again more recently in 2015, when supplies from India were blocked by Madhesis in the Terai protesting the discriminatory policies of the Nepali government. Even though the Indian government may not have been complicit, it certainly did not make any special effort to relieve the economic distress in the hill areas of Nepal created by the blockade. While the denial of transit is powerful negative leverage, it leads to hostile sentiments among the people of Nepal and this is then exploited by Nepali politicians for their own political ambitions. My own view has been that India should seek to become the transit country of choice for Nepal by offering it open access to its transportation network and ports, extending that country's efficient and economical services. This will create positive interdependency rather than negative leverage.

The Indian government has acceded to requests from Nepal to review the terms of the treaty, but so far only one round of such a review has been held at the foreign secretary level. During that round it was apparent that the Nepali side wished to retain elements that were advantageous to it but dispense with reciprocal obligations on itself. In practice, successive Nepali governments have abridged most of the 'national treatment' they were expected to extend to Indian citizens on a reciprocal basis, even while its own citizens continue to enjoy privileges on a par, almost, with Indian citizens in India. Unlike their Nepali counterparts in India, Indian citizens in Nepal require residence and work permits and cannot buy property there.

Nepal was in acute political turmoil when I landed in Kathmandu in October 2002 after spending only a year in Jakarta. A little more than a year had passed since the infamous palace massacre, in which the drug-crazed crown prince Dipendra slaughtered his parents, King Birendra and Queen Aishwarya, and several other members of the royal family as they gathered for dinner in the palace. Birendra's brother Gyanendra, who had been away from Kathmandu that fateful evening, succeeded to the throne amidst dark rumours, almost certainly untrue, that the massacre had been part of a conspiracy in which he himself was implicated.

Gyanendra went on to marginalize the political parties and gather power into his own hands. His command over the Royal Nepal Army gave him considerable authority, particularly at a time when the Maoist insurgency was beginning to spread across the country and its violent attacks had grown to frightening levels in scale and frequency. There were efforts to pursue peace talks with the Maoists but these did not succeed. The previous Nepali Congress–led government had dissolved Parliament in May 2002 but on 4 October that same year the king dismissed the government and began to rule through a succession of court-appointed prime ministers.

I arrived in Kathmandu soon after this development. When I visited Delhi on consultations, the late Brajesh Mishra, who was the NSA, told me my mandate was to attempt to bring the monarchy and the political parties together to neutralize the Maoists, who were threatening both institutions and creating political instability and economic distress in Nepal.

There was concern in Delhi over what the deteriorating situation across the border meant for India's security. If the Maoists could not be contained and defeated, there were fears that the result would be a 'red corridor' extending from the north all the way down to Andhra Pradesh. To counter the Maoist threat, the capabilities of the Royal Nepal Army through the supply of weaponry and training in counter-insurgency had to be upgraded – another task I was asked to oversee. It is another matter that I soon discovered that the king was in secret communication with the Maoists, just like some of the political party leaders.

Once the peace talks between the Nepali government and the Maoists were publicly acknowledged early in 2003, our agencies began to respond discreetly to feelers from the Maoist leaders. I was soon to discover how difficult it was to reconcile the glaring dichotomy between the often fraught and hostile state-to-state relations on the one hand and the many strands of people-to-people relations binding the countries together on the other. The political leaders I engaged with were nearly schizophrenic in their dealings with India, seeking favours and political intervention on their behalf in private but criticizing India for meddling in their affairs in public.

I was in Nepal for just twenty-two months, leaving the post in August 2004 to take over as foreign secretary, but the country continued to be high on my list of priorities. What began as a valiant and mostly frustrating attempt to promote accord between the mainstream political parties and King Gyanendra ended with us switching to a strategy of bringing the political parties together with the Maoists to neutralize an autocratic monarchy instead. The turning point came in February 2005, when Gyanendra assumed absolute power, arrested political party leaders and declared a state of Emergency. This was condemned by India, which called for the restoration of multiparty democracy, the release of political leaders and the restoration of civil liberties. As a point of pressure, military supplies to Nepal were suspended.

At the same time it was decided to actively promote an understanding between the mainstream political parties and the Maoists. It is on this basis that regular engagement began between the alliance of seven mainstream political parties and the Maoists, facilitated by our agencies. This resulted finally in the twelve-point agreement signed between the two sides in Delhi on 22 November 2005, which aimed at fighting an autocratic monarchical regime. The agreement was not authored by Indians; it was the handiwork of the Nepali interlocutors themselves. Our only advice to the mainstream political parties was to ensure that the Maoists accepted multiparty democracy. Though this was not formally acknowledged, India's role as guarantor for the implementation of the accord was implicit.

Shortly before this landmark agreement, King Gyanendra became openly hostile towards India. This was on full display at the thirteenth SAARC summit held in Dhaka on 12 and 13 November 2005. At the senior officials' meeting before the start of the summit, I had to confront a Nepali delegation which had instructions to oppose every proposal tabled by the Indian side. One proposal, for example, was for establishing a SAARC Disaster Management Centre in New Delhi. In Chapter 4, I had referred to an attempt by the Nepali delegation to propose membership of SAARC to China, which we opposed.

I had been against our prime minister meeting the Nepali king at the Dhaka summit but I was overruled. I did not attend the meeting. Instead, the NSA M.K. Narayanan accompanied the prime minister. Apparently the Nepali foreign minister Ramesh Nath Pandey had conveyed, presumably to Narayanan, that His Majesty did not want the Indian foreign secretary to be present. This was possibly because he attributed the Indian policy of the suspension of arms supplies to the Royal Nepal Army and the open support to the mainstream political parties to me.

I was briefed on the meeting later. It appears that we offered to review bilateral relations, including the suspension of arms supplies. Fortunately, no specific commitments appear to have been made from our side. The king reportedly offered attractive opportunities for hydropower cooperation, which had never taken off in the past. He also agreed to release political leaders and relax political curbs. After we returned to Delhi there was heavy pressure on me to have the arms ban lifted. It was with considerable difficulty that it continued to be in place. Without this sanction there would have been little pressure on the king to withdraw his draconian measures preventing all mainstream political activity. It was also a signal to the Maoists of India's changed attitude towards them. India began to consider favourably the prospect of an alliance between Nepal's mainstream political parties and the Maoists as a means of restraining an increasingly despotic king.

On 1 April 2006 the Nepali Congress leader G.P. Koirala was released. Later other political leaders were also freed. This was welcomed by the Indian government, whose statement put India squarely on the side of the popular forces in Nepal. It called for the 'removal of all curbs on civil liberties and fundamental rights and the lifting of media censorship and restrictions on movement to enable the people of Nepal to enjoy their legitimate constitutional and democratic rights'. India's formal position remained in support of the so-called 'twin pillars of constitutional monarchy and multiparty democracy'. As we shall see, this became untenable within the space of another three weeks.

The situation in Nepal continued to deteriorate, with increasing popular opposition to the monarchy. In April, a people's movement against the monarchy began to gather pace, not only in the Kathmandu valley but in other parts of

Nepal too. It was orchestrated by the political parties, and doubtless the Maoists also mobilized their cadres. There was a brutal crackdown by the Nepali security forces, including the army, but this only added fuel to the fire. There were worries in Delhi that the situation may spin out of control.

The effort now shifted to convincing the king that he should yield to democratic forces and retain only a ceremonial role. Dr Karan Singh, a distant relative of his, was asked to travel to Kathmandu as the prime minister's special envoy. I was asked to accompany him. The visit took place on 19 and 20 April 2006. Dr Karan Singh delivered this friendly advice to King Gyanendra. The king apparently asked for and was given assurance of his personal security and of his family's too. Dr Karan Singh met the king alone. I had agreed with him that this meeting should take place in private. When Dr Singh came back from the meeting he was very optimistic that the king would be ready to withdraw from an executive role, and agree to hand over power to a government constituted by the seven-party alliance and also withdraw all curbs on civil liberties.

While Dr Singh was with the king, I had my own series of meetings with the political party leaders who were now out of jail. I also had an important meeting with the chief of the Royal Nepal Army, General Pyar Jung Thapa, at the army headquarters. During my tenure as ambassador I had maintained very close and cordial relations with him and other senior military officers, and I felt I could be candid and forthright with him now.

I conveyed to him our assessment that the Jana Andolan or People's Movement should be taken seriously and that there was no alternative but for the king to give up his active political role. Any violence against the massing crowds, who were only a few kilometres away from the centre of the city, could result in a mass uprising which the security forces would not be able to control. The army chief said the demonstrators were mainly Maoist cadres and could not be allowed to overthrow the government. I tried to disabuse him of any such notion, pointing out that while there may be Maoists taking part, the majority of the protesters were ordinary citizens. I added that the army should not be seen killing its own people. I also expressed our fears that if the mass movement reached the centre of the capital and the security forces were unable to handle the situation, the king himself would be in danger. I said, somewhat provocatively, that he had a choice – to be the chief of the Royal Army or the chief of Nepal's army. He asked, with some irritation, what I was advising him to do. I said it was his duty to convey to the king that the situation was becoming dangerous and untenable, that the army could not risk a violent confrontation with massive crowds and that defusing the situation politically was the only way out.

I believe this message was conveyed to the king; it may have played a role in him announcing his intention to transfer all executive power to a government constituted by the seven-party alliance. The declaration by the king came the very next day, on 20 April, soon after Dr Karan Singh and I returned to Delhi.

From our informal interactions with leaders of the seven-party alliance, we gathered they were elated with the king's declaration and were ready to form a coalition government. It is on the basis of these talks that we issued a statement on 21 April welcoming the king's announcement as an affirmation of the twin principles of 'multiparty democracy and constitutional monarchy'. Little did we realize at this stage that the king's offer was too little too late. The Jana Andolan rejected the offer; it wanted nothing less than the monarchy itself to be abolished and the people's sovereignty to be recognized. The Maoists too were unhappy as they felt they could be sidelined despite the twelve-point agreement with the seven-party alliance.

Among the crowds that still massed around the capital, India's premature welcoming of the king's announcement began to be severely criticized. India was suspected of trying to protect an unpopular monarchy. Prime Minister Dr Manmohan Singh had already left for Germany on an official visit, and M.K. Narayanan had accompanied him. As the seniormost cabinet minister, Pranab Mukherjee, the defence minister, was in charge. On 22 April, as we briefed him on the fast-evolving situation on the ground in Nepal, he worked the telephones, speaking to Nepali political party leaders and senior aides to the king to avert a bloody denouement.

Towards the end of the day it had become abundantly clear that the worsening situation could only be defused with the king stepping down and the abolition of the monarchy. It was also clear that unless India quickly aligned itself with the prevailing popular sentiment in Nepal, all the political capital we had built up by unreservedly supporting the democratic forces would evaporate into thin air.

As reports poured in of crowds chanting anti-India slogans, I asked for Pranab Mukherjee's permission to hold a televised press conference the same evening. We would publicly abandon our erstwhile *mantra* of supporting the twin principles of 'multiparty democracy and constitutional monarchy'. We had to convey unambiguously that India would support any decision made by the people of Nepal; it was for them to decide what form of government they wanted. I also conveyed to Pranab Mukherjee that what I was saying would be at variance with a statement the prime minister had made the same day in Berlin to the Indian journalists accompanying him. He had said that India stood by the twin principles. This could lead to awkward questions later on. Pranab Mukherjee asked me to go ahead and do whatever was necessary to defuse the situation in Nepal and safeguard India's interests. He undertook to explain the situation himself to the prime minister when he returned.

So it was that on 22 April, late in the evening, I addressed a packed press conference, stating categorically that India was firmly in support of the democratic forces in Nepal and would accept whatever the people wanted. I was asked whether we were abandoning the twin principles. My reply was that the twin-principle objective was not an Indian creation or preference but one arrived at between the Nepali monarchy and the political parties; at this stage, I repeated, India would support whatever was acceptable to the people of Nepal.

We had alerted our embassy and political parties about the press conference. A very large number of Nepalis watched the televised proceedings, and I was told that cheering crowds greeted the statement. India was a 'good boy' again. But it had been a close shave.

A second proclamation from the king followed, in which he conceded that sovereignty now lay with the people of Nepal and not the monarch. Parliament was restored and the political roadmap put forward by the seven-party alliance accepted without reservation. The Nepal Army came under civilian control.

In the weeks that followed, the focus shifted to formalizing the peace process between the seven-party alliance and the Maoists. Preparations were being made to bring the Maoist leaders overground. In advance of this, I had an important meeting with the Maoist leaders, Prachanda and Baburam Bhattarai, in a safe house in Siliguri, arranged through our foreign intelligence agency, the Research and Analysis Wing.

I again assured them of our support for the peace process but reminded them of their commitment to give up the insurgency and commit themselves to multiparty democracy. I agreed that there would be a transitional phase before the revolutionary movement could transform itself into a political party like any other and contest elections. The Maoists came overground in June 2006, and in November 2006 the Comprehensive Peace Agreement was concluded between the political parties and the Maoists, declaring an end to the decade-old civil war and setting out a roadmap for elections to a constituent assembly.

On 28 May 2008 the Shah dynasty came to an end, and monarchy in Nepal was abolished by the newly elected constituent assembly. Nepal became a republic after 240 years of monarchical rule.

I believe Gyanendra had for quite some time had a premonition that his days as king were numbered. Three years earlier, just before I left Kathmandu for Delhi to take up my assignment as foreign secretary, my wife and I were invited by the king and his queen for a private farewell dinner at the palace. The conversation inevitably turned to the political situation in Nepal. When I asked him how he saw the future of the monarchy in Nepal, he replied, 'As an endangered species.'

In throwing its lot with the democratic forces in Nepal in 2006, India was re-enacting a drama similar to what had played out in 1951, when Indian intervention helped bring the monarchy back in a political role after a century of Rana rule behind a monarchical façade. The Rana aristocracy had ruled Nepal since Jung Bahadur assumed absolute power after the infamous Kot massacre in 1846, in which nearly the entire Nepali nobility was wiped out. The Shah dynasty monarch was reduced to a figurehead. Jung Bahadur became the prime minister, an office which he soon made hereditary.

When India became independent in 1947, Nepal was under the rule of Mohun Shamshere Rana. King Tribhuvan was a powerless figurehead confined to the palace. The Rana regime feared it could be undermined by ideas of democracy and political liberalism from across the border. There were several Nepali politicians, like the brothers B.P. Koirala and G.P. Koirala, who had taken part in India's own struggle for independence and looked to Indian support for political change in their own feudal country.

In 1949, the liberation of China by communist forces created another source of anxiety in Nepal, which only worsened with the invasion of Tibet by Chinese forces in 1950. India too was concerned about the security implications of these developments. This led to the two countries signing the Indo-Nepal Treaty of Peace and Friendship in 1950, which extended, implicitly, an Indian security cover over Nepal. Indian military presence was established at several locations along the Nepal–Tibet border (this was withdrawn in 1969 at the request of the Nepal government).

In 1951, King Tribhuvan, who, like his predecessors, chafed at being held a virtual prisoner in the palace, sought the help of the Indian ambassador Sir C.P.N. Singh to escape from the clutches of the Rana rulers. One day Tribhuvan and his family obtained permission to picnic in the outskirts of Kathmandu. On the way back, just as their carcade was about to pass Shital Bhavan, where the Indian embassy was then located, its gates swung open and the cars carrying the king and his family drove into the embassy compound. He was soon taken to Delhi, where he met Pandit Nehru.

A political deal was brokered, paving the way for an end to Rana rule, restoration of the monarchy and participation of political parties in the governance of the country. A constitution was to be drafted by an elected constituent assembly, providing for a multiparty democracy with a constitutional monarchy. Initially, a coalition headed by King Tribhuvan consisting of several political parties was set up. There followed a period of acute political instability and factional infighting within the most influential political party, the Nepali Congress. A new constitution was being drawn up but Tribhuvan died in 1955 and his son Mahendra became the king.

Mahendra continued to rule through an advisory council, like his father, with court-appointed prime ministers. The period of Mahendra's rule is important, since several steps were taken to establish Nepal's independent identity and international personality during his time. Diplomatic relations were established with China and Japan, and Nepal became a member of the UN in 1955. The long-pending constitution was finally adopted in 1959, establishing multiparty democracy and constitutional monarchy. But it was adopted as a document blessed by the king rather than as an outcome of deliberations in an elected and representative body.

General elections under this constitution were held soon afterwards. The Nepali Congress won an absolute majority and B.P. Koirala took over as the prime minister. One of the important achievements of the Koirala government was the conclusion of a border agreement with China in 1960, precisely at a time when the India–China border issue was becoming a source of rising tensions between the two Asian giants.

The deteriorating India–China relations created the space for Mahendra to take two major political decisions that influenced the course of Nepali politics and its foreign relations for years to come. First, on 15 December 1960, he dismissed the popularly elected government of Koirala, discarded the constitution and assumed absolute power. Political parties were declared illegal and, a couple of years later, a party-less panchayat system was put in place, with prime ministers and cabinets chosen by royal appointment. Second, the king promoted a nationalistic foreign policy emphasizing Nepal's independent and sovereign personality. Nationalism in the Nepali context could only be projected as resistance to India's pervasive political, economic and cultural presence in the country. Mahendra was confident that India would be diffident about reacting adversely to the new dispensation, both internal and external, precisely because of the Chinese factor. Thus his two decisions were mutually reinforcing.

In 1962, the India–China border war broke out, ending in defeat and humiliation for India. This enhanced Mahendra's room for manoeuvre vis-à-vis India. Waving the Chinese flag and, occasionally, the Pakistani flag too, Mahendra successfully constrained Indian leverages against Nepal.

Political authoritarianism and ultra-nationalism often go hand in hand, and one is used to justify the other. Mahendra embarked on reconstructing an identity for Nepal, projecting it as a relatively homogeneous nation, a mountain kingdom with a distinct identity and culture. This required a blurring of the reality of Nepal as a country made up of a number of very diverse ethnic groups, each with its own customs and traditions, professing different faiths and speaking different though related languages. It also implied an 'unlatching' from India. During the seventeen years of his rule, Mahendra sought to implant in his country a contrived hostility towards India, projecting it as an ever-present threat to Nepali independence and identity, which a patriotic and nationalistic monarchy alone could deal with. This policy continued under his successor King Birendra, who ascended the throne in 1972 on the death of his father.

During Tribhuvan's rule and later under Mahendra, India extended large-scale assistance to Nepal in several sectors. Airports were built in a number of Nepali towns, both near the India–Nepal border and in cities in the north. The Tribhuvan University campus was a gift from India. A number of roads, bridges and highways were built, including the greater part of the East–West highway. When I explored these projects, I found that the plaques commemorating India's contribution had either been defaced or blanked out altogether.

However, the 'unlatching' strategy has not really succeeded. India continues to be Nepal's major trade partner, and an overwhelming part of the country's trade continues to transit through India. The people-to-people links are as dense as ever, driven by shared religious, cultural and above all kinship ties. Despite the exhortations of nationalist elements, the recruitment of Nepalis into the Indian armed forces continues. Pensioners of the Indian Army are scattered across Nepal. The Kathmandu valley elite too, with their tendency to spout anti-India sentiments the most, maintain close ties with India, even owning property in several Indian cities. The Rana families still marry into the erstwhile princely families in India.

As mentioned earlier, six million to eight million Nepalis live and work in India, according to Indian home ministry estimates. They are a major asset for India, and are truly ambassadors of friendship between the two countries. But this ground reality is in constant contradiction to the recurrent tensions in government-to-government relations. While the rulers of Nepal have unable to alter this ground reality, India in turn has been succeeded in leveraging its considerable assets to influence the political calculus in Kathmandu.

Nepal has been undergoing a major transformation over the years – political, economic and social – and India must align itself with these changes. On the political side a landmark development happened in 1990 when absolute monarchy gave way to a hybrid political dispensation described as multiparty democracy and constitutional monarchy.

The king retained significant authority, in particular personal command of the armed forces. Political parties such as the Nepali Congress and the left-wing United Marxist Leninist (UML) party were dominated by the high-caste Bahuns and Chhetris. There was still only limited political space for the many ethnic groups and the Madhesis living in the plains of Nepal, who had been marginalized. The introduction of democracy provided them an opportunity to organize themselves, to assert their distinct identities and demand an end to discrimination. An acute expression of this was the Maoist movement, which soon became an armed insurgency threatening the Nepali state. The unwillingness of the political elite to allow for a more inclusive and plural democracy lies at the root of the Maoist revolt and continues to create political instability even today.

Nepal has also been undergoing a generational change. Its cohort of the young is larger in percentage terms than India's. The persistent lack of employment opportunities in their own country has forced them to seek their livelihood in India and other countries. There they are exposed to a very different world from Nepal's conservative and patriarchal society. They can be a major instrument of change in their country. None of the mainstream political parties has been able to articulate and respond to their aspirations. Even the Maoists, who profess a more progressive social and economic agenda, have slipped into behaviour patterns associated more with the established political elite. This is a tragedy.

It has been my view that among the countries of South Asia, Nepal has all the ingredients to be one of the most successful and affluent economies. Thanks to its open border with India and its privileged access to our rapidly expanding market, neither its size nor its population should limit its economic prospects. Given its pleasant climate and magnificent landscape, it could transform itself into a regional centre for high-quality education and health services, not to mention tourism. It can also be a large-scale exporter of power. Currently, despite its huge hydropower potential it is today an importer of power from India.

The root of its poverty and underdeveloped status lies in the mindset of its political elite, which prefers to see India as a threat rather than an opportunity. Any joint project of mutual benefit is immediately examined for what it brings to the Indian plate rather than for what it fetches Nepal itself. Even a morsel on the Indian plate is seen as irrefutable evidence that Nepal's crown jewels are being robbed by the scheming Indians. The success that Bhutan has achieved in utilizing its more limited hydropower potential to become the richest country in South Asia in per capita income terms by selling power to India is seen by the Kathmandu elite as evidence, not of mutually advantageous interdependence, but of Bhutan's subservience to India.

It is not at all surprising that India has a significant interest in developments in Nepal but the manner in which this interest is expressed and pursued is very important. My own experience is that we have been too focused on the political shadow play in Kathmandu and have paid little attention to engaging and cultivating constituencies with positive sentiments towards India, such as the vast network of Indian Army pensioners, the Madhesis living in the plains adjacent to India and the very large number of young Nepalis who study, live and work in India. The objective should be to work on these constituencies and make them instruments of real political influence.

As ambassador, I tried to make a start by connecting with

the Madhesis through small community-level development projects and by regularly visiting the Terai to directly meet their local leaders. This was done without reducing in any way the number of community projects we had going in the hill areas. It was obvious that the development projects promoted by the Nepali government and even by many of the international and Western aid agencies were almost entirely focused on these areas. The Terai plains were completely neglected until the Indian embassy began some community projects here. The Madhesis were subject to discriminatory citizenship regulations. They were not given citizenship papers despite being the original inhabitants of the plains. It was as a result of the Madhesi Jana Andolan that over four million Madhesis finally won citizenship rights in 2008. After decades of oppression, members of a disadvantaged community was now able to play a political role in their country.

The tendency in India is to regard Nepal's dependence on India for transit as leverage against it. But any exercise of this leverage only ends up intensifying anti-Indian sentiments in the country. It reinforces the sense of siege that Nepalis feel – 'India-locked', as they call it. In my view a better approach would be to offer Nepal 'national treatment' on the Indian transport network, allowing them the use of our roads and ports on the same terms as for Indian citizens and companies. The effort should be to convince Nepal that they are 'India-open', not India-locked.

At the same time, modern and efficient cross-border infrastructure in the form of highways, railways and state-of-the-art digital links must be built. Despite the India–Nepal border zone consisting of flatland for the most part, the cross-border roads on the Indian side are very bad. In fact, travelling from the Nepali side to the Indian side is like driving from a more developed country to a less developed one.

On the other side of Nepal, the Chinese have been busy building a number of highways from the Tibetan side into Nepal, all the way down to the East–West highway that traverses Nepal, hacking through high mountains and difficult terrain. The Tibet railway has now been extended from Lhasa to Shigaze and could well be extended to Kathmandu across the border in the next few years. In contrast, our plans to upgrade the existing highway and railway links between India and Nepal and create modern integrated checkpoints on the border have been on the agenda for years but we are bedevilled by a very slow process of implementation. I have always held that if you leave empty spaces behind someone else will walk in. This is what has been happening in several parts of our neighbourhood. China has seized the opportunity to walk in.

During my assignment in Nepal, I maintained a friendly relationship with the Chinese ambassador, sharing with him our assessment about developments in the country. The Chinese preoccupation at that time was mainly Tibet, and the possibility that an unstable Nepal may become a platform for countries inimical to China to create trouble in Tibet. They preferred to have India rather than any Western country, especially the US, playing the principal role in Nepal.

The situation today appears different, with China getting more directly involved in Nepal's domestic politics and significantly increasing its economic profile there. There is a willingness to contest Indian interests in cultivating local interest groups that could advance China's interests vis-à-vis India's. We have not been able to craft an effective counter strategy. As with our other neighbours, our engagement with Nepal tends to be episodic and crisis-driven, and not backed by the human and material resources that our neighbours deserve.

Driven by anxiety over our declining influence, the temptation to intervene in Nepal's domestic politics and label its political leaders as our friends or enemies has always proved to be counterproductive. Such intervention creates popular resentment and can turn friends into enemies. It is far better to adhere to positions of principle, and to advocate policies rather than persons. If India is seen as avoiding playing favourites and engaging with the widest possible political spectrum in Nepal, it has a better chance of influencing developments there.

Part Three

The Wider World

9

Tackling Energy Security and Climate Change

In managing its external relations, a country must constantly balance the different dimensions of its foreign policy. Traditionally, bilateral relations have been accorded primacy in the conduct of a state's foreign policy, since costs and benefits are relatively easier to calculate in a two-state context. But we are now living in an international landscape where a state's bilateral, regional and multilateral relations are intertwined in a complex dynamic with trade-offs being more difficult to determine.

The previous two decades were a time of growth and consolidation for the global economy. There was impressive economic growth, both in absolute and relative terms, in a number of major developing economies, most notably in China and India. This trend coincided with their rapid integration into the global economy. The consistently high growth paths charted by these two continental-size economies has been largely responsible for the shift in the centre of gravity of global economic power from the trans-Atlantic to the Asia-Pacific. The latter's share of global output was 16 per cent in 1950 and 34 per cent in 1998, and it is expected to rise to 44 per cent by 2030.

It is not only India and China that are dragging economic power away from the West. There are other significant emerging economies too, including Brazil, South Africa, Mexico and, more lately, Indonesia. They join countries like South Korea, which have during this period consolidated the impressive economic gains they had already made in the earlier decades. Economic capability has led to increased military capability and greater technological sophistication.

The world of today is populated by a cluster of major powers with growing economic and security assets, though there are considerable asymmetries still in the distribution of power among them. What is increasingly apparent is that it is no longer possible for a small cluster of advanced economies to impose global frameworks and rules on the rest of the world as they could in the past. Even if emerging economies are not able to have their say in the shaping of global arrangements in any particular field, they nevertheless enjoy the negative power to prevent these arrangements from being imposed on them. This has been apparent in the continuing deadlock at the Doha Round of trade talks under the WTO. The impression at the talks is that emerging economies have been obstructive in international negotiations, a charge hurled frequently at them. On the contrary, they have become more effective in safeguarding their perceived national interests.

The situation is complicated by the notable dichotomy shown by the economic structures of the newly emerging economies. For example, both India and China would qualify as major economies in overall GDP terms, according to their weightage in the global economy and trade, and in their overall technological and military capabilities. However, they would continue to be classified as developing countries in terms of per capita income levels and the incidence – now declining – of poverty, disease and illiteracy.

This has led to considerable ambivalence as these countries aspire to a global governance role because of their expanded capabilities but at the same time feel entitled to non-reciprocal benefits from global regimes to deal with developmental challenges. They are a different breed of major power from what was the historical norm. The developed countries of today had their domestic economic and social indices rising hand in hand with their overall GDP growth and international profile. This is not the case with the major emerging powers like India, China, Brazil and South Africa. They may be more appropriately described as 'premature powers' or 'transitional powers'. They have a larger global footprint than before but the economic welfare of their citizens has not kept pace with their growth.

Another significant feature of the current international landscape is the increasing number and importance of cross-cutting transnational threats that cannot be fixed by national or regional solutions. Some of these problems are international terrorism, maritime piracy, drug trafficking, global pandemics, climate change, and food and water security. To deal with these challenges – and equally, to manage what have come to be called the 'global commons', such as the high seas, outer space and cyberspace – the involvement of the major emerging economies is extremely vital. Global interconnectedness and interdependence are now a compelling reality whose management requires several hands working together at the helm.

All this makes global governance in the contemporary world a complex and difficult task. Nowhere is this more evident than in the ongoing multilateral negotiations on climate change.

Climate change and energy security are two sides of the same coin. Climate change is the result of the accumulation of greenhouse gases (GHGs) in the earth's atmosphere from the burning of carbon-based fossil fuels – coal, oil and gas. These emissions – chiefly, though not exclusively, CO_2 – have been increasing ever since the Industrial Revolution more than 200 years ago. They typically stay in the atmosphere as climate-forcing agents for a hundred years or more. This has important implications.

First, climate change is a stock and not a flow problem; current emissions add incrementally to the stock but it is the accumulated stock that is responsible for climate change. Mitigation through absolute reductions in global GHG emissions is necessary but not sufficient.

Second, even if emissions were to become zero, climate change would continue because the stock of GHGs in the planetary atmosphere will decline only gradually over many years. In the meantime, countries would have to cope with, or adapt to, the consequences of climate change. These consequences are higher temperatures, unpredictable weather patterns and rising sea levels. Clearly, adaptation is now of critical importance, particularly for countries most vulnerable to the impacts of climate change.

Third, climate change is a global threat that cannot be tackled by national or even regional solutions. Only a global regime can align the costs and outcomes to get the world to shift from its current reliance on fossil fuels to economic activity based progressively on nuclear or renewable sources of energy. Such a global regime must also deal with the challenge of adaptation as much as it does with mitigation.

India, which is likely to be one of the most vulnerable countries to the impacts of climate change, has much to gain from a robust global climate change regime which would bring about an early transition to a non-fossil-fuel-based economy through significant emission reductions globally. India would also expect strong global support in its efforts to meet its own adaptation burden, which is likely to grow in the coming years. But it is also wary of committing to contributions that may limit its development prospects. A premature and substantial limitation on its own use of fossil fuels could retard its economic development. These, then, are the twin challenges – how to reconcile, at least in the short and medium term, the objectives of significant reductions in global GHG emissions, and safeguard the country's energy security requirements for the future.

The Paris Agreement[1] adopted in December 2015 confirms that India abandoned the objective of obtaining an outcome robust enough to minimize the adverse impact of global climate change. In agreeing to a weak regime India may not necessarily have safeguarded its energy choices. The agreement happened primarily because at least since the climate summit (COP-15) at Copenhagen in 2009, India and other developing countries have been complicit in the relentless undermining of the existing climate change regime incorporated in the United Nations Framework Convention on Climate Change (UNFCCC) and its key principles and provisions. Since the Copenhagen summit constituted a critical turning point in multilateral negotiations on the subject, I have dealt with it in some detail in Chapter 11.

---

[1] Paris Agreement, unfccc.int/resource/docs/2015/cop21/eng/109.php.

The UNFCCC or the Rio Convention of 1992 was based on the global consensus that climate change was a potential threat to the very survival of humanity. A global, collaborative effort had to be mobilized to tackle it. It was agreed that the nature and scope of the threat, as well as the scale of effort required to halt and eventually reverse the increase in global temperatures resulting from climate change, would be determined in keeping with the scientific facts. This process would be guided by the reports of the Inter-Governmental Panel on Climate Change (IPCC), a body of international scientists under the UNFCCC. The international negotiations for this would be conducted under the UNFCCC on the basis of the principle of equitable burden sharing.

The Rio Convention recognized the historical responsibility of developed countries for the bulk of the accumulated GHGs in the planetary atmosphere. For this reason, only these countries were expected to take on absolute emission reduction targets and to assist developing countries, through finance and technology, to also contribute to the global effort. It is this key principle of 'common but differentiated responsibilities and respective capabilities' that has now been hollowed out in favour of a 'pledge and review' mechanism applicable to all countries. Now there will be only voluntary national contributions to meet the challenge of climate change, and they will have only weak linkages to the global effort that science prescribes as the urgent minimum required. This also marked the end of the Kyoto Protocol to the UNFCCC[2] concluded in 1997, which set out emission reduction targets for developed countries backed by strict international compliance.

---

[2] Kyoto Protocol to the UNFCCC, unfccc.int/kyoto_protocol/items/2830.php.

The fourth IPCC had pointed out that to limit the global temperature rise to less than 2 degrees centigrade over pre-industrial levels, global emissions must reduce by at least 25 to 40 per cent by 2020, using 1990 as the base year. Judging by current and anticipated pledges on emission reductions pre- and post-2020, it is unlikely that the 2 degree limit on temperature rise will be achieved. The implications for India are stark as it will have to bear a much higher burden in terms of adaptation in the years ahead. It is already experiencing some adverse effects of climate change as the frequency of both droughts and floods has increased. The Himalayan glaciers are receding and coastal areas are suffering relentless erosion. Higher temperatures are changing agricultural patterns. In Himachal Pradesh, apples could be grown at an altitude of 7000 feet in the past. Now the orchards thrive only at 9000 feet.

Was it good that India settled for a weak climate regime because it would safeguard its energy options? I don't think so. It is India that is more likely to see an upward growth in its emissions than the other major emitters – the EU, the US, Japan and China – over the next few decades. India has been a late starter and much of its infrastructure remains to be built. China's emissions rise is likely to flatten as its years of intensive growth will soon be behind it when it reaches its peak by 2030. China is already being seen as a positive contributor in meeting the global challenge, though its emissions will continue to increase for the next decade and a half.

The other major emitters are likely to record steady reductions in emissions, though not as much as they would have under a robust climate regime. The US recently committed to a 26 to 28 per cent reduction in its carbon emissions by 2030 from its levels in 2005. It will do this by shifting away from coal-based thermal power, the mainstay of its power supply, to gas-based power; it is flush with cheap shale gas. India has no such luxury and will continue to rely on cheaper coal for over 50 per cent of its power supply even in 2030. It will stand out as a 'problem country' that refuses to make a responsible contribution to the global effort. There are already signs that the US is seeking to penalize any new coal-based power and is using its voting clout in the World Bank to discourage the financing of thermal power projects in developing countries.

Since India has allowed the issue to be framed in terms of current emissions rather than the accumulated stock of GHGs in the atmosphere (for which the historical responsibility lies with the developed countries), it will now be difficult to deflect the pressures to curb emissions even though its energy needs are self-evident. This is why I do not see India's passive agreement to the US-led 'pledge and review' approach, which underlies the Paris Agreement, as helpful to itself. It will not allow a delay in its transition from a fossil-fuel-based economy, and will hurt its development prospects. It wil[l] ensure that those who already occupy the major part of the carbon space in the earth's atmosphere get to keep what they have because they got there first. Latecomers must be content with sharing the very limited carbon space that is still available before intolerable temperature rise kicks in and puts a cap on further GHG accumulation. According to some estimates, one trillion tonnes of accumulated GHGs in the atmosphere is the maximum level that can ensure even a 50 per cent chance to limit global temperature rise to 2 degrees centigrade by the deadline of 2030. Going by current trends this will be reached only by 2040.

What is India's current energy profile, and what will it evolve to in 2030?

The Integrated Energy Policy (IEP)[3] adopted by the

[3] IEP, planningcomission.nic.in/reports/genrp/rep-intengy.pdf.

Indian government in 2009 made certain projections, which indicate only a broad trend line since they are not based on comprehensive data and rigorous analysis. For example, assuming a roughly 6 per cent GDP growth rate it projected power generation to rise to 800,000 MW in 2030–31 from 160,000 MW in 2008. (Our capacity is currently around 270,000 MW.) It projected only a marginal shift in the current power source mix of 51 per cent coal, 36 per cent oil, 9 per cent natural gas, 6 per cent hydropower and 1.5 per cent nuclear. For 2030–31, it envisaged coal declining to 45 per cent and oil to 24 per cent, natural gas rising to 23 per cent, nuclear to 6.3 per cent and renewable to 6 per cent, and hydropower remaining unchanged. It is worth noting that coal imports are expected to cover more than 60 per cent of India's requirement, oil imports more than 90 per cent, and gas more than 30 per cent; much of the additional nuclear power too would come from imported reactors. India will be far more dependent on external sources than it is today if its energy mix changes little over the next two decades.

Another concern for India is that 70 per cent of our oil supplies come from the Gulf and West Asia, where political turmoil and disruption look set to escalate.

From these projections, it can be concluded that India will likely enjoy less energy security in 2030–31 than today. These figures also suggest India's emissions will rise from 4 to 5 per cent of global emissions to 7 to 8 per cent in the next decade and a half.

Keeping these projections in mind, the National Action Plan on Climate Change (NAPCC) adopted in June 2008 stated that for reasons of both energy security and climate change, India must move from its current fossil fuel-based growth towards one based increasingly on renewable and cleaner sources of energy – such as solar or nuclear. The Indo-

US nuclear deal was in part motivated by the compulsions of energy security and climate change, as we shall see in Chapter 10, which deals with the Indo-US Civil Nuclear Agreement.

If we examine India's current development strategy, including the Make in India initiative, it is implicitly oriented towards replicating the Chinese growth story. China's spectacular growth record is seen as a validation of the investment- and export-led model successfully pursued earlier by some of the East Asian economies, with a focus on low-cost labour-intensive manufacturing. This strategy has also been based on benign assumptions regarding energy and resource availability, which may not remain valid as the global economy undergoes a major restructuring after the global financial and economic crisis of 2007–08.

China's emergence as a low-cost manufacturing hub and leading merchandise exporter was enabled by a relatively extended period of unusually favourable international economic factors. The major consuming markets of the US, the EU and Japan were relatively open and expanding. Global trade grew at an average rate of 6 per cent per annum, double the rate of world GDP. Further, more than 50 per cent of Chinese export goods were generated by wholly owned subsidiaries of multinationals or joint ventures between Chinese and foreign partners. More recently, China has become increasingly integrated into the global supply chains of multinational conglomerates like Apple and Microsoft. The supply chains consist of production facilities spread across a number of countries, each manufacturing only some components, which are assembled together at a final location into finished products. India's participation in these supply chains is weak.

In the early phase, foreign companies invested in China to use it as a low-cost processing platform for products to be sold in Western markets rather than in the domestic Chinese market. Since China joined the WTO in 2001, its share of exports to the combined markets of the US, the EU and Japan has risen to 18 per cent. This extremely supportive international economic environment that helped China's economic rise, and which India to some extent also leveraged in the 1991–2008 period, no longer exists. It is unlikely to revive even when the global economy fully recovers from the consequences of the financial crisis. There are longer-term forces at play, which may transform global economic and trade architecture in such a way that India's investment- and export-led strategy may not deliver the expected outcomes.

Despite the economic slowdown, the US, the EU and Japan continue to be the most significant markets globally. But global trade, which has been growing faster than the global GDP, has now declined to equal global GDP growth rates, plunging even lower the last two years. And even though China is the world's second largest economy, it accounts for only 2 per cent of global imports. All this has left a global market that India finds less welcoming than in the past. The recent stagnation in its exports bears this out.

It has been argued that for accelerated growth India must seek to become part of global supply chains. But the major global and regional supply chains in Asia, centred on China, are already deeply entrenched and hard to penetrate, particularly since we still have problems on the infrastructure, delivery and quality fronts. In addition, technological changes such as 3-D printing are creating an incipient trend towards the relocalization of manufacture. Advances in robotics may also do away with the need for low-skilled, repetitive labour in industry.

China achieved a spectacular rise in its exports, from $17 billion in 1980 to $1.7 trillion in 2010. This was aided by a significant inflow of capital from Greater China (Taiwan, Singapore and Hong Kong), Japan and the West. The investments that poured into China were part of the global trend towards higher capital flows, both from and among the major economies. For example, in the US, foreign direct investment (FDI) grew from $19 billion in 1980 to $338 billion in 2013. For Japan the comparable figures are $2.3 billion and $135.7 billion. In the EU, investments rose from $21 billion in 1980 to a staggering $809 billion in 2000 before plunging to $250 billion in 2013. We are unlikely to see such massive flows of capital in the near future.

We are also beginning to witness a rise in protectionist trends, which portends the fragmentation of the global economy. India can welcome the Trump administration's decision to withdraw from the proposed new mega trade and investment blocs like the TPP in the Asia-Pacific and the TTIP covering north America and Europe.

From the Indian perspective these blocs are simply large trading and investment arrangements spanning the globe and excluding India. They would have made entering the world's largest markets more difficult for India particularly since they threatened to put in place a whole series of non-tariff barriers in the shape of new and more rigorous norms, standards and regulatory procedures. India would have been unable to conform to them. While the move gives India some breathing space, protectionist threats are cropping up across the world. The emphasis is now on nation-to-nation trade deals rather than regional arrangements. With global trade stagnant and markets shrinking, India will have to find additional drivers for growth rather than rely on just an export- and investment-led strategy.

Linked to this market-limiting trend is the growing resource crunch. China's growth has been highly energy-intensive and resource-intensive; it is already a major consumer of fossil fuels and raw materials from across the world. As a continental-size economy, India may find it difficult to compete with China for the same resources. This resources squeeze will intensify as concerns over environmental degradation and climate change intensify, as they already have.

Our current growth model also seeks to achieve the living standards and affluence levels of the West. We have welcomed the birth of a young, dynamic and aspirational India, and think it has the drive and energy to achieve these benchmarks. But it should be obvious that the pursuit of those levels of affluence for even a small fraction of the Indian population risks condemning the vast majority to a low-income trap – perhaps even poverty and deprivation. Here is one example of this, and several more can be cited.

Car ownership in the US is about 800 per 1000 people, and in Europe about 600. In India it is currently 30. If our car ownership were to rise to even a fraction of the European figure, our imports of oil, investments in roads and highways and land requirements just for parking cars would probably outstrip every other claim on resources. Even at the current low density of car ownership, we are battling traffic gridlock in our cities, road rage has become common and pollution from emissions is a major health hazard. Yet we continue to project car ownership as a mark of economic success and social status. And the state encourages and supports private car ownership, even providing incentives for car manufacture. Citizens have a right to mobility, not to vehicle ownership. The sooner we use financial measures to discourage private car ownership and invest heavily in efficient public transportation the more sustainable our economic development will be.

India does not have large fossil fuel reserves to sustain its current growth pattern without a progressive rise in energy imports. Again, access to these imports will be difficult, what with supply trailing demand and ecological concerns over both fossil fuel extraction and use. So the most important remedial measure is to swiftly improve the efficiency of use of our existing energy resources, substituting energy-intensive activities with energy-frugal processes.

India has neither a comprehensive energy plan nor an energy governance structure that can draft and implement such a scheme. The present government has made a start by putting the ministries of power, coal, and new and renewable energy under one minister but this is not enough to deliver a coherent energy policy. Neither is there a coordinated approach to tackling the twin challenges of climate change and energy security. One cannot be dealt with, either domestically or internationally, without reference to the other. I am not even taking into account the feedback loops that bind the domains of energy, water and food security. The result is that India has a fragmented energy infrastructure.

Its energy resource pricing is distorted, and these scarce resources are misallocated. The mobile towers cropping up all over the country use about 90,000 MW in diesel power at a costly ₹15/16 per unit because reliable power supply from the grid is not available. Transmission and distribution losses of electricity stand at over 20 per cent. When one considers the global benchmark of 3 per cent, this is a massive waste.

Energy security and climate change are, of course, related to ecological sustainability. The current production and consumption patterns across the world are based on an underlying assumption of unlimited resources, which investment and technology can continue to unlock. This has been the belief since the dawn of the industrial age. During the phase of history when only a small cluster of countries was industrially advanced and rich enough to access resources worldwide, such an assumption had validity. This no longer holds, given the explosive growth in global population – from 3 billion in 1960 to more than 7 billion currently. As incomes rise in large and populous countries such as China and India, expanding demand for land, water, food, energy and biodiversity will be the inevitable consequence.

By the year 2050, the global population will increase by 2 billion, of which India's contribution alone will be half a billion. The world is already consuming resources far beyond the earth's regenerative capacity, threatening planetary survival itself. India is particularly vulnerable because of its inability to contain its population growth and to adopt sustainable development strategies. A recent World Wide Fund for Nature study estimates that India is already using 50 per cent more ecological resources each year than can be replenished by nature.

Even if India's population were to stabilize earlier than mid-century, it will find mere survival a struggle. India's food, water and energy security is already severely strained by its growing population. Climate change will only worsen this. Intensive agriculture, required to feed a growing population, requires ever-increasing quantities of inputs such as water, commercial power, pesticides and chemical fertilizers, and more power to extract more water from surface or underground sources. To generate more power, the requirement of available water is greater. More recently, the large-scale use of fresh water for 'fracking' to unlock shale gas, or the substitution of food crops by varieties that can yield biodiesel as an energy source have adversely impacted food security. Food, water and energy security are bound together by powerful feedback loops that are not always apparent.

We are dangerously close to the threshold of the irreversible depletion of our resources. Let us look at water security as an example. Water tables are falling rapidly in almost all states in India from years of over-pumping subsoil water. More powerful pumps are required to reach water deeper in the ground. This has created more demand for power and for higher-capacity electrical or diesel pumps. The poorer farmers are left behind because they cannot afford to pay for power or diesel or buy the more powerful drilling machines now required. A downward spiral soon begins, leading to a water crisis. This is already evident in several states. The World Bank has estimated that about 175 million people in India are dependent on foodgrain produced by the over-pumping of subsoil water. This will mean a major decline in food output once these water sources dry up. And that will place us at the threshold of food insecurity.

It is estimated that 1000 tonnes of water is required to produce 1 tonne of grain. The additional grain we will need for the additional half a billion Indians who will inhabit this land in 2050 will call for staggering quantities of water and energy. The future looks truly daunting if we also take into account the likely consequences of climate change. Scientists say every 1 degree centigrade rise in temperature could pull down yield by 8 to 10 per cent in tropical areas. For India to persist with a growth strategy that continues to be resource intensive and depletes our precious ecological resources is a recipe for persistent poverty and social turmoil rather than a blueprint for prosperity.

Ecological deficit is not only an Indian phenomenon; the entire planet is under ecological threat. India is more vulnerable because significant numbers of its people live on the margins of survival already. This has been recognized in Sustainable Development Goals, adopted by consensus at the UN in December 2015. The goals point to a development strategy radically different from the current resource intensive and waste-generating approach.

In various parts of our vast country, ordinary citizens, concerned scientists and environmental activists have been creating and applying models of development sensitive to the need for sustainable solutions. These efforts need to become mainstream. If India can come up with an ecologically sustainable strategy of growth, based on its own traditional respect for nature as a source of nurture, it could help bring ecological sanity back into international discourse. In the multilateral negotiations India has adopted a mostly defensive stance instead of leading international opinion towards an alternative solution.

I now turn to two critical sets of negotiations I was involved in. The Indo-US nuclear deal was a landmark bilateral agreement but one located within a larger multilateral context represented by the NSG. The climate change talks were in a multilateral context but were heavily influenced by bilateral relations between India and the major powers on the one hand, and by relations between India and the larger constituency of developing countries on the other. These different sets of negotiations throw light on how India conducts its foreign policy in a rapidly transforming global political, economic and ecological environment, balancing its bilateral, regional and multilateral relations. My experience at these discussions also convinced me that the problems we are now confronting demand a much broader notion of national interest than a narrow reading of Kautilyan statecraft. The expansive Ashokan approach, which displays a greater sensitivity to ecology, may be a more relevant frame of reference.

10

The Road to the Indo-US Nuclear Deal

The two major diplomatic negotiations I was directly involved in were the Indo-US Civil Nuclear Agreement and climate change. Both were exceedingly complex and difficult. The nuclear deal was bilateral, but had a major and indispensable multilateral dimension. The negotiations on climate change were multilateral but we had to mobilize support by leveraging our relations with individual countries.

On 18 July 2005, India and the US announced their intention to conclude a bilateral civil nuclear agreement, marking a dramatic end to several decades of estrangement. It was an unprecedented initiative, reflecting a transformed relationship and signalling a significant shift in the regional and international geopolitical landscape. It took three years of complex, even tortuous, negotiations, often upended by sharp political controversies both in Delhi and Washington, to reach a successful conclusion. I was part of these negotiations throughout, first as India's foreign secretary, and later as the prime minister's special envoy.

For both sides, the encounter made for a sharp learning curve. The US was used to dealing with allies or adversaries, not with partners with claims to equality. For India too, this was a whole new experience, dealing with multiple centres of power and influence in Washington and coping with constantly shifting goalposts. This was also the first time that a foreign policy and security issue would became a major controversy in India's domestic politics, sharply polarizing political opinion. It was often the case that more diplomacy had to be expended at home than abroad. The multilateral dimension had to be dealt with at the IAEA and the NSG, which brought its own complications. To understand what made this landmark agreement possible one must first understand the setting in which it happened.

Indo-US relations fell into a recognizable pattern after India's independence. The US had all along regarded India as something of a given fixity or a predictable when crafting its policies for the Asia-Pacific region. There was an entrenched assumption that any collateral or adverse consequences for India as a result of US policy choices would not invite strong countervailing action – action that may hurt US interests. India might bark but would not bite – at least, not hard enough to jeopardize US interests. Similarly, there was a parallel, underlying perception, evident in successive US administrations, that returns on political investments in India would be modest, given India's attachment to a high degree of autonomy in international matters. This explains the US allergy to the policy of non-alignment, which India steadfastly pursued in the decades after Independence. So it was that even though both countries were vibrant and liberal democracies, their shared democratic values had not been able to prevail over their strategic dissonance, as was often the case. However, shared values could reinforce strategic convergence, if such convergence existed.

Our shared democratic values did not prevent the US from adopting policies hostile to us during the Cold War. After the Cold War, however, our common strategic interests, such as managing the rise of China, ensuring maritime security and confronting international terrorism, have been reinforced by the affinity we share as democratic countries.

There have been two exceptions to this general theme running through the saga of Indo-US relations, one negative and one positive. In 1971, India's action in Bangladesh threatened to undermine the newly established anti-Soviet US–China alliance. The US believed that if it allowed Pakistan to be defeated in a war with India, it would undermine its credibility in Chinese eyes. The American assumption that India would tamely acquiesce to the new regional dynamic created by this alliance was shaken by India's own countervailing (and perhaps unexpected) action leading to the defeat of Pakistan and the emergence of Bangladesh. The US sent its aircraft carrier *USS Enterprise* into the Bay of Bengal in a barely disguised attempt to threaten India.

Then US NSA Henry Kissinger had no qualms whatsoever in urging China to attack a fellow democracy, India, along the Sino-Indian border, as a diversionary measure to relieve pressure on their common ally, Pakistan.[1] Since then there has been a wariness in India about a possible collusion of interests between the US and China which may constrain India's room for manoeuvre. This wariness continues to exist, even in the changed environment of India–US relations. There are fears

---

[1] Memorandum of Conversation Between Dr Kissinger and Ambassador Huang Hua, 10 December,1971,White House papers.

that a US in relative decline may reach an understanding with China ceding to China's dominant role in Asia, to the detriment of Indian interests.

A more recent exception also has to do with China, but now as a US adversary rather than an ally. The US administration under George W. Bush became fixated on China as the new and increasingly threatening rival power in the Asia-Pacific. India, with its rapidly growing economic and military capabilities – in particular its naval capabilities – began to be seen in a new light. It was felt that as a strategic partner, India, for its own reasons, would parallel US efforts to limit Chinese influence in this region where US power had so far remained pre-eminent. The impressive performance of the Indian Navy in swiftly delivering relief to countries in South Asia and South East Asia after the tsunami of December 2004 was noted by the US and its allies. This strategic affinity was reinforced by a sense of partnership between the two countries in the 'war against terror', which emerged as a major US preoccupation after the terror attacks of 11 September 2001. It helped that a growing and more open Indian economy offered attractive economic and commercial opportunities to the US.

It was against this background that the Indo-US nuclear deal was conceived, to erase the negative legacies of the past and create a positive environment for forging a strong strategic partnership. However, within the US administration, there were officials who believed the US was making a big concession to India; they felt a suitable price would have to be extracted from India. One demand was that India vote with the US on UN resolutions, notably on Cuba. There were times during the discussions when the US urged India to make concessions to Pakistan on Kashmir. The explanation was that Pakistani president General Musharraf was making what the US saw as a genuine effort to curb cross-border terrorism. These demands, successfully resisted by us, added to the complexity of the civil nuclear negotiations.

India and the US announced a strategic partnership in January 2004 during Prime Minister Vajpayee's visit to Washington. One of the initiatives taken at the time was called Next Steps in Strategic Partnership (NSSP), covering three specific areas: civilian nuclear activities, the civilian space programme and high-technology trade. In addition it was agreed that the two sides would undertake a dialogue on ballistic missile defence (BMD). Cooperation in the civilian nuclear field was, however, limited to regulatory and safety issues.

On BMD, the US offered to brief India on its Patriot anti-ballistic missile systems in appreciation of the Vajpayee government's endorsement of the US administration's decision to develop and deploy systems to intercept and destroy incoming ballistic missiles. The Bush administration abrogated its Anti-Ballistic Missile Treaty entered into with the then Soviet Union in 1972, which had limited the deployment of BMD to the protection of each other's capital cities. Its abrogation was severely criticized by Russia and China, which feared their own nuclear deterrent would be undermined as a result. India's support to BMD came as a welcome gesture to the US. (India had earlier not taken a formal position on this matter.) The inclusion of potential cooperation in this area was the outcome. However, there has been no progress on this so far, and India appears to be working on developing its own indigenous BMD.

The NSSP was to be pursued in three phases; in each phase, a number of interlocking measures would be adopted by each side in response to matching measures by the other. The US committed to progressively relaxing its strict technology-denial regime, put in place after India's peaceful nuclear explosion in 1974 and greatly expanded since. India in turn would enhance its own export control measures, which would entail appropriate legislation to prevent the transfer of sensitive technologies to third countries. It would harmonize its export controls with the lists maintained by the MTCR and the NSG. The NSSP was acknowledged by both countries as being narrow in scope and leading only to a limited relaxation of US technology sanctions against India.

When I took over as foreign secretary in August 2004, I paid my first visit to Washington the very next month. This was the occasion for me to sign the End Use Agreement with the US Undersecretary of State Marc Grossman and Undersecretary of Commerce Ken Juster. This led to some relaxation of export controls against India and the removal of the Indian Space Research Organisation from the US Entity List, which contains the names of organizations to which export of high-technology items from the US is banned. This constituted the main content of Phase 1 of the NSSP.

The End Use Agreement incorporated commitments made by India not to use sensitive technologies received from the US for applications other than those specified in the contracts for the same. This was to assure the US that technologies of a dual-use character, that is, with both civilian and non-civilian applications, would not be used in non-permissible areas such as the defence or nuclear industry.

In November the same year, India and the EU too announced a strategic partnership at the fifth India–EU summit held in The Hague, Netherlands. What is important about this summit is the breakthrough achieved on the nuclear issue, which opened the door to the much more ambitious Indian initiative later with the US. In the preparatory talks leading to the summit, I had argued strongly that in pursuing a strategic partnership with India, the EU should review its stand on bilateral civil nuclear cooperation. I had pointed to India's impeccable record in non-proliferation, despite it not being a party to the NPT. India was expanding its nuclear power programme, I said, both for reasons of energy security and for dealing with the fallout of climate change. With international cooperation, we could expand our nuclear power significantly. But even without such cooperation, I added, India still intended to raise the nuclear component of its energy mix. I urged the EU not to be theological in its approach to nuclear non-proliferation but to recognize India's non-proliferation credentials, appreciate its daunting energy challenges and open the door to reviving civil nuclear cooperation.

The arguments seem to have resonated enough to enable an agreement to set up the India–EU Energy Panel headed by the EU director general of energy and the Indian foreign secretary. Nuclear energy was listed as one of the areas identified for cooperation, though its scope was not spelt out. India was also invited to participate in the International Thermonuclear Experimental Reactor (ITER) project, a nuclear fusion project sponsored by the EU, the US, Japan, China, South Korea and Russia. While Indian participation could only be actualized after getting the support of other participants, the EU invitation opened the door for civil nuclear cooperation, which had ceased completely since India's nuclear test in 1974.

I paid a second visit to Washington soon afterwards. I met with Condoleezza Rice on 18 November 2004. Rice was the NSA but was already slated to take over as Secretary of State in the second Bush administration. This proved to be a key meeting in opening the door to the resumption of civil nuclear cooperation between India and the US beyond the narrow limits of the NSSP. I made a pitch to Rice, similar to the one

I had made to the EU. I pointed out that energy constraints may hold back India's growth prospects. Despite the NSSP, I said, there had been little progress in operationalizing even the limited cooperation in nuclear safety that had been agreed upon. Even our nuclear scientists could not visit the US for any interaction with their American counterparts. If India was indeed a strategic partner to the US, I said, it should no longer be treated as a target. Rice replied that the two countries should engage in a 'deep dialogue' on the subject. She told me that even though this had not yet been publicly announced, President Bush had decided there ought to be a 'nuclear renaissance' in the US, which had not built a single reactor in the past twenty years. This, she said, may create room for the two countries to expand their cooperation in this field.

I referred to the India–EU Energy Panel, which had specifically included nuclear energy as an item for future cooperation, and the invitation India had received to participate in the ITER project. Rice turned to her aides and told them the US should consider a similar energy panel with India. This set the stage for Rice's subsequent visit to Delhi in March 2005, when a decision was taken to commence negotiations on a civil nuclear agreement going far beyond what had been intended in the NSSP. During the visit, Rice suggested that we conclude the NSSP in advance of Prime Minister Manmohan Singh's scheduled visit to Washington in July 2005. This would clear the decks for a much more ambitious initiative for nuclear energy cooperation between the two countries.

She also conveyed in unambiguous terms, both to External Affairs Minister K. Natwar Singh and to Prime Minister Manmohan Singh, President Bush's intention to enable civil nuclear commerce with India, including the sale of nuclear reactors. In public statements she was more reticent. However, in reply to a journalist's query whether 'specifically there will be sale of civilian nuclear technology', she was careful not to rule it out: 'Well, we can certainly discuss anything in this new relationship and I think we would want to discuss this issue.'

Condoleezza Rice was undoubtedly one of the major drivers of the new phase in India–US relations. She came across as a very energetic and focused person, clear in her objectives and determined not to give up even if the odds looked daunting. She could be forceful and demanding but would not hesitate to switch to deal-making if that advanced US objectives. These qualities were often on display during the difficult bilateral negotiations that followed.

The Rice visit launched an 'energy dialogue' between the two countries to explore how they could collaborate in meeting their growing energy requirements. And this became the framework for the negotiations for the civil nuclear agreement. It made for a major change in US policy, which had until then placed non-proliferation concerns at the top of its international agenda. However, it was not clear how such collaboration could take place within the existing parameters of US law and international regimes such as the NSG.

The answer came later, in April the same year, during a confidential one-to-one meeting I had with Philip Zelikow, counsellor in the US State Department and a close aide of Condoleezza Rice. Zelikow told me the American side wanted me to serve as a secure and confidential channel between the US president and our prime minister during the lead-up to the July 2005 prime ministerial visit. On the US side, the trio of Rice, Undersecretary of State for Political Affairs Nicholas Burns and Zelikow himself would be in touch with me. One key area for this dialogue, he said, would be nuclear energy cooperation. He suggested that we collapse the second and third phases of the NSSP into a single phase. This would mean fast-tracking the proposed Weapons of Mass Destruction (WMD) legislation mandated by UN Security Council Resolution 1540. This resolution commits member states to strengthen their legislative, administrative and regulatory regimes to prevent the proliferation of sensitive technologies that could assist state or non-state actors in the clandestine development of WMDs – nuclear, chemical and biological. It also implied harmonizing our export control regime with NSG and MTCR guidelines, putting in place relevant rules and regulations. Once the NSSP was out of the way, he added, the US would consider amending its own laws and that of the international regime – that is, the NSG – to enable civil nuclear cooperation with India.

Zelikow remarked that currently India was in a halfway house and had to steer its transition to a very different era. The aim was no less than choreographing a transformation in which India and the US would together take the lead in shaping the world agenda. This is what President Bush wanted, he added.

It was obvious to me that we were on the threshold of a major change in Indo-US relations. Just seven years after India's nuclear tests in May 1998, which the US had roundly condemned, it was not only recognizing India's de facto status as a nuclear weapons state but was ready to overturn the non-proliferation regime to enable India to participate in international civil nuclear energy commerce. It was ready to do so in view of a growing strategic convergence between the two countries.

My conversations with Zelikow were largely focused on the big-picture issues. I conveyed my view that while India would not be an ally of the US, it would, for its own reasons, pursue policies in the Asia-Pacific that would support US efforts to maintain a balance in a rapidly changing region. This balance was threatened by the emergence of China as a major power with substantial economic and security capabilities. India and the US also shared a common interest in containing international terrorism and upholding a liberal international order. There was a range of global issues which could not be tackled unless India was on board. For India, I said, the US could become an indispensable partner in the pursuit of economic and social development objectives.

While in Washington, I had conversations about China with several senior American interlocutors. Both sides were careful to forswear any intention to contain China and shared the view that expanded engagement with it was in our common interest. However, there was also a shared concern about how China may assert its new-found power in the region. This indicated a need for a countervailing strategy backed by close security consultations and coordination among the major friendly countries in the region, including India, the US, Japan and Australia. I must add that the US Department of Defence leaders, in their conversations with me, were far more upfront about their concern over China's growing power and saw India as an important actor in the regional and global balance of power.

On my return to Delhi I briefed Prime Minister Manmohan Singh on what had transpired in Washington. He agreed that I could serve as his personal representative to undertake the sensitive negotiations that would follow. However, he did inform Narayanan, the NSA, of what was being contemplated, and this caused some tensions because Narayanan felt that nuclear issues were his exclusive domain.

We began to work on getting the WMD legislation through and harmonizing our export controls with the guidelines of the NSG and MTCR. For this, one had to work closely with the departments of atomic energy, commerce and revenue, and with the Ministry of Law. The harmonized lists were then to be gazetted as formal government rules. The work was accomplished in record time, thanks to the efforts made at the MEA. When I met Zelikow and Burns in May, they were impressed that we had delivered so swiftly on the NSSP, which could now be declared concluded.

At this time it was still not clear what would be the nature of commitment the US was prepared to make to enable civil nuclear cooperation with India. It was in early July 2005 that we got, for the first time, an inkling of what it was looking for in terms of assurances to commit to a revival of bilateral civil nuclear cooperation with us. Among their expectations were the separation of civil nuclear facilities from our military facilities, acceptance of a high level of security on fissile materials such as enriched uranium and plutonium, the conclusion of an Additional Protocol with IAEA, which mandates more strict safeguards on civilian nuclear facilities, and the prevention of transfer of sensitive technology to third parties. The following weeks running up to the prime minister's visit to Washington were spent in negotiating the paragraph relating to civil nuclear cooperation with the Americans. Burns led the US side while I headed the Indian delegation.

These negotiations were unusually difficult. The mandate given to the Indian negotiating team by the prime minister was that we should not accept any limitation on our strategic nuclear weapons programme. However, the one inescapable element in our agreement was the separation of our civilian and military facilities, which I knew our Department of Atomic Energy (DAE) would be loathe to do. The civilian and the strategic programmes had, over the years, become enmeshed. India had first built its civilian nuclear sector;

the strategic weapons programme was a later offshoot of this civilian programme. It would be a complicated task to effect a separation, in terms of both facilities and activities. However, in the context of the proposed nuclear deal, the logic behind this separation was simple. There had to be a firewall between civilian and military facilities and activities to assure our partners that whatever we received as technology or material from them would not be diverted to support our weapons programme.

The other issue related to the recognition of India as a nuclear weapons state. As late as 7 July 2005, Burns informally told me in Gleneagles, where we were both attending the G-8/G-5 summit, that the US objective was to 'confirm India's status as a full-fledged nuclear weapons state with all the rights but also the obligations this would entail'.

Soon afterwards, in a phone conversation, he backtracked, claiming that as party to the NPT, the US could not explicitly recognize India as a nuclear weapons state. Instead, it would be ready to describe India as a state with advanced nuclear capabilities, with the same rights and obligations as other similar states, such as the US. This would obviously fall short of our original expectation though the new terminology would suggest a certain equality in status with the US in the nuclear domain. I reacted very negatively to this, seeing it as yet another attempt to move the goalposts. I complained to Zelikow, who tried to assuage my concerns but advised that we stay focused on the 'big prize', as he described it, rather than be sidetracked by terminological differences. After discussions amongst ourselves we agreed to the US formulation on the ground that this was a deal about civilian nuclear commerce and not about our strategic programme. Describing India as a nuclear weapons state was not necessary.

The vital aspect was that nothing in the deal should remotely constrain our weapons programme.

There were a few days of hectic negotiations in Washington before the arrival of the prime minister. Differences remained on two specific issues.

One related to the CTBT which would have banned all nuclear explosive tests without any link to the eventual goal of the complete elimination of nuclear weapons. India had been a strong proponent of the CTBT but had always seen it as a partial measure that had to be linked to the goal of nuclear disarmament. Otherwise, like the NPT, it would only perpetuate and even make permanent the division between nuclear weapons states on the one hand and non-nuclear weapons states on the other. India was not prepared to accept such a patently discriminatory treaty and had therefore refused to sign the CTBT when it opened for signature in September 1996. To US demands that India sign it, we maintained our opposition and agreed only to reflect that we would continue to adhere to our voluntary moratorium on further testing, a commitment we had made in the aftermath of our series of nuclear weapons tests in May 1998.

A second issue in the negotiations related to the Fissile Material Cut-off Treaty (FMCT) which was then under negotiation at the Conference on Disarmament in Geneva. Fissile material refers to nuclear material such as weapons grade uranium or plutonium used in the manufacture of nuclear weapons. A freeze in the production of such fissile material would have the effect of limiting the production of nuclear weapons. India had supported a proposed treaty to limit the production of fissile material and subject this limitation to a strict international verification. The US had also supported the proposed FMCT but was opposed to any international verification. We reached a compromise by committing the two countries to supporting the conclusion of the FMCT in negotiations then under way at Geneva but without reference to the verification issue. There were further efforts by the US to commit India to the CTBT, voluntarily freezing our fissile material production and accepting IAEA safeguards on all civilian nuclear facilities. We were successful in reiterating only a voluntary moratorium on nuclear testing. We rejected the expectation of unilaterally suspending further production of fissile material but referred to the fact that we were ready to pursue multilateral negotiations at the Conference on Disarmament in Geneva on the FMCT, which was already on its agenda.

Natwar Singh, the external affairs minister, arrived in Washington a day before the prime minister, and a meeting was arranged with Condoleezza Rice at our hotel in the afternoon, where the draft was subjected to further reading and amendments. For example, it was now agreed that in separating civilian from military facilities, it would be India that would determine the nature of any facility. It was also agreed that we would enter into an India specific safeguards agreement and an India specific Additional Protocol with the IAEA. The more stringent safeguards would be negotiated and concluded by India with the IAEA. This was to avoid India having to sign the standard format applicable to all non-nuclear weapons states that are parties to the NPT, which India was not. The US insisted, and we agreed, on a shared commitment not to transfer enrichment and reprocessing technologies (E&R) 'to countries which do not have them'. Most importantly, it was also agreed that the separation of civilian from military facilities would be carried out in a phased manner to avoid any dislocation or disruption.

When the prime minister arrived in Washington on 17 July 2005 with a large delegation that included the chairman of the Atomic Energy Commission Dr Anil Kakodkar, the negotiating team presented the final draft to the Indian delegation at Blair House where the prime minister was staying as a state guest. There was a very animated debate on the merits of pursuing nuclear energy cooperation with the US, given the bitter and negative experience of the past when it had put severe sanctions on the Indian nuclear, space and defence sectors after the nuclear explosion in 1974. There was scepticism among some delegation members over the prospects for civilian nuclear commerce for India opening up at all. Others pointed out that several of our nuclear power plants were running below capacity because of the shortage of nuclear fuel. Not enough uranium was being produced locally, and India could not import supplies because of NSG restrictions.

NSG guidelines prohibited the supply of nuclear materials, technology and fuel to countries that had not signed the NPT and which did not have all their nuclear facilities under IAEA safeguards. India did not qualify since it was not a party to the NPT and several of its indigenously built nuclear reactors were not under safeguards. The proposed deal would allow India to import uranium from the international market.

In fact, during our negotiations we had explored the possibility of the US supplying nuclear fuel to Tarapur as a special case. This was not pursued as the US felt it should await the changes to its law, which were anticipated, permitting full civil nuclear cooperation with India. Our arguments that the nuclear deal would serve to bring India into the nuclear mainstream, lead to the dismantling of the technology-denial regime operating against us and make for a significant diplomatic gain were not sufficient to dispel the serious reservations among some of the senior delegation members.

The meeting continued late into the evening, when the prime minister reluctantly decided to defer the consideration of the proposed resumption of civil nuclear cooperation with the US on the terms negotiated by the team I was heading. I was asked to convey this to my counterpart Burns. I called Burns to deliver the bad news: we would have to do without the paragraph on civil nuclear cooperation in the joint statement to be issued during the visit. I suggested a bland statement in its place, expressing the intention of the two sides to pursue deliberations on promoting civil nuclear cooperation between themselves. Burns was disappointed but said he would convey the message immediately to Rice.

Early the next morning Burns called me to say that Rice wanted to urgently call on the prime minister to deliver a message from President Bush. The prime minister was reluctant to meet her. He was afraid he would be pressured to proceed with the nuclear deal and that he would have to respond negatively to persuasion. So he asked Natwar Singh to receive her instead. Rice arrived at Blair House at around 8 a.m. She told Natwar Singh that President Bush had authorized her to meet Indian concerns as far as was possible, and that having got this far it would be a pity to give up on a truly landmark initiative at the final post.

Natwar Singh then took her to the prime minister's suite, where Rice repeated Bush's message. The prime minister then summoned Dr Anil Kakodkar, asking him to write down the changes he wanted to see in the paragraph to meet the reservations which the DAE may have had. The additions proposed by Kakodkar mainly related to committing both sides to full civil nuclear cooperation, clarifying that it would be India that would offer voluntarily those facilities it would determine as being civilian for the application of IAEA safeguards; these safeguards would be India specific, different from what was applicable to non-nuclear weapons states. The Additional Protocol too would be specific to India. It was only when Kakodkar said he was satisfied with the changes that the prime minister gave the go-ahead. Burns and I were then asked to finalize the wording of the statement in time for its public release after the summit meeting between the prime minister and Bush later that morning. There were still some last-minute glitches, this time from the US side because its legal experts were unhappy about some of the formulations. However, we were able to settle everything just before the prime minister and Bush emerged from their meeting to address the press.

While the joint statement was pretty broad-ranging, covering a number of areas for collaboration, it was the nuclear deal that became the centrepiece of the prime minister's visit. It caused considerable surprise among friends and allies of the US. China saw it as evidence of the US seeking to bring India into an anti-China grouping in the region and to boost Indian capabilities as a counter to its growing influence in the region.

The joint statement was no more than an expression of intent. Difficult negotiations still lay ahead, to give practical shape and substantive content to the agreement. A working group was set up to 'undertake on a phased basis in the months ahead the necessary actions mentioned above to fulfil these commitments'. It was decided in Washington itself that the working group would be led by Burns on the US side and by me on the Indian side.

When we returned to Delhi I was told that Narayanan had set up a separate apex committee consisting of DAE and PMO officials, from which I was excluded. The committee would deliberate on a brief for each of my negotiating sessions with Burns. I asked the prime minister to include me in the committee to ensure proper coordination but this never happened because Narayanan resisted it. It often turned out that I was negotiating with Burns on one side and the PMO on the other. Narayanan became the interlocutor between the negotiating team and the DAE, which seemed to be convinced that we were about to sell the store to the Americans.

The first phase of negotiations centred on India's Separation Plan, which would indicate which nuclear power plants and facilities would be put in the civilian category and then offered for IAEA safeguards. It would also contain a plan for the phased separation of these facilities and a schedule to bring them under safeguards. On the basis of the Separation Plan, the US would then move to bring legislation to exempt India from the application of those provisions of the US Atomic Energy Act of 1954 that prevented the US from engaging in civil nuclear cooperation with India. This would then be followed by the conclusion of a bilateral civil nuclear cooperation agreement under Section 123 of the Atomic Energy Act.

However, before the agreement could be made into law, India would have to negotiate an umbrella safeguards agreement with the IAEA, which would be applicable to all its civil nuclear facilities. In addition, the NSG would have to adjust its guidelines to permit its members to engage in civil nuclear cooperation with India, despite the country being outside the NPT and not having all its nuclear facilities under comprehensive international safeguards.

Though the Separation Plan was formulated by India as a voluntary exercise, it nevertheless had to be 'credible' for the US to convince its Congress to enact legislation permitting civil nuclear cooperation with India. The negotiations were expected to conclude before the first week of March 2006, when President Bush was to visit India. It had been informally agreed that the Separation Plan would be unveiled during the visit as a major step forward in actualizing the civil nuclear agreement.

The very first hurdle was on the number of reactors India would place in the civilian category. Our first offer was ten out of the existing twenty-two, while the US wanted to see all our reactors, excepting two, in the civilian category. After weeks of back and forth, it was finally agreed that fourteen of the twenty-two reactors would be classified as civilian and placed under IAEA safeguards in a phased manner over five years.

Another controversy erupted over the treatment of fast breeder reactors (FBRs). FBRs are nuclear reactors that generate more fissile material than they consume and can therefore, theoretically, provide fuel for an expanding nuclear power programme. A prototype FBR is currently under construction at Kalpakkam near Chennai. The DAE wanted them to remain outside safeguards, on the grounds that these were research and development facilities involving sensitive intellectual property rights issues. They could, however, be brought under safeguards in the future, if and when foreign-origin fuel was introduced into the facilities. The US kept insisting that the DAE itself had publicly classified them as civilian facilities, and so they should be brought under safeguards. It was with great difficulty and some creative argumentation that we were able to prevail on them.

A third issue cropped up rather late in the day. In February 2006, Burns and I had a long telephone conversation during which he sprang a fresh demand on us, insisting that we separate not only the facilities but also the personnel working in them. In other words, staff working in civilian facilities could not migrate to military facilities and vice versa. This would be subject to verification too, he said.

I replied that this would be politically unacceptable and practically impossible. It would entail a level of intrusiveness that would never be tolerated. I also pointed out that this was certainly not the practice in other states with advanced nuclear capabilities, such as the US itself. Burns insisted that this must figure in the Separation Plan, otherwise influential senators like Richard Lugar would reject the deal altogether. I replied that this was a red line I would not be able to cross.

Later in Washington I received a late-night visit from Ashley Tellis, advisor to the US delegation. He said our refusal to separate personnel could be a deal breaker. My reply was the same. This was a red line I could not cross. I did not even bring this matter to our prime minister's attention. I knew the DAE would throw a fit if this was even mentioned in our internal deliberations. Happily, it was never raised again by the US side.

The last and final issue, and perhaps the most difficult of them all, related to permanent safeguards. The US insisted that under its law, once a civilian facility had been put under safeguards as a condition for international cooperation, it would have to remain under safeguards in perpetuity. Our position was that we were prepared to accept permanent safeguards if there was an assurance of permanent and uninterrupted supply of fuel. If supply was interrupted then there could be no justification for the continuance of safeguards. We were unable to square this circle, even as President Bush was headed to Delhi on his first official visit to India.

Throughout the day there were several angry calls from Burns – from Air Force One, as he would have me know – insisting that the Indian side agree to permanent safeguards in return for vague assurances that there could be consultations in case fuel supplies were disrupted. I told Burns that it would not be politically possible for us to set ourselves up for another Tarapur type of situation, where the US had stopped fuel supplies despite a solemn contract between us, and we had been forced to seek supplies from elsewhere. He held out the threat that the whole deal could fall through on this issue. I insisted that we could not accept permanent safeguards unless fuel supplies were assured in perpetuity.

The delegation arrived in the evening of 2 March 2006. There was a late-night meeting in South Block, with Narayanan and myself on the Indian side and the US NSA Stephen Hadley and Burns on the American side. Dr Chidambaram, the principal scientific advisor to the prime minister, and Dr Kakodkar were in an adjacent room, ready for consultation if necessary. Despite several hours of difficult negotiations we were unable to reach a consensus. There was no way we could accept permanent safeguards and there was no way the US could dispense with what was a legal requirement on its side. We broke up at around 3 a.m. There seemed to be no satisfactory resolution in sight.

We resumed at Hyderabad House in the morning, President Bush met our prime minister in an adjacent room. Hadley conveyed a new formulation, which he said had been approved by President Bush himself. This offered to India multiple layers of fuel supply assurances, which would later be incorporated in the 123 Agreement word for word. Since these assurances were unprecedented, it is worth quoting them in full:

> To further guard against any disruption of fuel supplies the United States is prepared to take the following additional steps:
>
> i) The United States is willing to incorporate assurances regarding fuel supply in the bilateral US-India agreement on peaceful uses of nuclear energy under Section 123 of the US Atomic Energy Act, which would be submitted to the US Congress.

ii) The United States will join India in seeking to negotiate with the IAEA an India-specific fuel supply agreement.

iii) The United States will support an Indian effort to develop a strategic reserve of nuclear fuel to guard against any disruption of supply over the lifetime of India's reactors.

iv) If despite these arrangements, a disruption of fuel supplies to India occurs, the United States and India would jointly convene a group of friendly supplier countries such as Russia, France and the United Kingdom to pursue such measures as would restore fuel supply to India.

In light of the above understandings with the United States, an India specific safeguards agreement will be negotiated between India and the IAEA providing for safeguards to guard against withdrawal of safeguarded nuclear material from civilian use at any time as well as providing for corrective measures that India may take to ensure uninterrupted operation of its civilian nuclear reactors in the event of disruption of foreign fuel supplies. Taking this into account, India will place its civilian nuclear facilities under India specific safeguards in perpetuity and negotiate an appropriate safeguards agreement to this end with the IAEA.

For the DAE, the entitlement to build fuel reserves to last the lifetime of each Indian civilian reactor and the right to take 'corrective action' in case of disruption of fuel supplies provided them the assurance needed to agree to safeguards in perpetuity. We were now able to announce the Separation Plan[2] when the two leaders emerged after their summit. Another milestone had been crossed.

The scene now shifted to the US Congress, which had to

[2] Separation Plan, www.dae.nic.in.

pass legislation amending the US Atomic Energy Act to allow for civil nuclear cooperation with India. Our initial impression was that the legislation would be simple and brief, effecting the above amendments in the form of an unconditional and permanent waiver for India from the relevant provisions of the act. It soon became clear that the legislative process would, in reality, be long and complicated, with a number of extraneous provisions thrown in to satisfy the many different lobbies and interest groups in the US. Chairman of the House International Relations Committee, Henry Hyde, had a crucial role to play. There were several other congressmen and senators who would influence the proceedings. We decided to proactively engage as many legislators as we could to push for a favourable outcome for India. In the several visits I made to Washington, I made it a point to call on as many congressmen and senators as I could – as did Ambassador Ronen Sen and his colleagues at the embassy.

The first meeting I had with Congressman Henry Hyde was not encouraging. His staffers had briefed him to say the proposed deal would undermine US non-proliferation objectives. While he heard me out politely, he was non-committal. Barack Obama, then senator, was frank enough to express serious reservations on the matter and said he would probably vote against the legislation. Some others, like Senator (later Vice President) Joe Biden, were more supportive. For the first time, we mobilized the influential Indian diaspora in the US to lobby on our behalf with their respective congressmen and senators. US companies, in particular defence contractors eyeing a potentially significant market, also played a part. Finally, in November 2006, the Henry Hyde United States–India Peaceful Atomic Energy Cooperation Act of 2006[3] was

---

[3] Henry Hyde US–India Peaceful Atomic Energy Cooperation Act of 2006, www.dae.nic.in.

passed, amending the relevant provisions of the US Atomic Energy Act of 1954, thus enabling the conclusion of the bilateral civil nuclear agreement between the two countries. The scene would now shift to another round of negotiations on the bilateral civil nuclear cooperation agreement.

The Hyde Act had come in for criticism in India, and it was argued that irrespective of what the 123 Agreement may say, India would be subject to several onerous provisions.

The operative heart of the Hyde Act incorporates three permanent and unconditional waivers from relevant provisions of the US Atomic Energy Act of 1954. In layman's terms, the Hyde Act allows the US administration to engage in civil nuclear cooperation with India, waiving the following requirements:

i) that the partner country should not have exploded a nuclear explosive device in the past; (this waiver is necessary because India exploded a series of nuclear explosive devices in May 1998);
ii) that the partner country must have all its nuclear facilities and activities under full-scope safeguards; (this waiver is necessary because India has a strategic programme which would not be subject to international safeguards); and
iii) that the partner country is not currently engaged in the development and production of nuclear explosive devices; (this waiver is required precisely because there is no freeze or capping of India's strategic weapons programme. It is an acknowledgement that we will continue to develop and produce additional strategic weapons).

Irrespective of what else the Hyde Act contains, these three permanent and unconditional waivers are extremely significant because they acknowledge that India has an ongoing strategic programme. No restraint on this programme is envisaged as a condition for engaging India in civil nuclear energy cooperation. This is a significant gain for India and we should not lose sight of this. This can be appreciated if we just juxtapose this with the UN Security Council Resolution 1172 of 6 June 1998,[4] which called upon India to stop, roll back and eliminate its strategic programme and join the NPT as a non-nuclear weapons state.

I met Henry Hyde soon after the law carrying his name had been passed. He was full of smiles when I felicitated him on the passage of the legislation and for his efforts to make this day a reality. While shaking my hand, he said the proudest moment in his entire legislative career was the passage of this law carrying his name, and which would always be celebrated as a landmark in the history of US–India friendship. The contrast between this and my first meeting with him could not have been more stark; it reflected the long journey we had traversed in the past several months of intense diplomacy. Hyde unfortunately died a few months later.

In the subsequent months, negotiations proceeded on two parallel tracks. One was on concluding the 123 Agreement and the other on concluding the India-specific safeguards agreement with the IAEA.

In negotiating the 123 Agreement we soon came up against a number of difficult issues. I will cover only the key ones.

Under US law, a nuclear test by India in the future would trigger the suspension of civil nuclear cooperation between the two countries. However, since India was committed only to a voluntary moratorium on nuclear testing, it would not have been possible to acknowledge, in a bilateral legal document,

---

[4]UNSC Resolution 1172 of 6 June 1998, www.UN.org/press/en/1998/sc6528.doc.htm.

that India would agree to such suspension of cooperation in the event of carrying out a test. We were successful in keeping such a reference out even while conceding that cooperation may be suspended by either side should the terms of the agreement be violated. An explicit reference to a nuclear test was omitted. The issue of suspension of cooperation and the return of equipment and material upon cessation of cooperation was hemmed in by a number of caveats, including the need to avoid disruption of reactor operations, the practicability of return of equipment, and a provision for compensating any losses that may be incurred.

The agreement also provided for determining 'whether the circumstances that may lead to termination or cessation resulted from a Party's serious concern about a changed security environment or as a response to similar actions by other states which could impact national security'. In other words, if India were to resume testing in response to similar action by China or Pakistan, India's actions would be considered as having been done under extenuating circumstances. From the Indian point of view this matter was satisfactorily resolved.

Another contentious issue related to fallback safeguards in case the application of IAEA safeguards was no longer possible for whatever reason. The US wanted bilateral safeguards to be applied, in such cases, which India rejected. It was finally agreed that in such cases 'the supplier and the recipient should consult and agree on appropriate verification measures', without specifying what these measures would be.

The most difficult issue related to India's entitlement to reprocessed US-origin spent fuel. Radioactive waste generated by civilian nuclear reactors after using up uranium – in other words, the spent fuel – could be treated to produce plutonium, another fissile material, which India could use in its proposed

FBR. The US kept insisting that its law did not permit such an entitlement to be extended to India with respect to US-origin spent fuel. An upfront and permanent entitlement for India to reprocess US-origin spent fuel would require long and complex negotiations. Our point was that full civil nuclear cooperation, which the US had committed to, could not exclude reprocessing. For India, there was a political aspect to this too. We did not want another Tarapur, where the US was neither willing to allow the reprocessing of spent fuel accumulating at the reactor nor allowing it back into the US for disposal. It was finally agreed that India would have a permanent entitlement to reprocess US-origin spent fuel but this would be carried out in a specially designed and dedicated reprocessing facility under safeguards, and administrative arrangements for this purpose would be worked out by the two sides within a period of six months.

Once these issues were resolved, negotiations on the 123 Agreement were successfully concluded on 27 July 2007.[5]

The India-specific safeguards agreement with the IAEA did not pose much of a problem. The IAEA director general, Mohamed El Baradei, was supportive throughout, and it helped that India had an excellent reputation for compliance at the IAEA. The text of the safeguards agreement was finalized after several rounds of consultations between India and the IAEA, starting November 2007. The Pakistani delegation did try to stall the process but the board of governors approved and passed the text of the agreement on 1 August 2008.

The NSG waiver was the only critical component left to be tied up before the 123 Agreement would be put before the US Congress to be passed into law. At this point it may be worthwhile to reflect on the reasons why it was decided

[5] 123 Agreement of 27 July 2007, www.dae.nic.in.

to persist with the initiative despite its complexity and the sharp political controversies it was generating at home, threatening even the survival of the United Progressive Alliance government. And, from the wisdom of hindsight, did India make any significant gains from the deal?

Since 1974, India had been the target of an increasingly restrictive, rigorous and continually expanding regime of technology denial, not only in the nuclear field but in many other areas involving dual-use technologies. Any technology or equipment that had mainly civilian uses but could conceivably assist our nuclear programme in any way was proscribed. In the 1980s, when India wished to purchase a US-made supercomputer for weather forecasting, we were refused; it was argued that the machine could also assist India's nuclear weapons programme. It was our aim to seek the dismantling of these inequitable regimes, which were becoming progressively more detrimental to India's maturing economy. Our key sectors required constant technological upgradation and sophistication. The same was true of our defence sector.

In pursuing this objective, we were acutely aware of the following ramifications:

- The role of the US would be imperative to remove India as the target of multilateral technology-denial regimes such as the NSG and the MTCR. The US was after all their principal initiator and leader. It was also still the world's pre-eminent source of new and innovative technologies.
- Since our first nuclear explosive test in 1974, technology denial was initially limited to nuclear-related technologies and then progressively expanded to cover a growing range of dual-use technologies. For this historical reason, it was clear to us that unless we resolved the nuclear

issue, we would not be able to obtain access to other useful technologies. It is only by turning the nuclear key that we would open the door to enter international trade in other dual-use and sophisticated technologies in the field of advanced materials, precision instruments and metallic alloys.

- Another important consideration behind the initiative we took in July 2005 was that India's growth story would soon begin to suffer from a serious energy constraint. Concerns over climate change would further limit our access to and use of fossil fuel resources. We had to adopt a strategy of diversifying our energy mix and make a graduated shift away from fossil fuels and towards renewable and clean power. Nuclear energy occupies a key place in this strategy, and for good reason. Despite the technology denial we had to contend with, our scientists had succeeded in putting in place a comprehensive, sophisticated and innovative nuclear industry, with a highly trained manpower capable of sustaining a major expansion in nuclear power. We had succeeded in mastering the entire nuclear fuel cycle, from mining to reprocessing. What retarded the expansion of this nuclear power was the non-availability of domestic uranium.

In addition, our technological capability was still limited to smaller-capacity reactors of about 700 MW, while the world was embracing 1600 MW reactors. If we were to target a major increase in nuclear power in the medium term to, say, 60,000 MW-plus by the year 2030, then the import of higher-capacity reactors and uranium fuel would be essential. According to the Integrated Energy Strategy document of the Planning Commission issued in 2007, India's power needs were expected to total 900,000 MW in 2030.

In no way does all this detract from the continued pursuit of the visionary three-stage nuclear energy development plan laid down by Dr Homi Bhabha, who is widely acknowledged as the father of India's nuclear programme. The plan is capable of yielding significant breakthroughs in the longer term, with the possibility of generating 475,000 MW of nuclear power by mid-century on the assumption that the second stage of establishing FBRs and the final stage of putting up thorium-based reactors would have been successfully accomplished. But in the short and medium term, a significant expansion of nuclear power would be possible only if the constraints we faced on the import of uranium and large-capacity reactors were removed.

Indigenous development is not in contradiction to international collaboration. In fact, they are integrally and symbiotically interlinked. Each cycle of international collaboration prepares the ground for higher levels of indigenous development at the next stage. A higher level of indigenous technological sophistication then enables a much more discriminatory and productive new cycle of technological collaboration and, eventually, productive international partnerships. Dr Bhabha himself vigorously promoted international cooperation in nuclear energy, which enabled India to lay the foundations of its current nuclear programme. He was, in his time, one of the most highly respected scientists among the international nuclear community.

In entering the negotiating process, therefore, our objectives were to seek the dismantling of the multilateral technology-denial regimes targeting India and the accelerated development of our nuclear power generation capability to significantly shore up our energy security in an ecologically sustainable manner.

The negotiators were also given a firm guideline: in seeking the above objectives we would not accept any limitation whatsoever on our strategic weapons programme. That would remain inviolate and fully autonomous. In practical terms, this implied that it would be outside the purview of any international safeguards regime or any form of external scrutiny.

It implied also that our ability to further develop and produce such weapons would not be constrained in any manner.

Finally, it implied that we would retain our legal right to conduct a nuclear test should that at any time be deemed necessary in the overriding national interest. We would, in our negotiations, not extend ourselves beyond reaffirming our current policy of observing a voluntary and unilateral moratorium on further testing.

The negotiating team was also instructed to ensure that India's indigenous research and development programme – the three-stage, long-term nuclear development strategy of Bhabha's, in particular, the FBR programme – would also proceed uninhibited and not be subject to external scrutiny. It was argued that as this was a technology with major potential for commercial exploitation of thorium-based nuclear energy in the future, the intellectual property generated on it should be safeguarded. But we acknowledged that when reprocessed fuel from a safeguarded reactor was introduced into an FBR, the latter would also be subject to IAEA safeguards.

While the Indo-US bilateral agreement has come under intense focus, much of the commentary on the subject has lost sight of the multilateral regime, whose adjustments in favour of India were what we were aiming at. Our objective was not merely to seek the US as a partner but to have a wide choice of partners in pursuing nuclear commerce and high-technology trade. But we could not attain this objective without the US taking the lead on our behalf. Yes, Russia and France are friendly and extremely keen to engage in nuclear commerce with us. But there should be no doubt that neither they nor others would have made an exception for India unilaterally unless the NSG adjusted its guidelines in the same manner as the US was prepared to do.

Whatever be the reservations that have been expressed about our relations with the US, no other friendly country which is a member of the NSG had the necessary standing to lead the process of opening up the existing multilateral regime to accommodate India. The US is in a unique position precisely because it initiated these restrictive groupings in the first place and also because it remains the pre-eminent source of new sensitive technologies. It was the intense diplomatic effort mobilized by India with the NSG countries, and supported by the US, which finally realized the promise of India becoming a full partner in international civil nuclear commerce. And without in any way compromising its strategic programme.

This initiative of Prime Minister Manmohan Singh represents a significant and unprecedented effort to expand India's choices, create a more conducive and supportive international environment to advance India's developmental goals, and mark the country's emergence as a major global player in a rapidly transforming international landscape.

India has signed agreements for civil nuclear cooperation with a number of individual countries. India and Russia are already collaborating on two 1000 MW reactors at Kudankulam. Four additional reactors of Russian design at Kudankulam itself, and two more at another site, also of 1000 MW capacity each, have been agreed upon.

With the US, a letter of intent promises to result in 10,000 MW of additional nuclear capacity at two designated sites.

Bilateral agreements have been concluded with Argentina, Australia, Canada, France, Kazakhstan, Namibia and

Mongolia, covering all aspects of civil nuclear cooperation, including the supply of nuclear fuel. A similar agreement with Japan was made in 2016 after difficult negotiations.

Nuclear fuel constraints no longer hamper our capacity utilization and expansion. India has broken out of the confines of the international non-proliferation regime and is being seen as a partner in promoting both non-proliferation objectives and in leading a renaissance of civil nuclear power, notwithstanding the setback and slowdown caused by the unfortunate Fukushima nuclear disaster in 2012.

What enabled India to even attempt such a major and path-breaking initiative? In embarking on it in 2005, India took advantage of a marked change in international (including US and Western) perceptions of India.

Four broad developments led to this change.

First, fifteen years of accelerated and sustained economic growth, coupled with the steady globalization of the Indian economy, saw India merged as an economic powerhouse. It was also a powerhouse whose democratic structures gave it a reputation for political stability. The prospects for the continued and steady growth of India's economy made it a crucial partner for countries across the globe.

Second, a globalizing world found itself confronted with a number of transnational, cross-cutting threats, such as international terrorism, drug trafficking, global pandemics and the twin challenges of energy and climate change. In seeking solutions to such global challenges, the active involvement of India as a large, populous and continent-size economy has become indispensable. This is another reason why its global profile has increased.

Third, India is a country with significant defence capabilities and has an enviable record of activism in UN peacekeeping. In December 2004, its swift response to the tsunami disaster and its assistance to affected countries demonstrated its capabilities in maritime security and in tackling natural disasters.

Fourth, despite a four-decade effort to put India in a technological corral and stifle its nuclear and space capabilities, Western countries led by the US had failed to achieve their objective. Technology denial might have slowed down development in some respects but did not halt its growth into a country with a wide range of sophisticated and sensitive technologies. Isolating it made no sense, particularly at a time when engagement promised much political and economic gain. There was the opportunity to partner its outstanding scientists in the collaborative development of cutting-edge technologies, such as the ITER project. India was able to get a clear message across to the world – you cannot continue to treat India as a target even as you seek to engage it as a partner.

India was able to move with a sense of confidence to leverage these favourable developments – not merely to seek the upgradation of its relations with key regional and global players but also to mobilize them collectively to reflect India's emergence in multilateral regimes. This explains India's success in obtaining a waiver from the non-proliferation guidelines of the NSG in September 2008 against very difficult odds. That is the subject of the next chapter.

11

Running the NSG Gauntlet

On my retirement from the foreign service in September 2006, I was appointed Special Envoy of the Prime Minister for the Indo-US nuclear negotiations. In this capacity, I continued to be associated with the negotiations on the nuclear deal. However, my successor as foreign secretary, Shivshankar Menon, gradually began to focus more on the bilateral aspects of the negotiations while I concentrated on lobbying for approval of the deal at the NSG.

There are forty-eight countries in the NSG, and its decisions are taken by consensus. Its genesis itself is linked to India's nuclear test in 1974, when the US gathered together a number of supplier countries to lay down a set of guidelines governing the export of nuclear technology, equipment and materials to non-nuclear weapons states. Such exports were to take place only if certain non-proliferation concerns were met, including through the imposition of international safeguards. The original grouping was known as the London Club, since all its initial meetings were held in the British capital from 1975 to 1978. No meetings were held thereafter until 1991, when suspicions of an Iraqi nuclear weapons programme and the first Gulf War led to further restrictions on technology exports. The curbs now extended to dual-use items – items that had both civilian and military applications. The 1991 meeting had twenty-six participating countries. Later the group expanded to the current forty-eight. The London Club then became the NSG.

The task of persuading forty-eight countries to agree to an India specific waiver of its guidelines was daunting, to say the least. According to the US-India joint statement of 18 July 2005 (on the occasion of Prime Minister Manmohan Singh's visit to Washington), it was the responsibility of the US to persuade its 'friends and allies' to change the guidelines to permit full civil nuclear cooperation with India. But we knew that a great deal of the heavy lifting would have to be done by us. We had to independently engage with the NSG members and convince them of our case. If there was no NSG clearance, the Indo-US deal would not go through. The deal was conditional upon the conclusion of a safeguards agreement with the IAEA and clearance from the NSG.

From 2007 to the middle of 2008, I travelled to as many as twenty NSG member countries as the prime minister's special envoy. These included Sweden, Denmark and Norway in West Europe; Japan, South Korea, Australia and New Zealand in East Asia; Argentina, Brazil, Chile and Mexico in Latin America; and Germany, Ireland, the Netherlands and Russia. Some other countries I approached on the sidelines of multilateral meetings. For example, at climate change forums too, I would press our case for NSG clearance. In some capitals, I was given access to heads of state or governments. In others I met the foreign minister or senior officials.

We had to use different arguments with different interlocutors. However, some common themes were

India's long-standing and demonstrated track record in non-proliferation, its continuing commitment to nuclear disarmament despite having become a nuclear weapons state, and its willingness to join a new international consensus on non-proliferation, which could deal with challenges not foreseen by the NPT, such as international terrorism. That India had harmonized its export control lists with the NSG and the MTCR was a powerful argument in our favour, as was the adoption of the WMD Act, pursuant to UN Security Council Resolution 1540. This resolution, it will be recalled, enjoined all member states of the UN to put in place strict legal, regulatory and administrative measures to safeguard fissile material and sensitive technologies to minimize their proliferation.

I experienced both good and bad moments during my visits to NSG member countries. I recount here some of my encounters that give a flavour of the interactions I had. In Japan, Foreign Minister Taro Aso solemnly read out his ministry's brief on why it would be difficult for Japan to support NSG clearance for India unless India signed the NPT as a non-nuclear weapons state and adhered to the CTBT. It also referred to public opinion in Japan being strongly against nuclear weapons, it being the only country to have suffered a nuclear attack. However, the meeting over and his formal brief delivered, Aso accompanied me to the lift, and during that short walk asked me to convey to our prime minister that Japan may have to 'make a lot of noise' at the NSG but would not oppose a consensus in favour of India. He said he was conveying this on behalf of Japanese prime minister Shinzo Abe.

In Brazil, Foreign Minister Celso Amorim was at first quite discouraging. He said Brazil originally held a position similar to India's in regarding the NPT as an unequal and discriminatory treaty. It endorsed the possession of nuclear weapons by a handful of states, while denying them to others. However, Brazil had later changed its position and, together with Argentina, not only signed the treaty but also accepted full-scope international safeguards on all its nuclear facilities. If Brazil now supported a waiver for India at the NSG, he argued, Brazilians would want to know why their own country had given up its weapons option when India got to keep its nuclear weapons and also gain access to international civil nuclear commerce. He complained that the US was putting pressure on Brazil to abandon its nuclear submarine programme and to agree to limits on E&R. And here, he said, was the US, giving India, which had nuclear weapons, a huge carve-out from the international non-proliferation regime.

Despite its initial reluctance, Brazil became one of our strongest supporters at the NSG, with President Luiz Inácio Lula da Silva himself giving an assurance to our prime minister in this regard.

Sometimes luck played a part in paving the path forward for India. When I landed in Buenos Aires, I discovered that my chief interlocutor was Acting Foreign Minister Roberto Garcia Moritan, a close friend from my days as India's alternate representative at the Committee on Disarmament (later the Conference on Disarmament) in Geneva between 1980 and 1983. Those days we were on the same side of the fence, criticizing the NPT, pressing for nuclear disarmament and, in general, upholding the interests of the non-nuclear weapons states. Moritan was then a young diplomat like me. He was intelligent and articulate, with a warm and engaging manner.

I was welcomed by him as an old friend and we spoke at length about our time in Geneva, the colleagues we had worked with, the battles we had won and the battles we had lost. Moritan was impressed by what India had been able to extract out of the US and echoed Celso Amorim, saying the waiver for India would be regarded with envy because it was getting to have its cake and eat it too. He told me that China had already made a démarche to Argentina arguing against an India-specific waiver, describing it as contrary to the international non-proliferation regime anchored in the NPT. In the end Moritan assured me that while Argentina may ask a few tough questions, it would do nothing to harm India's interests and would not create difficulties for us. 'You can count on our friendship,' he said. He was true to his word.

As should have been expected, I had very positive feedback from Russian foreign minister Sergey Lavrov when I called on him in Moscow in August 2007. Having been a career diplomat himself, and having earned an enviable reputation for his professional diplomatic skills, Lavrov was familiar with the intricacies of the exercise being undertaken at the NSG. He assured me that Russia would support a clean and unconditional waiver for India at the NSG. He said he would pass on the necessary instructions to Vice Minister Sergey Kislyak, who was handling the NSG. Russia was a constant support at Vienna when the NSG was deliberating the waiver.

Australian prime minister John Howard was unambiguously supportive when I met him in Canberra in April 2007. He said Australia would also consider the sale of uranium to India, though under stringent safeguards.

Prime Minister Helen Clark of New Zealand received me in her office in Wellington and heard me out politely. She smiled throughout but made no commitment. She said New Zealand was part of a group of like-minded countries at the NSG, which included some Scandinavian countries, Austria, Ireland and Switzerland, which attached great importance to upholding the NPT. They were all deeply concerned about the Indo-US nuclear deal, she said, because of its negative implications for the NPT. She also revealed that the Chinese had made several démarches to the group, opposing an India-specific NSG waiver and expressing worry about undermining of the NPT.

As it would turn out, at the NSG meeting later in 2008, it was the 'like-minded countries' that led the charge against India.

The 123 Agreement between India and the US having been finalized on 27 July 2007 and the IAEA board of governors unanimously approving the text of the proposed India-specific safeguards agreement on 1 August 2008, the way was now clear for taking up the final piece of the jigsaw: the NSG waiver for India.

The US had asked for an NSG plenary meeting to consider the draft waiver decision it would be tabling. This draft was shared with us by the US late in July 2008. We offered several amendments as it did not conform to what we had already agreed in principle – that we would stick closely to the template of the 18 July joint statement and India's Separation Plan of 6 March 2006.

For example, there was language suggesting that the application of full-scope safeguards on India would continue to be an objective for NSG members. We could hardly accept that since there was no possibility either now or in the future of us putting all our nuclear facilities under international safeguards. Further, an implicit commitment was being sought from India to adhere to any future and additional guidelines and modifications. We could not be expected to give such a commitment unless we were part of the consultations leading to such amendments or modifications. The draft was suitably modified to take care of our concerns.

The NSG meeting to consider India's case was scheduled to take place in Vienna on 21–22 August 2008. I was part of the delegation led by Foreign Secretary Shivshankar Menon. The US side was led by John Rood, the US undersecretary for arms control and international security, and included David Mulford, the US ambassador to India. At a late-evening meeting on 20 August, the two delegations took stock of the situation. Rood told us that during his interactions with various delegations, they had raised a number of concerns. Among them was a demand to include explicit language for withdrawal of the waiver in case India carried out a nuclear test. Some wanted India to sign and ratify the CTBT, while others wanted a moratorium on India's fissile material production. Still others wanted a specific prohibition on the transfer of E&R technologies to India. Rood said the countries that had raised these issues would need 'something to point to' in return for their support.

We told him we would be unable to go beyond the draft decision already circulated by the US. Some of the issues raised by the countries were already provided for in the existing NSG guidelines, which called for consultation among members in the case of violation of its norms. The guidelines also called for restraint in transfer of E&R technologies. We did not see any need for specific and expanded restrictions on India.

Rood felt it would be best to let the various delegations have their say so they could report to their headquarters that they had spelt out their positions formally. Once this was out of the way, then the stage would be clear to get down to brass tacks.

We left the meeting feeling somewhat apprehensive that the US delegation was trying to get through the NSG what it had failed to get through bilateral negotiations with India.

The next two days were not encouraging. There were three plenary meetings of the NSG members and a separate session where the Indian delegation briefed the NSG members on the steps taken so far by India with the US and with the

IAEA. The case for a clean and unconditional waiver was also argued most persuasively by Foreign Secretary Menon. But the meeting ended without any decision on the US draft.

The US and other friendly delegations regularly briefed us on what had been happening at the plenary meetings, which were restricted to NSG members. We were told that some countries had tabled several killer amendments to the US draft, knowing well that these changes would be unacceptable to India. The group of like-minded countries – Austria, Ireland, the Netherlands, Norway, New Zealand and Switzerland – had made a joint statement strongly criticizing the nuclear deal, characterizing it as the death knell for the NPT.

Over sixty amendments had been tabled by various delegations, some minor or cosmetic, others designed to overturn the entire initiative. In some of the national statements there were demands that India sign the NPT as a non-nuclear weapons state, sign the CTBT, accept a freeze on fissile material production and be denied the transfer of E&R technologies. There were also calls for an annual or at least regular review of India's adherence to the commitments it had made. Discovery of non-compliance would then trigger cessation of cooperation.

It was also apparent that in putting forward these amendments some delegations were hoping to delay the whole process beyond the very limited time available to obtain approval for the 123 Agreement from the US Congress. With the US presidential elections looming, the plan may have been to delay the process until election time, which would have sent the deal into terminal orbit.

The plenary decided to hold another meeting on 4 and 5 September, when the US was expected to present a fresh draft.

During the intervening period, we engaged in hectic diplomatic activity. We urged the US to get politically active at the highest levels to ensure success for the draft at the September meeting. A number of strong démarches were made by Indian diplomats in the capitals of countries opposed to the waiver, conveying that the position they adopted at the NSG would impact their bilateral relations with India.

However, when we reassembled in Vienna on 4 September, the outlook was not good. The US delegation, now led by the new undersecretary of state William Burns, was not particularly hopeful. They felt some reference to cessation of cooperation on future testing by India and a ban on transfer of E&R technologies may be inescapable to obtain a consensus on the waiver. The group of six like-minded countries were particularly active in persisting with killer amendments, with China lending strong support.

On 5 September, as a result of conversations between US NSA Stephen Hadley and his Indian counterpart M.K. Narayanan, External Affairs Minister Pranab Mukherjee issued a one-page declaration reiterating India's policies on non-proliferation and nuclear disarmament. The declaration also reaffirmed India's voluntary moratorium on nuclear testing and its continuing readiness to engage in multilateral negotiations on the FMCT at the Conference on Disarmament in Geneva. All the points that featured in the 18 July 2005 statement were repeated in the declaration. No new elements were added.[1]

This declaration allowed some members of the like-minded group to break ranks and support the US draft unconditionally. Some delegations who supported the draft were able to use the declaration to persuade others to withdraw their amendments.

---

[1] Statement by External Affairs Minister of India Shri Pranab Mukherjee on the Civil Nuclear Initiative, mea.gov.in/in-focus-article.htm?718806.

By the end of the day, the holdouts were Austria, Ireland, New Zealand and China. The US now put real pressure on its allies while India made a further démarche with the Chinese. The French, the British and the Russians also pitched in.

On the morning of 6 September, while breakfasting at our hotel, we received an urgent written message from the Chinese mission to the IAEA in Vienna. It said China would support the draft decision in its present form at the final plenary scheduled for 11 a.m. When the plenary convened, the NSG adopted the decision contained in the US draft by consensus and without amendment.[2] This was truly an extraordinary turnaround. That we had achieved success against all odds took some time to sink in.

As the delegates came streaming out of the conference hall, some of them came up to congratulate our delegation. One of them said, 'Believe me, this could only happen because it was for India.'

There is little doubt that on this occasion the US played a decisive role. Its delegation in Vienna headed by William Burns was much more supportive than Rood had been in August. It is to the credit of the US delegation that it steadfastly refused to accept any amendments to the final draft it had agreed to with us. There was undoubtedly some heavy-duty arm-twisting of recalcitrant allies, which the allies clearly resented but in the end gave in to.

We also benefited from the consistent support received from South Africa, Brazil, Argentina and Mexico – out of a certain sense of solidarity, I suppose, among the emerging powers.

[2] Communication dated 10 September 2008 received from the Permanent Mission of Germany to the Agency regarding a 'Statement on Civil Nuclear Cooperation with India', www.iaea.org/sites/default/files/publications/documents/infcircs/2008/infcirc734.pdf.

And China finally climbed down because it did not want to be the last one left standing!

With the NSG clearance achieved, the 123 Agreement was passed by the US Congress on 1 October 2008, beating the deadline of the impending US presidential elections by a very thin margin indeed. It became part of US law when President Bush signed it on 8 October, just weeks before the end of his second term in office. The agreement was signed by Pranab Mukherjee and Condoleezza Rice on 10 October in Washington. It was with deep satisfaction that I witnessed this historic event, which had taken three years of complex, often tortuous, negotiations.

The Indo-US nuclear deal was a top-down initiative driven by the political leadership of both countries. It was not the result of inter-agency and bureaucratic processes, which are inherently wedded to cautious and incremental steps. On a number of occasions, the leaders of the two countries intervened personally to overcome what at first appeared to be insuperable roadblocks. On fuel supply assurances and giving India upfront and permanent entitlement to reprocess US-origin spent fuel, it was President Bush who ensured that the deal was not derailed by technical or legal difficulties.

Right from the moment I came back from Washington in April 2005 and reported to him the initiative that could transform India's position in the world and its economic prospects, Prime Minister Manmohan Singh never looked back. He established a personal equation with President Bush, and this helped us overcome many difficult moments in the long-drawn negotiations.

An unlikely rapport developed between the hearty, voluble and outgoing Texan who was the president of the US and the very reserved, soft-spoken and cerebral Manmohan Singh. Bush appeared to have a genuine regard, even affection, for

Singh. And the Indian prime minister was unusually relaxed and communicative in the presence of the US president. This personal chemistry between them played an important role in helping the diplomats of the two countries iron out several kinks in the negotiations.

Dr Manmohan Singh never lost faith, and despite the many twists and turns, navigated the political shoals at home with a rare and under-appreciated dexterity. At critical moments, he stood his ground against political detractors, both among coalition partners of his government and his own party colleagues. Those opposed to the deal, including the left-wing parties, continue to nurse deep suspicion of US intentions. Others expressed apprehension that in being seen as close to the US, the Congress might lose support among Muslims. Their assessment was that US policies in West Asia were regarded by Muslims throughout the world as anti-Islamic, and that any cooperation with the US would be seen by the community as insensitivity to their interests.

The Bharatiya Janata Party (BJP) opposed the deal only for partisan reasons. It could not bear the thought that a Congress-led government would walk away with a prize that should have been theirs to begin with. After all, it was the BJP government under Vajpayee which had initiated a new and more positive phase in Indo-US relations. While briefing BJP leaders on the deal, Manmohan Singh had remarked to Vajpayee that he was only carrying forward an initiative that Vajpayee himself had started.

In September 2008, the US was in the midst of its worst financial and economic crisis since the financial crash and depression of 1929. Yet Bush found time to host a private dinner for the Indian prime minister at the White House. It was held in a smaller, more private dining area. The atmosphere was both relaxed and intimate, and conversation flowed free and easy. Bush was accompanied by Vice President Dick Cheney, Secretary of State Rice, NSA Hadley and Burns. Our prime minister was accompanied by NSA Narayanan, Foreign Secretary Shivshankar Menon, our ambassador to the US Ronen Sen and myself.

During the course of the dinner, Rice said the US Senate was about to pass the 123 Agreement and, turning to Dr Manmohan Singh, expressed the hope that India would reciprocate the 'heavy lifting' that the US had to do on India's behalf by placing orders for reactors with American firms. Before the prime minister could respond, Bush cut in, saying he did not care if India did not buy a single reactor. The deal was not about selling reactors to India; it was about the larger significance of the US–India relationship.

When the dinner was over, Bush accompanied the prime minister down the stairs to the White House portico where the Indian carcade had lined up. Before rushing to my own vehicle some way back in the carcade, I stopped to shake hands with Bush and bid farewell to him. He gripped me by my shoulders, pointed to the prime minister already seated in the car, and said, 'This man is my friend. You take good care of him.' Bush had been good to India, and his affection for Dr Singh was always an asset. During his visit to India in March 2006, President Bush had observed, 'What this agreement says is that things change, times change, that leadership can make a difference.'

There are moments in history when decisions taken by leaders can turn the tide. Both Bush and Dr Singh created one such moment.

12

One Long Day in Copenhagen

At the Copenhagen Climate Summit, no country could set aside its selfish interests to set up a robust framework for global collaboration to deal with the elemental threat staring humanity in the face. Neither the developed industrialized countries nor developing countries like India were able to rise above their narrowly defined and near-term interests. Instead, the negotiations had a competitive dynamic, each country yielding as little as possible and extracting the maximum. It was inevitable that this would lead to a least-common-denominator outcome, and that is what happened with the Copenhagen Accord.[1]

In the forenoon of 17 December 2009, I was on my way to the Indian Air Force technical area to join the prime minister's special flight to Copenhagen. We were flying to the Danish capital to participate in the High Level Segment of the fifteenth Conference of Parties to the UNFCCC, better known as the Copenhagen Climate Summit or COP-15. A large number

---

[1] Copenhagen Accord, unfccc.int/meetings/Copenhagen_doc_2009/items/5256php.

of heads of state and government leaders were expected at the summit, as the effort was to conclude an international agreement on dealing with global climate change.

En route to the airport, I received a call from the PMO telling me that the Chinese premier, Wen Jiabao, had requested a meeting with him on the sidelines of the summit. However, as he was short on time, the prime minister was not meeting bilaterally with anyone. We were arriving only late that evening and the summit plenary was scheduled for 9 a.m. the next day. The prime minister was to return home the same evening. Nevertheless, when he asked for my views before a response was conveyed to the Chinese, my instant reaction was that he should agree. Only an early morning meeting at around eight was possible, just before the plenary. I advised that we offer this time slot and leave it to the Chinese to decline. By the time I boarded the flight the Chinese had already conveyed their readiness to have the meeting at that early hour.

I insisted on the meeting because of the recent strains in India–China relations. There had been incidents at the border and the Chinese had reacted negatively, even threateningly, to the tour of Arunachal Pradesh by His Holiness the Dalai Lama as well as to our prime minister's own visit to the state later in the year. The proposed meeting in Copenhagen, I felt, would help in reducing some of the prevailing tensions. It would also strengthen coordination among Brazil, South Africa, India and China – the BASIC group – at the climate summit. Throughout the two years of multilateral negotiations leading up to the summit, these four emerging countries had worked together to uphold the UNFCCC and its principles and provisions against Western attempts to undermine them.

Soon after the flight took off, Foreign Secretary Nirupama Rao and I were summoned to the prime minister's cabin.

He was not enthusiastic about meeting Wen Jiabao and was apprehensive that contentious issues like Tibet would be raised. Nirupama and I assured him that we would work on some talking points for him during the flight so that he could respond appropriately if these matters did come up. My own feeling was that the Chinese premier wanted India's support, as a member of the BASIC group, against what was turning out to be a concerted effort by the US and its Western allies to isolate China at the climate summit.

This was a big change from our experience of the previous two years, when China was projected as the poster boy for tackling climate change while India was pilloried for being 'recalcitrant' and 'obstructionist'. The irony was that the Chinese were often taking more hard-line positions than we were in the negotiations. I remember pointing this out in a meeting with the British foreign secretary David Milliband, who was lecturing me about India being in denial and standing in the way of a successful outcome at Copenhagen. But Milliband claimed that while China may be taking a strong public posture, it was conciliatory and accommodating in private interactions!

One witnessed a change in the West's attitude towards China soon after Obama's first official visit to China as US president in November 2009. Instead of inaugurating what the Americans believed would be a new era of 'strategic trust' and cooperation between the established and the rising power, the Chinese treated the visitor as a supplicant.

There were humiliating restrictions on his public activities and interactions – restrictions that had not been placed on his immediate predecessors. Obama's 'town hall' style meeting with Shanghai students was not permitted to be televised and broadcast. His press conference with Chinese president Hu Jintao was limited to only set statements and a fixed number of questions and answers. In fact, the visit did not live up to the tone and substance of the US–China joint statement[2] which had been negotiated in advance of the visit. The Obama administration had already been projecting it as a significant strategic convergence between the two countries, based on mutual respect for each other's 'core interests'. The statement regarded them as a new Group of Two (G-2) working together to manage regional and global affairs. Here is what was supposed to represent the G-2 moment:

> The two sides agreed that respecting each other's core interests is extremely important to ensure steady progress in US-China relations.[3]

American eagerness to construct a positive narrative of US–China relations may have led the Chinese to believe that the US was in a weak and vulnerable position and that this was China's opportunity to press its advantage politically and psychologically. But the Chinese had made a miscalculation, and US anger surfaced soon afterwards, in the run-up to Copenhagen. And it had its impact on Indo-US relations, too.

Prime Minister Manmohan Singh visited Washington later that same November, shortly after Obama's China visit. Much pomp and ceremony surrounded the visit, intended to assuage Indian concerns over the growing alignment in US–China relations. The special attention shown to our prime minister was in the nature of a consolation prize. Behind the scenes the new US administration did not accord India the same priority as the previous one. There was an early hiccup when Obama

---

[2] US-China Joint Statement, November 17, 2009, www.whitehouse.gov/the-press-office/us-China–joint-statement.

[3] Ibid

announced a special envoy who would cover India as well as Pakistan and Afghanistan in his mandate to foster regional peace in the region. India was removed from the special envoy's ambit only because of a very strong and negative reaction in New Delhi. There was, moreover, considerable unhappiness at the inclusion of a paragraph about South Asia in the US–China joint statement:

> The two sides are ready to strengthen communications, dialogue and cooperation on issues related to South Asia and work together to promote peace, stability and development in the region.[4]

During the preparations for the Indian prime minister's visit to Washington, the US side also played hardball, insisting that India align its negotiating position at Copenhagen with the US, believing perhaps that China would drift away from BASIC. There was a video-conference on 11 November between Obama's chief economic adviser of the time, Lawrence Summers, and his climate envoy, Todd Stern, on the US side and Planning Commission deputy chairman Montek Singh Ahluwalia and myself on the Indian side. Summers adopted an overbearing and threatening tone, virtually demanding India's alignment with the American position and a reflection of this in the joint statement. My suggestion that we should only have a general statement committing the two countries to work for a successful outcome at Copenhagen was summarily rejected.

But the prime minister's Washington visit turned out to be more substantive and positive than expected, thanks to the Chinese overplaying their cards. Much of the visit was devoted to an exchange of notes on the China challenge.

---

[4] Ibid.

This must not have gone unnoticed in Beijing, and the request for a meeting between the two leaders at Copenhagen was probably related to this change in the geopolitical equation. Also, rightly or wrongly, the Chinese were worried at what they saw as a shift in the Indian position on climate change indicated by recent statements from India's environment minister, Jairam Ramesh, who had sought to introduce a degree of flexibility in India's negotiating brief.

Our delegation arrived in Copenhagen on the evening of 17 December, and Jairam Ramesh reached the hotel to brief the prime minister on the results of the ministerial segment he had been attending. The Danish chairman had circulated a draft of the Copenhagen declaration, which would be in the nature of a political declaration, and this was to be discussed at an informal meeting that same night among a Friends of the Chair group of twenty to twenty-five leaders, soon after the formal banquet by the Danish queen. Jairam had been invited to take part even though he was not a head of state or government, and he was confident that India's equities would be safeguarded in the deliberations.

I joined the meeting in the early hours of the morning of 18 December. A virtual who's who of the world's top leaders was present – Angela Merkel of Germany, Gordon Brown from the UK, Kevin Rudd from Australia, Nicolas Sarkozy of France, Mexican president Felipe Calderon, Jacob Zuma from South Africa and US Secretary of State Hillary Clinton. China was represented by its vice foreign minister, He Yafei. The UN secretary general, Ban Ki-moon, was seated next to the Danish prime minister, who was presiding. Representing the Least Developed Countries (LDCs) were President Nasheed of the Maldives, the Bangladesh prime minister, Sheikh Hasina, and the Ethiopian president Meles Zenawi.

A draft of the possible outcome document was circulated

and was then considered paragraph by paragraph. The formulations deviated substantially from the BASIC group's positions. While there was consensus on limiting global temperature rise to 2 degrees centigrade, the European countries also wanted to include a target of reducing global GHG emissions by 50 per cent by 2050. This was accompanied by an offer from the developed countries to reduce their own emissions by 80 per cent by the same date. The implicit assumption was that the developing countries would also have to achieve absolute reductions in their emissions by at least 20–25 per cent by that date to meet the 50 per cent reduction target for global emissions.

China, Brazil and India, predictably, opposed this proposal. There was a sharp reaction from the European countries. They alleged that this opposition could jeopardize the interests of other developing countries for which the developed world was ready to provide $100 billion in climate-related finance by 2020. At one stage, Jairam Ramesh suggested that the 50 per cent target could be included so long as it was linked to the equity principle. But this was categorically rejected by the Chinese delegate. By now we knew that without its substantive content being spelt out, equity would be a mere slogan.

The Europeans then suggested that while the global goal of 50 per cent reduction in global emissions could be omitted, there should continue to be a reference to the developed countries' commitment to reduce their own emissions by 80 per cent by 2050. This too was opposed by the Chinese, who argued that inclusion of this target, along with the 2 degree centigrade temperature limit, would again imply that the balance reductions would have to come from developing countries. There was a storm of protest from the Western leaders.

Another controversy erupted over the treatment of voluntary mitigation actions by developing countries. This was sought to be put in the same category of commitments as those of the developed countries and subjected to some form of international verification. This would have blurred the distinction between developed and developing countries, whose obligations are as different as their entitlements in the UNFCCC.

The final controversy was over the legal nature of the 'agreed outcome'. The Western countries wanted a specific reference to a legally binding outcome. India and other BASIC countries insisted that the nature of the outcome be determined by the content of the agreement and not be prejudged.

The discussions were still in progress when I left to cover our prime minister's meeting with his Chinese counterpart at 8 a.m. at the hotel. In the meantime, President Obama had made an entry into the negotiating room and was pressing for mitigation actions by the major emerging economies and the need for transparency in evaluating these actions.

Prime Minister Manmohan Singh's meeting with the Chinese premier lasted for about forty-five minutes and is worth describing in some detail.

Wen Jiabao welcomed the prime minister, saying he regarded Dr Singh as his 'guru' and a wise elder brother. He said he wanted to acquaint the prime minister with the very disturbing developments that had been taking place over the twenty-four hours he had been in Copenhagen. The US and the West European countries had been working conspiratorially to cook up an outcome behind China's back. He had not been invited by the Danish chairman to the informal Friends of the Chair meeting (convened by the chairman) after the formal banquet the previous night. His vice foreign minister

He Yafei had gone instead. It had been reported to him that the Danish draft was completely against the consistent positions held by the BASIC group. Wen requested our prime minister to extend support to China against this well-orchestrated Western attempt to undermine the UNFCCC and to openly attack the interests of developing countries.

Our prime minister suggested that the leaders of the BASIC group meet informally before the plenary to coordinate their positions, and Wen Jiabao welcomed the suggestion.

There followed an interesting exchange on India–China relations. Wen recalled that during his visit to India in April 2005, the two leaders had agreed to a strategic and cooperative partnership, and that their bilateral relations had acquired a global dimension. India–China cooperation was necessary to safeguard their respective interests as well as the interests of developing countries on several global and regional issues. The Chinese premier added that China would never harm India's interests and recognized India's leadership role in South Asia.

Then he made an extraordinary assertion. He acknowledged that his 'Indian friends' had been unhappy with the reference to South Asia in the China–US joint statement issued after Obama's visit to Beijing in November (from which I have quoted above). He said he wanted to clarify that the formulation was not China's but put there by the US side! He again emphasized that China would not interfere in South Asia and harm India's interests.

Whether this was true or not, it certainly put India–China relations thereafter on an even keel for a period, and Wen made a successful visit to India later in 2010.

Our notes to Prime Minister Manmohan Singh on Tibet and the India–China border remained unused.

After the meeting with Wen Jiabao, the prime minister asked the Indian delegation how this plan for coordination among the BASIC countries should be followed up. I suggested that he ask Jairam Ramesh to work in close coordination with China and the BASIC countries, and avoid taking any contrary positions.

This was done, and we then went on to the plenary where the prime minister was scheduled to deliver his address. Just before the plenary began, the BASIC leaders – Premier Wen, President Lula of Brazil, President Zuma of South Africa and our own prime minister – met in the delegates' lounge. This was the very first such meeting of the BASIC leaders. In the brief exchange, each of the leaders criticized the conduct of the Western countries and the partisan role played by the Danish chair. They deplored the attempts to create a division between the developing countries and the BASIC countries. More importantly, they agreed that their negotiators would work in close consultation and coordination, holding firmly to the well-known BASIC positions on outstanding issues. They also agreed that the leaders should not be expected to engage in negotiating the outcome draft.

This informal meeting attracted considerable interest among the delegates and the international media assembled in the plenary hall.

Meanwhile, the Friends of the Chair had completed the first reading of the draft put forward by the Danish hosts. There had been no consensus and the chairman had agreed to prepare a fresh draft for consideration, taking into account the deliberations held in the early hours of that morning. There was no effort by the chair to brief the very large number of heads of state and governments who were whiling away the hours on the conference premises. It was, in fact, fairly late in the afternoon that the restricted meeting among the leaders reconvened and a new draft was circulated.

Jairam Ramesh had apparently been engaging in

consultations with several of the leaders and their aides. When we reassembled he handed me the fresh draft document and requested me to handle the negotiations as he had to meet and brief our prime minister. The draft was deeply problematic, and I pointed out to him that several of the formulations would be unacceptable to the BASIC group. He said that nothing had been agreed in the informal consultations and everything was ad referendum. I could seek amendments as we deemed fit. For the rest of the session it was Ambassador Chandrasekhar Dasgupta and I who engaged in what proved to be difficult, unpleasant and acrimonious negotiations.

The points of contention were no different from those raised in the morning session. The goal of 50 per cent reduction in global emissions was retained, along with the 2 degree centigrade temperature rise limit. I immediately objected to it. Gordon Brown accused the Indian delegation of bad faith, insisting that Jairam Ramesh had agreed to the formulation in the morning. Merkel also chimed in, saying that positions agreed in consultations among leaders should be respected.

I explained that the 50 per cent target carried the implicit assumption of substantial emission reductions by developing countries without any indication of the financial resources and technology transfers necessary to enable such mitigation action by them. I also pointed out that such expectations were in complete contradiction to the overriding objective of poverty eradication and social and economic development, which was recognized without qualification in the UNFCCC.

Once again, as they had in the morning session, the West Europeans insisted that along with the 2 degree centigrade temperature rise limit, the commitment of developed countries to reduce their own emissions by 80 per cent by 2050 should be recorded in the document. I had to point out that this would not be acceptable for the same reason, that is, it implied that the developing countries would have to contribute the balance of absolute emission reductions required to attain the global temperature goal; they could not take on this commitment without a clear and definitive indication of the financial and technological resources available to them under the proposed climate regime.

Subsequently, I had to repeat these arguments for President Obama, who came in later and demanded to know why India was saying no to every proposal without offering any alternative. After hearing me out, he said he understood our position but could not agree with it.

The discussion then moved on to the issue of transparency. Obama insisted that the voluntary mitigation actions by developing countries should be in accordance with international guidelines and subjected to international evaluation. While developed and developing countries may have differential commitments, the same legal template should apply to all.

Here, again, I had to point out that the obligations and entitlements of developed and developing countries were clearly differentiated in the UNFCCC. This was the essence of the principle of common but differentiated responsibilities and respective capabilities, or the so-called CBDR principle, enshrined in the agreement. I added that developing countries were ready to use their already existing responsibility to provide details of their climate action as part of their National Communications (NATCOM). This could be made more detailed and more frequent but it was not the same as the evaluation of absolute emission reduction obligations of developed countries.

This set off another storm in the room, with Sarkozy accusing India and the 'emerging big countries' of indulging in a charade. He went on to threaten to expose the obstructions posed by them, adding that if agreement could not be reached on the global goal and transparency, no money would be available for poorer countries. He added for good measure that it was because of these 'big countries' that the Maldives and Bangladesh would be deprived of the money they would otherwise have received from developed countries.

There was a subsequent discussion on finance. The Mexican president proposed a Green Climate Fund, which could be subscribed to on the basis of accepted criteria. There were some queries about whether major developing countries would also contribute funds. I pointed out that it was the legal responsibility of the developed countries to provide both finance and technology to developing countries to enable them to undertake climate action. Developing countries had no such obligation. This was greeted by much smirking among Obama, Gordon Brown and Sarkozy.

It was during this session that the developed countries agreed to provide $10 billion a year for three years, from 2010 to 2012, to the LDCs, Small Island Developing States (SIDS) and African states. A firm commitment from the developed countries to provide $100 billion by 2020 was shot down by Obama, who said that the term used should be 'mobilize' rather than 'provide'. He said he could not make a firm commitment without US congressional approval.

When Ambassador Chandrasekhar Dasgupta was occupying the Indian chair and taking part in the drafting, Sarkozy, at one point, shouted that leaders should not have to negotiate with 'junior officials'. Ambassador Dasgupta reacted strongly to this, pointing out that he was representing India and his credentials should not be questioned. Sarkozy did subside after this, apologizing for his remark.

I left the negotiating room soon afterwards to brief the prime minister and also to prepare for our departure that evening for Delhi. It was already past five in the evening, and it seemed unlikely that an agreement would be reached in time for a closing plenary, when we received a message that Wen Jiabao was requesting an urgent meeting with our prime minister. He had also invited the other BASIC leaders to the meeting to take stock of the day's deliberations. The prime minister conveyed that he was about to leave for the airport and a meeting may not be possible. There was another call repeating the request and urging our prime minister to agree, as a personal gesture to the Chinese premier. We had no option but to defer our departure. The meeting was set for 6 p.m. in a small conference room at one end of the hotel.

When we arrived, Wen Jiabao was already waiting, and we were soon joined by Presidents Lula and Zuma. Our delegation consisted of Jairam Ramesh, Environment Secretary Vijay Sharma, Ambassador Dasgupta and myself. The Chinese premier was accompanied by Xie Zhenhua, vice minister at the National Resource Development Council and China's chief climate change negotiator. The Chinese vice foreign minister, He Yafei, was also present. Despite his role as chief negotiator, Xie had been conspicuously absent from the negotiating room throughout the day, leaving it to He Yafei to hold the fort. Both Lula and Zuma were accompanied by their senior aides. While Wen Jiabao and our prime minister sat on one side of the table, Lula and Zuma sat on the opposite side.

Wen Jiabao welcomed his fellow leaders and said he wanted to discuss the manner in which BASIC should handle the impending failure of the summit, which the developed countries would squarely blame on the BASIC countries. He suggested a coordinated strategy to deal with the negative fallout. He also said the US president had asked to see him before his departure, and the meeting with him had been set for 7 p.m. So he also wanted advice on what he should convey to the US president.

An inconclusive discussion followed on what the BASIC leaders should say about the summit. It was agreed that while regretting the failure of the summit, a commitment to continuing the negotiations should be conveyed to the international community. It was also agreed that BASIC needed to strengthen their consultations and coordination in the negotiating process. The leaders agreed with the positions taken by their negotiators in the Friends of the Chair meeting. Wen was asked to convey all these points to the US president.

It was at this juncture that President Obama arrived at the glass door of the conference room, accompanied by Hillary Clinton and other senior aides. The deputy NSA for economic affairs and later the US trade representative Mike Froman was there, as was Stern, the US special envoy on climate change. Obama called out to Wen Jiabao from the door, asking whether he should come in or wait for the meeting to conclude. Wen Jiabao looked questioningly at his counterparts, who readily agreed to invite the US president to join the discussions. Obama was invited to sit next to Zuma. The room had become very crowded, and several accompanying aides had to stand.

The US president began by saying that a failure of the Copenhagen summit would be a very serious setback and every effort should be made to salvage it. He said most of the proposed Copenhagen Accord had been agreed on except for the impasse on a few remaining issues. For the US, the issue of international review of mitigation actions undertaken by developed and developing countries was most important, he said. For him to persuade the US Congress to approve significant financing for developing countries, the transparency of action taken by all parties was crucial. He conveyed that if acceptable language could be found on this issue, then the accord could be saved. If not, he was prepared to go ahead with an agreement with those willing to join the accord. The rest would have to explain to the world why they were standing outside the agreement.

Wen Jiabao conveyed the willingness of the BASIC countries to record their voluntary actions in their respective NATCOMs, which could meet the transparency objective. However, Obama said this would not be sufficient. He suggested an attempt be made to find some acceptable language. He asked Mike Froman to consult with the representatives of the BASIC leaders to see if a compromise could be reached. Froman was joined by He Yafei from China, Jairam Ramesh from India, Lula from Brazil and Alf Wills from South Africa. They went into a huddle in a corner of the room while the leaders continued to discuss other issues. After about ten minutes, the group returned with the formulation 'technical analysis and assessment' as applicable to developing country mitigation actions to meet the transparency criterion.

Obama was not satisfied with the wording and wanted a stronger, more explicit, formulation. After some further back and forth, he suggested the phrase 'international analysis and assessment', but the Chinese looked sceptical. At this point Jairam proposed 'international consultations and analysis', which Obama seemed inclined to accept. He turned to Wen Jiabao to ask whether the latest formulation would be acceptable to China. Wen Jiabao in turn looked around to see if the others had any reservations. When the other leaders kept their counsel, he nodded his head in assent.

It was at this point that all hell broke loose. Xie Zhenhua, China's chief climate negotiator, who had been following the exchange with increasing distress, got extremely agitated and began to loudly and angrily berate his own premier. Since I knew Mandarin, I could broadly follow what he was saying. Xie wagged his finger at Obama, exclaiming that the

American president had brought nothing to the table and was making outrageous demands on China. He then banged the table with his fist and warned his premier against accepting any compromise that would be akin to selling out the country. Obama asked Wen Jiabao's interpreter to translate what Xie was saying. She was extremely flustered and said she could not translate what had been said. Wen Jiabao sat impassively and did not retract his acceptance of the compromise formulation.

Xie's outburst was most unusual and unexpected. For an official to angrily disagree with his own premier in public would be unthinkable in any country, and more so in an authoritarian and strictly hierarchical system like China's. However, Xie continues to serve as China's chief climate change negotiator to this day and does not seem to have been taken to task for his public outburst at his premier at Copenhagen.

Having pocketed what he had been looking for, Obama proceeded to sell his European allies down the drain. He agreed to have all references to the 50 per cent reduction in global emissions dropped from the final draft outcome document as well as the reference to the developed countries' commitment to 80 per cent emission reduction by 2050. He also agreed that there need not be any reference to a legally binding outcome that the European countries had been insisting upon. He then left to consult with his allies still waiting in the main negotiating room. After about twenty minutes, he emerged to announce to the gaggle of American and international press: 'We have a deal.'

For a leader representing a country that had brought nothing to the negotiating table, this was indeed a public relations coup. The Europeans were given no opportunity to demur.

Earlier when we were exiting the small conference room

after Obama's departure, Xie Zhenhua, whom I had worked with closely during the past two years, came up to me, held my hand and declared with barely concealed frustration: 'The UNFCCC and the Kyoto Protocol have been buried at this meeting and we will learn to regret this day.'

The process of attrition and systematic hollowing out of the UNFCCC had begun. The Paris Agreement of 2015 represents the culmination of the dismantling exercise. And India dare not acknowledge that it has been complicit in it.

13

Shaping the Emerging World Order and India's Role

In his celebrated poem, 'The Passing of Arthur', the poet Alfred Tennyson writes the following lines when the dying King Arthur is set on the royal barge to take him to the nether world:

> The old order changeth yielding place to new/
> And God fulfils himself in many ways/
> Lest one good custom should corrupt the world.

There is little doubt that the world today is at an inflection point, when the old and familiar order is crumbling but it is not clear what it is yielding place to. If history is any guide, a new order will emerge. The question is whether this will be born from the ashes of a debilitating war or through a gradual process of adjustment. And if the frenetic pace of change will even allow a more leisurely construction of a new architecture of global governance with stable and effective institutions and processes. We may be able to identify the key drivers of change but not the manner in which they could lead to an outcome that will be stable and conducive to peace among nations. Tennyson's words do convey an important insight: the multiplicity of societies and the extraordinary variety of human thought and endeavour cannot be encompassed in a singular blueprint.

The modern state system on which an international order is built originated in the Peace of Westphalia which brought a debilitating thirty-year war in Europe to a close in 1648. It inaugurated a European order based on the inherent equality of states and the recognition of a state's monopoly over coercive power within its territorial limits. Thus were born the concepts of political sovereignty and territorial integrity of independent states and, as a consequence, a multipolar order held together by a set of agreed rules of the game and a balance of power among its participants. As Kissinger has observed in *World Order*:

> ...the structure established in the Peace of Westphalia represented the first attempt to institutionalize an international order on the basis of agreed rules and limits and to base it on a multiplicity of powers rather than the dominance of a single country.

An attempt by any country to upset the balance and seek dominance would trigger responses from other players to restore the equilibrium of power. And this is how the system operated in subsequent decades.

After Westphalia the concept of European order received a further elaboration at the Congress of Vienna convened in 1815. The objective of the Congress was to restore peace in Europe by constructing a new balance among the major powers after another bout of nearly continuous warfare for almost twenty-five years due to the French Revolution and the Napoleonic Wars. The main players were Austria, Britain, Russia and Prussia which had allied against Napoleonic France. However, at the Congress, France also became part of the order and played a role in maintaining European balance. The Congress of Vienna may be regarded as a maturation of the concept of multipolar order, with the development of a more elaborate set of rules of engagement among sovereign states. The Congress was followed by a series of regular meetings amongst its main participants, which became known as the Concert of Europe, inaugurating the age of multilateral diplomacy. The Concert of Europe created the template which led to the setting up of the League of Nations after the First World War which may be considered the early precursor of the UN established in 1945 after the Second World War.

In the century of relative peace which followed the Congress of Vienna, several international organizations were created by common consent to enable and promote cooperation among countries in a number of domains. These include the Universal Telegraph Union set up in 1865, the Universal Postal Union set up in 1874 and the Permanent Court of Arbitration set up in 1899. These institutions were testimony to the fact that technological change was forcing nations to collaborate to manage a more interconnected world. It is the Concert of Europe which created the basis for a new architecture of global governance based on shared interests, which is now taken for granted as part of the UN system.

The emergence of independent and sovereign states after the Peace of Westphalia gave rise to the requirement of constant engagement and communication. Diplomacy as an organized and structured activity with its own protocols and norms of behaviour among representatives of states also dates from this period. These norms were further elaborated and codified at the Congress of Vienna and the Concert of Europe. This also marks the beginning of the adoption of official titles for different classes of state representatives and the alphabetical order to establish an order of precedence among equal states.

One must not lose sight of the fact that the international order which germinated and grew into maturity between the seventeenth and twentieth centuries was a European construction and its principles and norms did not apply to relations between the European countries and their colonial possessions across Asia, Africa and Latin America.

There was no question of equality or observance of any norms in the treatment of colonized peoples. But in the aftermath of the Second World War, when wave after wave of colonized countries emerged as independent states, the Westphalian principles of political sovereignty and territorial integrity were universally affirmed as the basis on which they would enter the international order. The Westphalian imprint is apparent in the Panchshila or the Five Principles of Peaceful Coexistence which were codified as the basis for interstate relations within the community of the decolonized states of Asia, Africa and Latin America. The principles of international law and the codes of conduct to be observed in interstate relations, which were elaborated over the past four centuries since Westphalia, were also accepted by the new entrants into the international system. The UN Charter codified these into universal principles.

The legacy of Westphalia, in a very real sense, is that international legitimacy demands adherence, in appearance if not in substance, to the rules of the game codified over the centuries of Western dominance, first in Europe and then in its Atlantic extension in the US. These rules establishing a multipolar order among roughly equal states found universal application in the post–Second World

War era and international legitimacy, in theory, required multilateral sanction.

However, such appeal to legitimacy remained in constant tension with a very asymmetrical and skewed distribution of economic and military power. The US emerged from the ravages of the war as the most powerful economic and military power. It helped create multilateral institutions like the UN, the World Bank, the International Monetary Fund and the General Agreement on Trade and Tariffs but ensured that these were dominated by the West. The UN label was useful in its interventions in countries far and near but unilateralism would often be resorted to if the label was not forthcoming. But even as the most powerful military and economic power after the Second World War, the US had to contend with the parallel hegemony of the Soviet Union and the resistance of a large number of emerging states to participation in its security system.

It was not until the collapse of the Soviet Union in 1990 and the end of the Cold War that the US and the West in general would enjoy a brief unipolar interlude. During this interlude which lasted up until the global financial and economic crisis of 2007–08, the US was a true hegemonic power which could set aside the established multilateral structures and processes and ignore the Westphalian norms in the pursuit of an interventionist strategy dictated by its own intent. Other powers had to acquiesce either by choice or compulsion. It is this interlude which is coming to an end.

The US remains a pre-eminent power against any metric of economic and military might. Its status as the chief source of technological innovation and creativity remains undiminished. But it is no longer a hegemonic power. Its relative power has declined as other powers, chiefly China, have steadily accumulated significant economic and military capabilities. More importantly, even if its power remains formidable there is a decline in popular support in the US for an expansive engagement with the rest of the world. Trump's slogan of 'America First' is a symptom of that change.

The narrowing of America's vision is paralleled by the fragmentation of Europe, a key pillar of Western ascendancy. The EU is strained by the emergence of a unified Germany at the heart of Europe as its strongest power. That Germany has emerged unscathed from the economic and financial crises which have severely weakened other states of Europe has only sharpened these strains.

Brexit may well lead to Britain once again seeking to play the role of an offshore presence to uphold a balance of power in continental Europe as it did through most of its recent history. This may set off countervailing developments in Europe with Germany expanding its room for manoeuvre in partnership with Russia and, or, with China. The weakening of US engagement with Europe, which Trump has already embarked upon, may only reinforce these trends. In any event it appears unlikely that the promise of a cohesive Europe playing the role of an influential international actor, either in its own right or as part of a powerful trans-Atlantic partnership, will be realized in the foreseeable future, if ever.

In *World Order*, Kissinger posed different scenarios which may unfold in Europe. Would Europe, he asked, 'relate itself to its recent past of Atlantic cohesion or its long term history of manoeuvring for maximum advantage on the basis of national interests?' On present indications the latter prospect is the most likely.

Russia retains its position as one of the great powers of the world. It has rich natural resources, a long history of mastery over science and technology and a sense of its own civilizational uniqueness. It has also been nursing a grievous sense of loss and resentment over the loss of its Soviet empire in Eastern Europe and Central Asia. The erstwhile Soviet republics remain its 'near neighbourhood' and a target of renewed influence, if not control. This brings it into confrontation with the US and Western Europe and may eventually do so with China as well. At the same time there has been its long-standing urge to be accepted as part of the West and accorded respect as a fellow European power. When this is not forthcoming the sense of grievance is only heightened.

In its current state, however, it is unlikely that Russia will emerge as one of the key architects of the emerging world order. Its relative economic and military power has diminished, its demographics are against it and in its isolation from the West it has to acquiesce to an alignment with China, despite its anxieties over long-term Chinese penetration into its 'near neighbourhood'. However, if its relations with the US and Western Europe normalize, there could be a major shift in geopolitical alignments, constraining Chinese calculations. It is interesting to note that Russia is today one of the vocal champions of a multipolar order.

It is in Asia that the new world order is likely to be shaped. There are good reasons for this. Over the past three decades and more, the Asia-Pacific region has replaced the trans-Atlantic as the centre of gravity of the global economy. Asia is home to the second and third largest economies in the world, namely, China and Japan. In purchasing power parity terms India is already the fourth largest economy in the world although it still lags behind at seventh place in nominal terms. In addition there are other substantial economies in South Korea, Australia, Taiwan and the ASEAN countries as a whole. This cluster of major Asian powers also deploys a formidable array of security capabilities, in particular maritime capabilities, though still modest in comparison to US military presence in the region.

At a time when the economies of the US and Western Europe continue to be sluggish, Asia has in India and China two of the fastest growing large economies in the world. They are likely to remain the key growth drivers of the global economy. The major powers in Asia have managed to sustain relative political stability and social cohesion and this, too, enables them to exert expanding influence on both regional and global affairs.

What kind of regional order is likely to emerge in Asia given these trends? The answer to this question is important because the shape of the regional order in Asia will greatly influence the new global order precisely because Asia has now emerged as a key fulcrum of power in the world. There can be no multipolar world order without a multipolar Asia. An Asian hegemon will inevitably aspire to global hegemony.

There are a number of scenarios which could emerge and each will be defined by the distribution of economic and military power among countries in the region and the perceptions among them concerning the implications of such power distribution. There may often arise a disconnect between the reality of power and how it is perceived. The US continues to be the most formidable military power in Asia. On the eastern flank, constituting the Asia-Pacific, the US Pacific Command deploys by far the most powerful land, air and naval forces and is allied to countries which themselves have significant capabilities of their own, such as Japan, South Korea and Australia. In addition, the US has strong security arrangements with India and several ASEAN countries, which augment its capabilities and geographic reach.

However, its economic profile in the region has diminished even as China's has grown. And the perception, if not the reality, of capabilities and more importantly the willingness to use them has diminished among the countries of the region even as Chinese economic and military capabilities have steadily advanced. Despite the continuing gap in security capabilities vis-à-vis the US, China has shown a willingness to assert its power against the countries of the region, through unilateral occupation of the offshore islands it claims in the South China Sea or through the creation of artificial islands and the deployment of military assets on them. The unwillingness of the US to confront these actions has led to a pervasive sentiment in the region that China's ascendancy is becoming an inevitability. This is reinforced by Chinese diplomacy using a mixture of threats and blandishments, which echo the Kautilyan instruments of *sama*, *dana*, *danda* and *bheda*.

On the western flank of Asia, which includes West Asia and the Gulf and Central Asia, it is again the US which, through its Central Command and network of bases, deploys the strongest military presence in the region. No other power comes close. However, the availability of overwhelming power is inhibited in its use for a variety of reasons, including war fatigue, the reduced dependence on the Gulf for energy supplies and a growing domestic sentiment against expansive external engagement.

This has coincided with visible Chinese activism in Central Asia, the appearance of its naval forces in the Indian Ocean and its establishment of naval bases in Djibouti on the Horn of Africa and the Pakistani port of Gwadar. The perception of US decline has been further reinforced by the tactical assertiveness of Russia, which is backing Bashar al-Assad in Syria and Iran. Any objective assessment would reveal that China is still a modest player in the region even though its presence is expanding.

The Chinese presence in Central Asia has been expanding most rapidly with an emphasis on infrastructure development, investment in energy resources and trade. The security element remains less visible but as Chinese assets gather in scale, security capabilities will follow. The Central Asian component of China's ambitious One Belt One Road initiative should be seen in this perspective. Here it is not the US that is the likely countervailing power but Russia, which has important stakes, as has been described earlier, in its 'near neighbour'. At the moment, Russia's concern over China's inroads into this 'near neighbourhood' may be muted for tactical reasons but when looking at the prospects of China emerging as a new global hegemon, this essential incompatibility of Chinese and Russian interests in the region must be kept in mind.

In terms of this analysis it is clear that on neither flank of Asia does China have military capabilities anywhere near the scale deployed by the US. In the Asia-Pacific region, in addition to the US, there is a cluster of major powers with substantial military capabilities and these are being significantly expanded in response to a perceived Chinese security threat. India, Japan, South Korea, Vietnam, Indonesia and Australia fall in this category. Even without a substantial US military presence in the region, these capabilities together would easily surpass what China can deploy.

In terms of economic calibre, China is admittedly the most important trade and investment partner for a number of South East Asian and Central Asian countries, but there are other important players such as the US, Japan, South Korea and India itself. On the economic and commercial side, Chinese prosperity is very much a creature of strong interdependence in the shape of extended value chains. Disrupting them for political reasons would also impose a cost on China.

China has also tried, with some success, to characterize its emergence as a front-ranking power in Asia as a return to its ascendant status through much of history until it became a victim of Western imperial depredations and later Japanese aggression. This interlude of about 150 years is described as a period of national shame and humiliation from which China has now re-emerged to take its place, once again, at the top of the hierarchy of nations, first in Asia and then in the world. This is, in the Chinese telling, a return to the natural order in Asia that needs to be universally acknowledged. The One Belt One Road initiative tries to project that it is a revival of ancient maritime and caravan routes with China at the centre, but in a modern context.

The historical narrative of China as the pre-eminent Asian and global power is mostly contrived and imagined as is the projection of China being at the centre of global trade through history. But the narrative is useful in mobilizing national pride and energy, and in creating a sense of awe among the countries of Asia and beyond. The Belt and Road Forum convened by Chinese president Xi Jinping in Beijing in March 2017 was designed to demonstrate that Chinese centrality in the contemporary world was being accepted by friend and adversary alike. The Indian refusal to be present was seen as an impertinence.

It is true that sections of Asian and international opinion have already begun to concede this central role to China with the corollary that it is best for the rest to acquiesce to this inevitability. What careful analysis points to is that we are, in reality, neither in a China-centric Asia nor in a world destined to become China-centric. China may continue to expand its economic and military capabilities and may even become the most powerful country in the world but the world which is emerging will still be populated by a number of substantial powers both old and new. This includes Asia.

Furthermore, the Chinese economy is slowing down, as has been the case with every major economy in history. A simple linear projection of China's current growth rate into the future may not be realistic. China also remains a brittle polity and the rising insecurity within its political leadership sits uneasily with overweening arrogance of power. Its historical insularity is at odds with the cosmopolitanism that the densely interconnected contemporary world demands of any aspiring global power.

The US was, for most of the post-war period, a pre-eminent power, but its power was contested militarily and ideologically by the Soviet Union. Even among the constituency of newly independent but mostly poor countries, the hegemony of the two superpowers was contested by the NAM. It is only in the quarter of a century after the end of the Cold War in 1990 that the US may be regarded as a true hegemonic power, capable of imposing its will in virtually any part of the world. But we must acknowledge that the US presided over a world order which had been in the making over several centuries under extended Western dominance. We have seen how the modern state system and rules of the game and its norms of state behaviour have evolved since the Westphalian Peace of 1648, traversing successively through the Congress of Vienna, the Concert of Europe, the League of Nations and finally the UN. In that sense the US was a legatee of Western dominance, not its progenitor, though it did expand and extend that dominance in several aspects. For any non-Western aspiring hegemon there is no such legacy to build upon and, as has been argued, Chinese claim to even pre-eminence in Asia is mostly myth.

What lessons does the history of the world since the birth of the Westphalian state system hold for us? A stable world order needs a careful balance between power and legitimacy; and legitimacy is upheld when states, no matter how powerful, observe the various established norms of behaviour and codes of conduct and act through institutions which have been accumulated and put in place over the past four centuries, layer by layer.

The Westphalian system by its very nature is multipolar in character and is based on the assumption that any attempt by a state or a group of states to gain hegemony will always invite countervailing action by other states in the system and in, extreme cases, war. The is what happened when Napoleon tried to bring the whole of Europe under French domination. The Napoleonic Wars ended with the restoration of balance at the Congress of Vienna. The balance was again sought to be upset by an ascendant Germany and this led to two debilitating world wars. In our own time, the period of US hegemony from 1990 to 2007–08, when the global financial and economic crisis broke out, reducing the West to prolonged and debilitating stagnation and psychological pessimism, lasted only for a generation. This may have been a period when there were no wars among major powers but there were conflicts in several parts of the world in which interventions by the West eventually proved to be damaging to itself.

Hegemony often leads to hubris which in turn leads to overextension and then to exhaustion and sometimes war through miscalculation. We are facing chaos and uncertainty precisely because the period of Western hegemony and the reliance on power with scant attention to legitimacy weakened both international institutions and processes which could allow a degree of flexibility in adjusting to changes in the balance of power. The long period of European peace between the Congress of Vienna in 1815 up until the outbreak of the First World War in 1914 shows that as long as all key actors generally observe mutually agreed rules of interstate relations and norms of state behaviour, a stable order can be maintained. The current shifting international landscape where states continue to be cast in the Westphalian mode lends itself more appropriately to a twenty-first-century version of that multipolar world order and not the hegemonic interludes which have mostly ended in tragedy.

There are even more compelling reasons why the contemporary world needs a multipolar order. Most of the challenges we confront as an interconnected and interdependent world are cross-cutting in character and global in dimension. These include global warming, health pandemics, cybercrime, drug trafficking, proliferation of WMDs and international terrorism among others. They are often cross-domain in nature with strong feedback loops. We explored some of these issues in the chapter relating to climate change and we shall encounter them again in the Epilogue.

These challenges cannot be dealt with through exclusively national responses; and even national responses have to contend with the fact that there are external dimensions which must be taken into account while devising national solutions. The most effective way to deal with them are collaborative responses and this was already apparent in the century of building international institutions to deal with new domains spawned by the advance of technology such as the Universal Postal Union, the International Telegraph Union and the International Association of Railway Congresses. The emergence of new technologies with an even greater global reach and penetration makes such international collaboration a compulsion today rather than a choice. A hegemonic order can constrain other states; it will rarely be able to promote collaborative action which can be effective only if based on consent and consultation, not coercion.

Despite this compelling logic of multipolarity, it is possible that hegemonism will hold an attraction for some aspiring power or powers. China certainly appears headed in that direction and at some future date the mood in the US may change leading it to believe that its unipolar interlude, in fact, was the natural order of things. Neither the Chinese version of national rejuvenation nor American hopes of revivalism are realistic, precisely because the diffusion of economic and military power and the horizontal and accelerated spread of scientific knowledge and technology point to what author Thomas Friedman has called the Flat World.

It is also possible that an ascendant power may temporarily be ready to accept a dyarchy with what it sees as a declining though still powerful country. A China–US condominium is possible especially if there is some understanding, even if temporary, over their respective spheres of influence. China may be ready to accept a US-dominated Western hemisphere if it is conceded power over Asia-Pacific and Central Asia. This is what several US and even Chinese analysts suggest for avoiding the so-called Thucydides trap. (Thucydides was a Greek thinker who in his celebrated history of the Peloponnesian War between ancient Athens and Sparta in the fifth century BC had drawn attention to how a contest between an established power and an aspiring one usually led to a war for dominance.) This is also the essence of what China calls the 'new type of great power relations' between China and the US in order to avoid the Thucydides trap. But by its very nature it will be unstable as there will remain zones of contestation between China and the US, and each will seek uncontested dominance.

There could also be cases of the 'tail wagging the dog' as we see in the rising tensions on the Korean peninsula. The US may feel compelled to launch a strike against the nuclear and missile installations in North Korea because of the direct threat these may pose to the US itself. China may respond not because it supports North Korea's nuclear adventurism but because the loss of North Korea or its incorporation in a more powerful united Korea may be seen as a major threat to China's security.

Even during the Cold War, neither superpower was able to fully control its respective allies and this can happen with more tragic results in the unsettled world today. And it is unlikely that even if the US concedes a Chinese sphere of influence in the Asia-Pacific that the other Asian powers will acquiesce. The withdrawal of US security guarantee over Japan will almost inevitably lead to its acquisition of nuclear weapons. The same may happen in South Korea. As a substantial and growing power itself, it is unlikely that India will accept junior league status in a Chinese-centric world. Therefore China faces the same dilemma as other emerging powers in history: what Bismarck referred to as *le cauchemar des coalitions* or the nightmare of coalitions. There will always be a countervailing coalition to constrain a rising power.

It is the third scenario of a multipolar order with a template which came into being in Europe in 1815 which is likely to be more stable and enduring and capable of adjustment as the distribution of power changes as it always does. This is valid even if there exists a degree of asymmetry of power. But this order will require its own rules of the game and norms of interstate relations appropriate to the contemporary international landscape. It also needs a spirit of internationalism with some shared sense of humanity and human values. What we do not need is the relapse into assertive and competitive nationalism and the narrowing of political vision which is sweeping the world.

There is something of a backlash against globalization but the economic and technological drivers which lie behind it are now so deeply embedded in our lives as individuals, communities and nations that they cannot be unravelled. We cannot do without the Internet. We cannot think of a world without smartphones. Rather than trying in vain to put the genie back into the bottle and reassert national control over forces which by their very nature are cross-national, there is a need to embrace governance at the international scale. This implies multilateral institutions and multilateral processes which must be informed by a spirit of internationalism. Otherwise they will degenerate into platforms for competing nationalisms.

Assertive nationalism also shrinks the space for diplomacy. Diplomacy can operate effectively in areas of grey; its role gets marginalized when there is a tendency to frame issues in black and white. In *World Order*, Kissinger has described how in the run-up to the First World War, diplomacy lost touch with emerging technology and its corollary warfare, and the military in European countries 'ran away with diplomacy'. There is a danger of this happening again as political leaders fail to understand the implications of modern technology.

Diplomacy is also constrained by advances in digital technology and the growth of social media including Twitter and Facebook. There is a premium on instant communication and political leaders themselves post reactions on social media, unmediated by professional and carefully deliberated processes that lie at the heart of successful diplomacy. This is as true of Trump's America as it is of Modi's India. There is little or no room for the '*mantra-shakti*' or sage counsel which Indian exponents of statecraft placed ahead of military and economic strength as sources of a country's power and influence. The potential for conflict among states due to misunderstanding and misperception as a result of unmediated messaging has greatly enlarged. We truly live in a world where a single tweet may launch a thousand riots. This is yet another reason why we need a multipolar order which can create a new template and a new common platform for a densely interdependent and instantly connected world. No hegemonic order could possibly hope to control these unregulated and in some ways unregulatable domains.

It is evident that for India it is a multipolar order which will be most aligned with its interests. It is an emerging power which seeks to expand its own room for manouevre unconstrained by either a latter-day hegemon or a return to a bipolar system dominated by two major powers. Its developmental challenges need a supportive, peaceful and stable international environment. Therefore India's best interests are served by its assistance in shaping a multipolar order with the support of other major powers. It should not hesitate in promoting and participating in a countervailing coalition to constrain any aspiring hegemon even while it expands its own economic and military capabilities.

But this cannot be the whole of India's story. India possesses the civilizational attributes which could contribute to the success of a new international order attuned to contemporary realities. Its culture is innately cosmopolitan; it embraces vast diversity and plurality and yet has an underlying sense of being part of a common humanity. There is a deep conviction that to achieve greatness a nation must stand for something more than itself. These are assets which it should leverage in helping shape a new world order. The mindless eruptions of narrow nationalism, communalism and sectarianism detract from the credibility of its role. We should certainly seek to advance India's interests but not without a constant awareness of our place in a larger, interlinked and interdependent world.

Epilogue

India and the New Global Landscape

We live in a world that is changing. And rapidly at that. This is the Age of Acceleration, where the only constant seems to be the certainty of even more change. As children we played the game of 'joining the dots'. Today we live in a world where the dots keep shifting as we try to join them. The challenge before us is to draw a map even as the terrain it is meant to represent is constantly changing shape. This is the new global landscape which individuals, communities, societies and nations must learn to navigate.

The key driver of change is technological advancement. The computing power of a microchip in our mobile phones is equivalent to that of several acres of mainframe computers of a generation ago. The volume of data and the speed with which it can be sent across great distances is constantly increasing, and we are still far from reaching the limits of this technology. There are other domains where potentially disruptive technologies are in the making. These include the domains of nanotechnology, advanced materials (such as graphene), biosciences and artificial intelligence, which are pushing the frontiers of knowledge. We do not know how the new domains will interact with social and political systems, or affect psychological attitudes that change only very slowly.

Technological change has altered our global landscape. The global environment is no longer amenable to management by instruments and processes that were fashioned to deal with an altogether different reality. Yet our predisposition to familiarity and precedent makes us reluctant to set them aside and craft tools more appropriate to the new challenges we face. For example, our energy systems are still fossil fuel-based. Our current production and consumption patterns are inevitably resource-intensive and waste-generating, and therefore ecologically unsustainable. While these older patterns of economic activity still survive, it is only a question of time before new domains of activity disrupt and eventually overwhelm the old economy.

Despite its rapidity of change, the new landscape does have certain defining characteristics. It has three critical domains:

- A terrestrial domain that is increasingly defined by maritime space,
- An extraterrestrial domain, which is related to outer space, and
- Cyberspace, encompassing both the terrestrial and the extraterrestrial.

As globalization becomes more entrenched, and as the interconnectedness and integration of economies across the world continues apace, the maritime sphere becomes a critical factor, impacting directly on the overall security of nations. Consider the following: export of goods and services as a proportion of world GDP went up from 20 per cent in 1990 to 31 per cent in 2012; the FDI stock, as part of world output, rose even faster, from 9 per cent in 1990 to 33 per cent in 2012. Ocean-going trade now constitutes well over 90 per cent of total world trade. Dependence on maritime trade is only intensifying, if we consider the global movement of energy resources, particularly oil, and of other strategic commodities, such as iron ore, coal and, more recently, rare earths. Resource security is now integrally linked to maritime security.

The maritime domain is also in flux. The melting of Arctic ice due to global warming, for example, is opening up new and much shorter sea routes between Europe and Asia, reducing shipping distances by over 40 per cent. From just over four cargo vessels in 2010, the number using the north-east passage along the Russian Arctic coast had crossed 200 in 2014. New ports and infrastructure are planned along the Russian and Norwegian Arctic coasts. If the melting of Arctic ice continues at the current pace, it is estimated that by 2030, over 25 per cent of world shipping may be traversing this route instead of the traditional passage through the Suez Canal. The Arctic may also hold over 40 per cent of the world's known energy and mineral resources, which the melting of ice is making accessible. The economic profile of the Arctic littoral countries, in particular the US, Russia, Canada, Norway and Denmark, would increase, and so will their global importance. This could retard or even reverse the ongoing shift of the global economic hub from the trans-Atlantic to the Asia-Pacific region. In a few decades from now, the pecking order among nations may begin to look very different.

The critical importance of the maritime domain also implies that countries with significant maritime capabilities will be the more influential nations of the future, rather than those nations that continue to allocate resources to large and increasingly less effective land forces and weaponry.

Space is another key domain. Much of the world's communication systems, its information and media infrastructure, navigation and surveillance systems, and resource survey platforms are based in space. The number of operational satellites orbiting in space has grown from just a handful fifty years ago to about 5000 now. These space-based assets are vital to modern economies but they are also vulnerable. This was brought home to the world by China's unannounced test of an anti-satellite (ASAT) weapon in 2007, when it used a space launcher to destroy one of its own defunct satellites still orbiting in space. China's obvious intent was to demonstrate that it had the capability to destroy the space-based assets of other countries.

The space domain is now completely woven into the fabric of our lives on earth, though few fully comprehend this reality. In the none-too-distant future, space travel may become as commonplace as air travel today. The colonization of other planets, the exploitation of rich and rare minerals that lie buried in their soil, and their use as remote platforms for future explorations of outer space, are no longer in the realm of fantasy. The countries which have mastery of the space sciences and have deployed ambitious programmes for future growth will be significant players in any future world order. Among the developing countries, only China and India make the grade today.

Cyberspace is a complex hybrid of the terrestrial and extraterrestrial domains. It is terrestrial in that it relies upon a vast and dense network of fibre optic cables that gird our planet, running under land as well as seas. It is extraterrestrial because it is also connected to all the space-based systems referred to in the previous paragraph. The virtual reality maintained and created by cyberspace activities depends upon both land-based (including maritime) and space-based platforms, which are interconnected and enmeshed in a dense, complex and continually expanding system.

It is difficult to comprehend how much our current day-to-day functioning is dependent on this interconnected cyberspace. Even a temporary disruption of this network can wreak havoc on countries and on the global economy. And yet, it is only a little over fifty years since the satellite age was born and only thirty years since personal computers and portable phones came into existence. The worldwide Internet, which created a global cyberspace, is only a little over a generation old. The world still has a generation or two who have lived through an era when there was no television, let alone the computer, no mobile phone and no Internet. Today we cannot conceive of a modern economy and a modern society without these devices and technologies.

This also implies that countries with advanced cyber capabilities will possess a most powerful means to both economic and national security advancement. Cyberspace is a unique resource, being not material or tangible. It is, nevertheless, a virtual network that no nation or society can opt out of and survive as a viable entity. Interconnectedness is no longer a choice. It is a fundamental condition for modern life.

Cyberspace is also different in another aspect from the maritime and space domains. It is both a platform as well as a resource in itself. And, unlike the other two domains, it also generates knowledge. It is a force multiplier. It enables swift accumulation of vast amounts of data, increasingly on a real-time basis. Collation of large amounts of data generates information. Advanced software allows one to analyse this information and to discern patterns in them. This yields knowledge, which in turn leads to insights, which then trigger the next cycle of even more complex and value-added processes. These capabilities have propelled companies like Google, Apple, Amazon and Facebook to the very front ranks of the global economy.

We cannot fully imagine the power cyberspace has placed in the hands of modern humans. It could propel civilization to unprecedented advancement by providing it instant access to information and knowledge across the human spectrum. It could lead to enhanced freedom for individuals and societies. But it could also lead to immense oppression through pervasive intrusion into individual privacy. The ability of states as well as of multinational corporations to engage in mass surveillance of individuals across the world destroys any notion of individual privacy. It exposes people to blackmail and manipulation. It can be used to spread distortion and discord through what has become known as 'fake news'. The IS, for example, has used the Internet to spread its message of hate and violence to recruit foot soldiers from across the globe. Different malevolent forces may come together bringing us – individuals, societies, nations, the whole world – face to face with the unpleasant and the unfamiliar.

Our institutions of governance, both domestic and global, are based on sector-specific knowledge and management systems. These systems are unable to collaborate to deliver responses that can cut across domains and disciplines, which is what an interconnected and globalized economy requires. This is the first challenge we face. The global financial crisis of 2007–08 was attributed to failures in the financial and banking sectors. We deploy the instruments specific to those sectors to deal with the crisis, including both fiscal and monetary responses. We fail to understand that the financial overleveraging which triggered the crisis was only a symptom of a much deeper crisis – the mismatch between the real economy and the financial markets, and the outdatedness of regulatory instruments, which were lagging behind changes in the global economy. We also fail to understand that instant transmission of information, as well as misinformation, made possible through the cyber domain, creates networks of shared perceptions across borders. These networks are not subject to any domestic or international control. That is why domestic governance structures have become increasingly ineffective. International governance structures either do not exist or are lacking in the capacities needed for coping with these new predicaments.

The global economic crisis, which is now eclipsed by a deeper ecological crisis, has also exposed the interrelationships among different resource areas. It is now clear that it is impossible to deal with food security without, at the same time, considering water security. Both food and water are in turn impacted by energy security. All these factors will be impacted by climate change. Each is no longer an independent variable but impacts and is impacted by what happens in other interlinked areas.

In Punjab, for example, maintaining, let alone increasing, the production of wheat, rice and sugarcane requires a progressively greater use of chemical fertilizers and pesticides, which in turn need higher volumes of water. The water table in the state is going down precipitously from overextraction. Now, more powerful diesel or electric pumps have to be used to access the deeper aquifers. We are caught in a vicious cycle, where increasing food production is leading to water stress, and water stress is leading to power shortage. Unless there is a comprehensive cross-domain strategy which factors in these feedback loops, we shall be unable to meet this interlinked crisis. At present we have neither such interdisciplinary approaches nor institutions and systems that can work across domains.

As we have discussed earlier, domestic responses are no longer sufficient to cope with these pressures. Because our world is so closely interconnected and resources are so unevenly distributed, national or regional boundaries are becoming increasingly nominal. Our national interventions are impacted by what happens in the rest of the world. The world itself is affected by what may happen even in its remotest corner. We have to invent instruments of domestic and global governance to deal with this reality.

Take the example of the oil market. Since India imports over 70 per cent of its oil, and mostly from the Gulf, any supply disruption, say, due to political unrest or a natural disaster in the region which blocks the narrow Hormuz Strait, could cause a major dislocation in the Indian economy. At the same time, India's oil demand is the fastest growing in the world, and the oil market will be influenced by a slowdown in the Indian economy resulting from a lack of reforms, political and social unrest, or a series of bad monsoons affecting food production. Just as India needs an energy strategy that provides for likely trends in the international oil market, so too must major oil suppliers and companies closely follow trends in the Indian economy.

The next challenge lies in changing the notion of competition among nation states as a means of enhancing national security, which we now understand in a much more comprehensive sense than in narrow military terms. Cross-cutting problems, as we have discussed earlier, are not amenable to national or even regional solutions. For example, global health pandemics such as Ebola or Zika may arise in a remote part of the world, but spread across vast regions in a very short time. Drug trafficking and international terrorism, maritime piracy and environmental pollution are other cross-border challenges that require a collaborative response.

The most urgent of all challenges is the climate change emergency. Regional and national actions are only aggravating the situation by perpetuating resource- and energy-intensive patterns of production and consumption. But in creating a global mechanism to manage the crisis, the negotiating remains competitive, with each country trying to maximize its own benefits and minimize its perceived costs. If every country follows the same principle, this would result in a least-common-denominator result rather than in a response of a scale appropriate to the challenge. The global dimension of the issues we confront requires a mindset change that gets nations working together rather than racing each other for selfish advantage. But there is little evidence of such a collaborative approach in our world today.

There are many dangers in applying a narrowly nationalistic and competitive framework in managing the maritime, space and cyber domains that will become crucial in the future. If maritime security is sought through a competitive build-up of our respective naval forces or through unilateral actions, as China is doing in the South China Sea, it will plunge us all into insecurity. We would be better off creating a framework of mutual reassurance so that our shipping lines are safe. The components for such an architecture have been under discussion for several years. They include:

- A commitment by all states using the maritime space to adhere to the principles and provisions of the Law of the Seas and other principles of international maritime law.
- The establishment of a regional, and eventually global, facility for real-time maritime domain awareness, enabling states to have an accurate picture of all shipping movements, civil and non-civil, which would reduce, if not eliminate, disputes over the violation of territorial and exclusive economic zone limits of states.
- The formulation of a code of conduct for the use

of maritime space, including procedures to handle encounters at sea, accidents and threats from piracy.

- The creation of institutions to foster regular exchanges, both civil and naval, among maritime countries, to promote personal- and institution-level contacts, confidence building and cooperation.

In the space domain, we need to recognize that space-based assets are now critical to our functioning as modern societies and their disruption may have disastrous consequences for the economic and social welfare of people across the world. To acknowledge this should lead the way to establishing a space regime which ensures the safety of space-based assets, prohibit the deployment of space-based weapons and enable cooperation in dealing with problems such as space debris. The alternative would be a competitive build-up of ever more sophisticated offensive capabilities such as ASAT weapons, which would exacerbate mutual distrust and suspicion.

Similarly, in the field of cyberspace we need to arrest the slide towards the anarchic and even dangerous use of this powerful capability, as evident in the increasing frequency of cyberattacks and the widespread violation of individual privacy in the name of counterterrorism. Instead we should agree to draw up and follow norms and guidelines for the beneficial growth of cyberspace, carefully balancing security and privacy needs.

To repeat what I have said earlier in this chapter, cyberspace is unique in that it is both a platform as well as a resource, though an intangible one. It has brought into existence large networks of interconnected individuals across national borders. It has created an ever-expanding knowledge pool, which has unleashed a surge of creativity and innovation across the world. In this sense, it is liberating, democratic and life-enhancing. However, it is also a powerful instrument for a predatory state to violate the privacy of its own citizens and that of citizens of other countries. It could become an invisible, unregulated medium for shaping perceptions, feeding prejudices, preaching hatred and violence. We are aware of the manner in which non-state actors like Al-Qaeda and IS, also known as Daesh, have used social media to spread their language of hate and violence. There are suspicions that Russian intelligence may have used hackers to leak confidential emails of US Democratic Party functionaries, thereby influencing the presidential elections in favour of Donald Trump.

The capabilities available in cyberspace allow powerful surveillance networks to operate without visibility, giving the state and its agents the means to control the lives of ordinary citizens, threaten their freedoms and, worst of all, subjugate their minds. This capability in the hands of a state that sees security as requiring control over its citizens' thoughts, relationships and political persuasions may lead to a new, more oppressive and tyrannical version of authoritarianism than ever seen before. The state assumes such power and authority by sustaining the fear of terrorism. But the dangers of such authoritarianism may eclipse any danger from terrorism. Democratic and liberal societies encourage fraternity and fellowship among their citizens. Instead, we see fear being spread to make citizens complicit in the restriction of their own freedoms. The reaction of the US administration to the Edward Snowden affair, for example, is a grim warning of what may await citizens of democratic societies when a fear psychosis is artificially created to justify the state's use of powerful tools of control.

So where does India belong in this transformed landscape?

India is, and will remain, an influential actor in the emerging global order, precisely because it has demonstrated capabilities in all three critical domains of the future. It is already a maritime power with a strong regional reach. Our global footprint is still modest but our maritime capabilities are expanding, though maybe not as much as a long-term strategy would dictate. India is one of the handful of space powers in the world, and despite its frugal resources, has developed sophisticated capabilities comparable with the best in the world. The outstanding success of the Mangalyaan or Mars project illustrates this. And lastly, in cyberspace, India's capability is well established and internationally acknowledged; India is among the few countries that has defensive and offensive cyber capabilities.

It is precisely these capabilities that qualify India to lead the world in creating global governance structures that are not based on the competitive principle but on a recognition that only collaborative responses will be able to deal with the interlinked challenges posed by these emerging domains. India has a stake in the norms and standards to be adopted by the global institutions. As India will be a key player in each of these domains, the world too has a stake in it being a part and parcel of these regimes. India's absence from these regimes will make them ineffective. This is powerful leverage in our hands to safeguard and promote our interests.

It is not certain if India will continue to develop its capabilities in the cyber and space domains as these technologies advance to very high realms. It is more likely that India will advance, perhaps in fits and starts, if it remains a plural, diverse and extraordinarily interactive society. Cellphone technology, the Internet and social media are enabling Indians to converse and interact among themselves and with people across their borders on an enormous scale. Over 900 million of our 1.2 billion population have mobile telephones, currently the most powerful tool for information gathering and networking.

Harnessing the creative and innovative energy of India's people requires leadership that understands the altered global landscape in which we live. This leadership must put in place institutions and processes appropriate to this changing landscape.

It is an advantage that we are not already locked into the pattern of energy- and resource-intensive economic development on which hinges the success of China and much of the world today. This is a model which belongs to the past. The future will be built upon its deconstruction.

India has the opportunity now to fashion a model of development which draws upon the country's pool of capabilities in the new domains. If India can lead and ride the changes that are necessary rather than become overwhelmed by them, its future as a front-ranking country in the world of tomorrow is assured.

Our capabilities in these three domains are one aspect of our preparedness for the future. The values India will stand for are another.

There are two competing and often clashing forces at work in the contemporary world. At one end of the spectrum, the technological revolution has bonded humanity much closer than it has been at any other time in history. There are vastly greater opportunities to directly experience other cultures or learn about them through virtual media. There is continual exposure to different ways of life, cultural norms, traditions and even cuisine. This is leading to a growing appreciation of the best that every country and culture has to offer, making us more aware of the cultural particularities of peoples the world over. This awareness is the basis on which we develop sensitivity to and respect for the deeply held beliefs and convictions of people different from us.

However, there is another, darker force that has been unleashed by the very same proximity, leading to fears of loss of identity and a sense of being culturally adrift in a world transforming with bewildering speed. We see this in the emergence and spread of fundamentalist interpretations of religious ideas, the assertion of narrow ethnic, regional and national identities, both real and imagined, and the rising intolerance of ideas, beliefs and even ways of living different from our own. This retards engagement and dialogue not only between cultures but within cultures and among generations too.

The global war on terrorism has spawned an environment of fear and suspicion, which only breeds even more intolerance and prejudice. This in turn feeds the coercive power of the state and its innately predatory instincts. We are becoming societies where security agencies increasingly exercise a veto over the choices of elected governments. This is justified by the state and increasingly rationalized and accepted by its citizens as the price they must pay to be safe in a world threatened by terrorism. This slide towards authoritarianism may become imperceptibly internalized.

In the midst of this churn, where do we seek a reliable compass? I believe that open and liberal societies – in particular plural democracies like India – are far better equipped to deal with the emerging new world. India has the ability to manage diversity and adapt to different cultures, and this will be the hallmark of a great and successful power of the future. As pointed out in the introductory chapter, India is a classic crossroads culture with an innately cosmopolitan spirit. We need to be careful not to devalue the very strengths we possess as a confident and accommodative culture. We must reject a political culture that feeds on division and exploits the fear of loss of identity among its people, creating in them a sense of siege. We must reject the intolerance we see towards the expression of views different from our own or towards depictions in art supposedly disrespectful of culture or religion. If we are to engage other cultures in productive dialogue we must reaffirm confidence in our own, accepting and celebrating the diversity that lies at the heart of our democracy.

I would like to conclude this book by revisiting the first chapter on the sources of India's world view. I pointed to the modesty inherent in Indian cosmology, which located India in a realm beyond which existed several other progressively higher realms. Our view of the world is not India-centric, unlike that of other cultures, including the Chinese. There is an acceptance of different, coexisting and equally valid realities, which is encapsulated in the ancient Sanskrit *sloka* from the Rig Veda: '*Ekam sat vipra bahudha vadanti*' – 'Truth is one but sages call it by different names'. This lies at the heart of India's expansive cultural sensibility, in the Argumentative Indian's[1] delight in open discourse and debate and, above all, in India's embrace of humanity with all its quirks and eccentricities. These traits have been the hallmark of a civilization that has mostly seen itself as a journey, not a destination.

The Constitution of India built upon these civilizational attributes to aim for a society based on the inalienable right of the individual to choose his or her own destiny and to live life the way he or she chose to. It was left to individual choice to conform to their community norm or reject it. The institutions

---

[1] Amartya Sen, *The Argumentative Indian*, Penguin UK, 2006.

of the state were obligated to safeguard this right, whether threatened by another individual, group or community, or by the state itself.

Steadily and relentlessly, however, community-based entitlements have become the norm, not the exception they were meant to be – to such an extent that the very concept of individual choice now appears almost illegitimate. In setting any boundary to define what is permissible and what is not, every prejudice of the most bigoted in each community must be pandered to for keeping the peace. Would it be possible now to sustain the creative ambience which made India the repository of the most sublime music and sculpture, the most profound literature in a variety of languages and a highly developed and subtle understanding of aesthetics?

India is in danger of being reduced to a mere agglomeration of narrowly conceived communities with closed minds, hostile to each other and stifling to their own lot. How Indians relate to one another influences how the country handles interstate relations. A shrinking vision at home cannot sustain an expansive vision abroad.

The constitution envisioned the India of the future as an enlightened society of free citizens, where diversity among its people was celebrated, where no monochromatic ideology could reign and where the people's creative impulses would take the country to the front ranks of the modern world. That vision is blurred today, even as the world, at once densely interconnected but deeply conflicted, gropes for a solution to successfully manage the multiplicities which rapid technological change is forcing humanity to confront.

The Indian spirit in its most refined articulations has been an outstanding example of the sharing of diverse cultures, traditions, and ways of thinking and living; coexisting harmoniously for centuries. But we are in danger of losing this unique cultural inheritance even though much of the world still comes to our shores to seek the wisdom which could restore humanity amidst a rising tide of extremism, cruelty and barbaric violence.

And what about the Indian state? Do Kautilya's *Arthashastra* or Kamandaki's *Nitisara* still hold lessons for their navigation of a world so different from theirs? I believe the attributes of a successful state as laid down by Kautilya remain relevant.

Both Kautilya and Kamandaki counsel prudence in managing interstate relations. For a relatively weak king, Kautilya has this practical advice: 'One should neither submit spinelessly nor sacrifice oneself in foolhardy valour. It is better to adopt such policies as would enable one to survive and live to fight another day.'[2]

Resorting to *danda* – coercive power or war – is advised only once the other means of *sama* (conciliation), *dana* (placating through gifts) and *bheda* (creating dissension) have been tried and have failed. Kamandaki attaches higher value to wise counsel (*mantra-shakti*) than to ruler-led military or financial power. The ruler is enjoined to make a clear determination between what is attainable and what is not through cool and intelligent deliberation (*mantra-shakti*). (*Sarga* XII, *Prakarana* 7).

Hundreds of years later, these principles are valid even in our transformed world.

[2] Kautilya, The *Arthashastra*, trans. L.N.Rangarajan, p. 508, Penguin India, 2000.

Acknowledgements

I wish to acknowledge the support and encouragement I have constantly received from family, friends and colleagues in taking on the unfamiliar task of writing a book. Particular thanks are due to Nandini Mehta, who acted as friend, mentor and guide, and without whose constant urging I may never have written this book.

This book is dedicated to my wife, Anita, and to my children, Nakul and Indrani, who have been my cheerleaders throughout.

Index

Praise for the Book

'Part history, part memoir, *How India Sees the World* is an illuminating and at times controversial insight into the thinking of one of India's great diplomats and civil servants. A vigorous defender of India's national interests, Shyam Saran offers us a unique and candid view of policy deliberations at the highest levels of the Indian government. He rightly argues for a deeper understanding of China and the historic factors which inform and shape its strategic behaviour today. Moreover, Ambassador Saran provides a timely overview of the contemporary challenges facing global politics, including but not limited to cyberspace, climate change and outer space. This is a strong contribution from a fine strategic thinker' **Kevin Rudd**, Former Prime Minister of Australia

'As an insightful, acute and erudite description of the well-springs of Indian foreign policy, Shyam Saran's *How India Sees the World* is unmatched. Drawing on his deep experience in crucial positions and his undoubted intellectual gifts, this book is required reading for anyone interested in India's role in the world, and the future of Asia and the world. His familiarity with traditional Indian statecraft, and his focus on China — a country he is familiar with and has studied for over forty years — makes for fascinating and thought-provoking reading. A must read and an essential addition to any library on modern India' **Shivshankar Menon**, Former National Security Advisor of India

'Arguably the most brilliant Indian diplomat in the past four decades, Shyam Saran's breathtaking command of the ancient foundations and Cold War dimensions of India's foreign policy provides an indispensable frame of reference for the country's current external challenges. His discussion of the rise of Chinese power and its muscular strategic applications should be required reading for every head of government and foreign minister in the world. And his penetrating analyses of adversarial Pakistan and unpredictable America are as insightful as they are troubling. If you can only read one book on how India should conduct itself as world order fractures, read this one' **Robert D. Blackwill**, Former US Ambassador to India and Senior Official at the White House

'Drawing on his exemplary career as one of India's shrewdest and subtlest diplomats, Shyam Saran's penetrating tract is at once strategic road map, policy handbook, and practical manual: a magnificent, sophisticated statement of the axioms and skills that must guide us in confronting the opportunities and wicked challenges ahead as we make our way in an uncertain world' **Sunil Khilnani**, Avantha Professor and Director, King's India Institute

'Shyam Saran's *How India Sees the World* is a thoughtful reflection on the deepest wellsprings of Indian foreign policy. By integrating his own rich experiences with a careful analysis of India's strategic circumstances, he has produced a magnificent book that interprets Indian grand strategy as a persistent struggle for autonomy characterized by a humane realism. It will be indispensable reading for better understanding not simply India's recent diplomatic history but also how its efforts to relate to the modern international system bear the deepest traces of its ancient and venerable ethos' **Ashley J. Tellis,** Tata Chair for Strategic Affairs, Carnegie Endowment for International Peace

'Nowhere else but in India do religion, culture, history and recent developments come together to define a nation's relations with the world. Shyam Saran is a unique guide to the long lines in Indian foreign policy. His practical statesmanship, eye for a good story and intellectual force offer refreshing insights into India as a critical Asian and global power' **Erik Solheim**, Executive Director, United Nations Environment Programme

'A work of erudition . . . highly recommended' ***Mint***

'Saran . . . is a superb raconteur . . . eschews strategic and diplomatic jargon, explaining complex issues and incidents in language that the lay reader can enjoy . . . brings to light several issues that have remained undisclosed so far . . . excellent' ***Business Standard***

'Timely, lucid and eloquent' ***Outlook***

'Nobody can be more eloquent than Shyam Saran when it comes to reflecting on the evolution of the Indo-US Civil Nuclear deal' ***Tribune***

'A riveting account of critical events and shifts in Indian foreign policy in the post-Independence period' ***Economic Times***

'An impressive disquisition on foreign policy . . . a liberal, humane and far-sighted perspective on India's place in the world many decades into the future' *India Today*

Given his inside knowledge of the policy deliberations that went on behind closed doors — and which he has freely shared — Saran's renderings of events . . . are as insightful as they are thought-provoking' *Deccan Chronicle*

'Fascinating . . . Lucid enough for a reader merely interested in global politics . . . provides new insights for a foreign policy expert' **IDFC Institute**

'Engaging . . . enjoyable . . . provides a perceptive account of the compulsions and motivations driving India's foreign policy' *Print*

'Anyone even remotely interested in India's foreign policy must read Shyam Saran's book . . . a treasure trove of anecdotes that give you terrific insights into how diplomacy and negotiations are conducted . . . an absolutely riveting account of how the Indo-US nuclear deal unfolded and was eventually signed' *Swarajya*

'Written in an easy story-telling style . . . A must read for those interested in an authentic yet quick reference on contemporary trends in India's foreign policy' *The Hindu*

'As one of our leading China hands, Saran offers an incisive look at the challenges that the rapid rise of the Middle Kingdom poses for us' *Indian Express*

'An important book' **Quint**

'The really delightful bits are . . . Saran's descriptions of his interactions with Chinese culture' **Wire**

'Offers an instructive view of the world from the vantage point of a pillar of the establishment' *National Herald*

Reader Reviews on the Juggernaut App

'Well articulated. A must read for all those seeking to understand Indian foreign policy: its past, present and future' **Rajat Ubhaykar**

'The book is really interesting and has something new to learn. I never felt that I am reading a foreign policy book rather it was like a story told by grandfather...☺' **Venkatesh Bamne**